Martin Erdmann

Millennium
Historical & Exegetical Debate

Verax
Vox Media

Greenville, South Carolina
2016

Verax Vox Media
225 Barbours Lane • Greenville, SC 29607
VeraxVoxMedia.com

Millennium
Historical & Exegetical Debate

Copyright ©: 2016 by Martin Erdmann
ISBN: 978-069262-643-6
Publication Date: Juni 2016
Cover design: Estelle C. Erdmann
Cover image: Detail of an ancient byzantine fresco of the council of Nicaea. From the church of St Nicholas, Demre, Southern Turkey. Copyright: mountainpix / Shutterstock

All rights reserved. No part of this publication may be reproduced or transmitted in any form or by any means, electronic or mechanical, including photocopying, recording, or any information storage or retrieval system, without prior permission in writing form the publisher.

Endorsements

Martin Erdmann has provided us with an extremely helpful study of the early church's beliefs about the millennial kingdom. He demonstrates persuasively that from the very beginning belief in a literal, earthly thousand-year reign of Christ was common among Christians who understood the prophetic passages of Scripture without any interpretive embellishments. Other approaches to understanding the millennium all began with serious hermeneutical missteps. The history of how these views arose and gained popularity makes a fascinating study.
This is a book well worth reading for anyone who wants a better grasp of the history and development of early millennial views.

> ❖ John MacArthur
> Pastor-Teacher of Grace Community Church in Sun Valley, California; President of The Master's College and Seminary.

Dr. Erdmann's treatment of the various millennial views is thoughtful and courteous. His scope of research and documentation is very impressive. He has concisely, clearly, and graciously opened this issue to its core values and given us a valuable tool to aid in correct Biblical teaching. His presentation of the various methods of interpretation is very helpful. He insists on holding the text of Scripture as critic of the human attempts to interpret its meaning.
It is helpful to be reminded of how deeply the early Church Fathers held to the Biblical teaching about the return of Jesus and His millennial Kingdom on earth. I appreciate so much his showing that the influence upon their thinking was their expectation of a literal, physical fulfillment of the promises made by the OT prophets [and Jesus Himself] to the descendents of Israel. Right on! Martin Erdmann has done such a good job of letting the various teachers speak for themselves, showing how other influences moved them from handling the text fairly.

Congratulations on a marvelous work – worthy of the widest and most diligent reading by anyone interested in the Truth of Scripture and how we can "rightly divide the Word of Truth" and not "twist the Scriptures". I wholeheartedly endorse this book, its conclusions, and its spirit and recommend it to those who wish to get to the roots of this controversy in eschatology.

❖ Dr. Jim Custer
Teaching Pastor, Senior Pastor Emeritus, Grace Polaris Church, Columbus, Ohio

I am grateful for this scholarly treatise emphasizing the premillennial return of Christ. The discussed historical debate among the Church Fathers brings a fresh perspective to ministers of the Gospel today.

❖ Prof. Dr. Gordon Elliott
formerly Senior Pastor, Grace Bible Church, Jacksonville, Florida, Pastor-at-large with S.I.M., Professor of Biblical Studies at Fruitland Baptist Bible College

Martin Erdmann has produced an exceptionally thorough volume of the history of interpretation of Revelation 20:1-10. Anyone serious about accurately interpreting God's Holy Word regarding the thousand year kingdom of which the Apostle John wrote will benefit immensely from this careful work. Dr. Erdmann brilliantly substantiates premillennialism while avoiding denigration of those of differing viewpoints. Opponents of a literal understanding of this passage must now face and deal with this persuasive research and argumentation. It is a privilege to endorse enthusiastically this thoughtful and well-reasoned study.

❖ Prof. Dr. Roger D. Peugh
Associate Professor of World Missions at Grace Theological Seminary, Winona Lake, Indiana

Martin Erdmann's comprehensive study on millennialism in the early church is a welcome contribution to this complex issue. He objectively sifts through the available evidence and presents the case for premillennialism in a way that is historically astute. Though not all readers will agree with the conclusions of Erdmann's study, they will nonetheless profit from his thorough research. His book will prove to be a valuable reference work on this subject for New Testament students.

> ❖ Prof. Dr. Terry L. Wilder
> Associate Dean of PhD Programs, Wesley Harrison Chair of New Testament, Southwestern Baptist Theological Seminary, Fort Worth, Texas

Martin Erdmann's *The Millennial Controversy in the Early Church* is a lucid, rigorously studied, easy to read defense of premillennial eschatology. After careful examination of Revelation's relationship to early Jewish apocalyptic literature, Dr. Erdmann traces the development of millennial eschatology from Revelation itself through the major Church Fathers up to the millennial views of Augustine. The author's exegetical and church historical analysis concludes with the judgment that premillennialism best accounts for all of the biblical phenomena that relate to the millennium, particularly the two resurrections spoken of in Rev 20:4-5. Dr. Erdmann is to be congratulated for this fresh, important contribution to the ongoing study of Christian eschatology.

> ❖ Prof. Dr. Edward P. Meadors
> Professor of New Testament and Program Director of the Bible Department, Taylor University, Upland, Indiana

Dr. Martin Erdmann is one of today's most capable researchers and religious writers. His intellectual giftedness combined with an insatiable desire to reveal truth produces an extremely high level of scholarship. Dr. Erdmann is dedicated to the inerrant Word of God. Indeed, his writings and teachings are worthy of international interest.

> ❖ Dr. Clyde M. Narramore
> Author and Founder of the Narramore Christian Foundation, Arcadia, California

Dedication

This book is dedicated to those I love most

Joy E. Erdmann,

Estelle Chérie Erdmann, Johannes Luc Erdmann,

Edgar & Alide Erdmann,

Beate L. Gsell

Acknowledgements

While writing this book in Aberdeen, Scotland, I have experienced the inestimable assistance of various people whose friendship and kindness were a constant source of joy to me. The list of names would be too long to mention them all. There are, however, some who will always have a special place in my heart.

Noel and *Catharine Evans.* Your hospitality and practical help were exemplary and refreshing.

Woody and *Elena Hingle.* We cherished your friendship and the many hours we spent in each other's company.

Terry and *Denise Wilder. John* and *Elaine Phillips. Ed* and *Kathy Meadors.* Your presence in Tillydrone was wonderful. Thank you for the memorable times we laughed and talked together. We will remember you all.

Joy E. Erdmann. I am especially grateful to my wife, Joy, whose love and support during the time of research constituted the greatest source of encouragement and inspiration to me.

Foreword

Prof. Dr. Trevor Craigen, The Master's Seminary

When Martin Erdmann sent me a copy of his manuscript for this book on the millennial debate in the Early Church and graciously invited me to write its foreword, I accepted with alacrity since this debate has long been of interest to me. A sampling of a few pages in each chapter noted the extensive footnoting and marks of in depth research.

The millennial debate of today had its seed in the early centuries of the Church. Even those who have only an elementary acquaintance with the writings of that time period would readily recognize this to be the case. Names such as Augustine, Eusebius, Jerome, Justin Martyr, and Chrysostom, for example, are familiar ones, with Augustine being recognized, perhaps, as the most prestigious and influential of the Church Fathers. He has exerted, and still exerts, a powerful and long lasting influence over others who sought to write on the millennium and Revelation 20. One whole chapter is devoted to the amillennialism of Augustine, as is one given to the anti-millennialism of the Alexandrians.

The disparate hermeneutics of the day, the reader will quickly realize, resulted in substantially different interpretations of Revelation 20. In a forty-three page chapter, Dr. Erdmann deals with the millennialism of the Apostle John. He also focuses attention on this crucial chapter in John's Apocalypse. Methodically, the proposals put forward by both amillennial and postmillennial exponents for what they understand of the binding, release and judgment of Satan, the two resurrections, the period of one thousand years, the saints reigning with Christ, the deceiving of the nations, and the non-futuristic nature of these events, are shown to be totally inadequate interpretations of John's words. Although Dr. Erdmann has irenically dealt with the propositions of both amillennialist and postmillennialist, the reader may very well inquire a bit more polemically as to why it is that writers and commentators from these two schools of eschatological thought should make such an effort to convince each other and the reader that Revelation just cannot be futuristic. Is it because a highly revered writer and theologian would not allow it to be so? To this very day, the premillennialist finds this to be an enigma.

By the time the conclusion to the whole study is reached, the reader has begun to realize that just because a giant of intellect makes a reasonably good contribution to theology and exegesis, it does not follow that all his conclusions will be equally good. Indeed some might very well be flawed. What should the exegete and theologian of today do then? Applaud the accurate exegetical work done, of course, but reject the inaccurate and the incorrect, then study it out again and restate it. Sound doctrine suffers if the inadequate analyses and conclusions of the past are considered sacrosanct and thus protected from wise alteration, exegetically informed. Frankly, the millennial debate is at a stalemate, and nothing more can be said to move it forward. Revelation 20:1-10 still stands as the great divide between premillennialism and its two opponents, amillennialism and postmillennialism.

Usually, a reader bypasses a book's preface, but Dr. Erdmann's six-page preface should be read before starting into the informative content of the book. The time taken to read this study will certainly be no loss – it's worth it!

Preface

The millennium was a source of controversy during the first post-apostolic centuries; it has become even more so in later times. Ever since its Christian inception[1] by the pen of John, the author of Revelation, it has remained, and in all likelihood will remain, an exegetical battle field among theologians and church authorities.[2] At times the controversy was fought with a ferocity almost unimaginable today. At other times it has lost momentum and millennialism has become an accepted part of Christian eschatology. There was never a time, however, when millennialism has been universally accepted as a valid doctrine of the Christian Church. During the second and third century the Church party which rejected its validity was gaining in strength, until this party occupied a prominent place at the ecumenical council of Nicaea in A.D. 325. From then on the majority of Christians accepted an anti-chiliastic position for the next 1000 years.

Yet in the midst of a prevailing anti-chiliastic atmosphere in the fourth century, especially fostered by Augustine, Jerome, and Eusebius, there was always a minority who kept the teaching about Christ's future reign on earth alive. Although at times pushed against the wall and almost crushed, this group, nonetheless, asserted its legitimacy in the orthodox Church. It could not, however, prevent the final triumph of the anti-chiliastic elements in Christendom. Still, this triumph could not eclipse the fact that the outstanding characteristic of the patristic era was the Church's

---

1 Christian chiliasm has to be clearly distinguished from similar Jewish or Gnostic ideas. To prevent any confusion about the meaning of the particular terms used in this study, I will use the following terminology. "Chiliasm", "millenarianism", and "millennialism" are interchangeably used to mean "the Christian doctrine of a literal millennium", unless otherwise indicated. The expression "Golden Age" refers to the Jewish hope of the messianic times. The pagan idea of a blissful future is called "paradisal Age".

2 Although, in an academic setting, it might be preferable to quote the passages written by the Greek and Latin Church Fathers in their original languages, the author decided either to translate them or to provide English translations taken from standard reference works.

pronounced adherence to chiliasm. Most of the early Church Fathers anticipated the bodily resurrection of the righteous and the inauguration of a millennial kingdom at the Second Coming of Christ. This kingdom would last one thousand years and find its conclusion in the resurrection of the unrighteous, their judgment, and condemnation. God would then destroy the old order of things and usher in his eternal kingdom.

Critical theologians in the 19th and 20th century have contended that millennial ideas were introduced into the early Church primarily by the influence of Jewish apocalyptic literature on Christianity. They also have discussed the possibility of a pagan origin of some of these apocalyptic ideas. To a certain degree they have been able to substantiate their assumptions, inasmuch as Jewish and pagan converts to Christianity were acquainted with chiliastic speculations long before they espoused the Christian faith. The religious traditions of antiquity cherished ideas about a paradisiac Age which would be established on earth at a future time. That these ideas took on different forms, and were often perpetuated under the cloak of esoteric knowledge, did not prevent their wide-spread dissemination over the ancient world. It would be wrong to conclude, however, that the concept of a paradisiac Age originated exclusively in pagan mythology. On the contrary, the Jews developed their own millennial tradition apart from any other outside source. Although the contention of an exchange of similar concepts between pagan and Jewish traditions is certainly plausible, especially in the last pre-Christian centuries, it would be erroneous to understand the messianic hope of Judaism as derived exclusively from pagan origins. The whole thrust of pagan influence was probably never more than just a fanciful elaboration of the blissful condition during the Golden Age.

Considering the chiliastic tradition of the early Church Fathers it would appear doubtful that they deliberately appropriated elements of pagan mythology. It is, however, undeniable that their thinking was strongly imbued with apocalyptic ideas of Jewish origin which played a facilitating role in the development of Christian millenarianism. Therefore it is not difficult to understand why scholars such as J. A. MacCulloch believed that the Jewish concept of a messianic kingdom exercised more influence on the formulation of the chiliastic dogma than the writings of the apostles. MacCulloch expressed it thus:

> In spite of the fact that, save in the Apocalypse, the New Testament did not speak of the Millennium, and that Christ does not connect the Parousia with the establishment of an earthly Kingdom, this belief had an extraordinary hold on the minds of Christians. Doubtless a misunderstanding of the Apocalypse gave the belief a certain authority, but it is rather from its Jewish antecedents that its popularity and the elaboration of its details are to be explained.[3]

The most obvious example of a direct influence of apocalyptic literature on the millennialism of the Church Fathers can be seen in the description of the extreme fertility during the millennium. Irenaeus popularized the motif of the vine with ten thousand branches and clusters of ten thousand grapes, etc. on the authority of apostolic tradition. Papias, from whom Irenaeus might have heard this motif initially, attributed it even to Christ himself. Undoubtedly, however, its origin can be directly traced back to Jewish speculations about the abundance of vegetation at the time of the messianic kingdom.[4]

Yet regardless of the particular scholarly emphasis given to questions about the origin of the chiliastic material, millenarianism has remained a subject of controversy. Its ambiguous potential has generated an atmosphere of tension filled with strong emotions and convictions on either side of the controversy. Therefore anyone who is interested in the chiliastic debate during the patristic epoch will immediately be confronted with a diversity of different viewpoints. It

---

[3] J. A. MacCulloch, "Eschatology", in *Encyclopedia of Religion and Ethics*, vol. 5, J. Hastings, ed., Charles Scribner's Sons, New York, 1928, p. 388.

[4] Cf. *Apocalypse of Baruch* 29:5ff; *1 Enoch* 10:19.

could even be said that a certain controversial tone seems to underlay the patristic literature in general, because it was written by persons who had to formulate their belief against a background of a pagan culture. They contended with their pagan and Jewish neighbors for the superiority of their Christian faith. Moreover, they had to preserve the purity of the orthodox doctrines handed down to them by the Apostles against many heresies. As a result they became famous for their apologetic and polemic literary achievements. To study their writings, even in the 21th century, is still a rewarding exercise. Yet to limit oneself only to the study of the literature itself is to divorce the author's writings from the historical setting in which they were composed. To prevent such a purely analytical approach the historical context will have to play a prominent part in this study.

To assume that the Church Fathers were only slightly conditioned by theological currents and historical events, as they interpreted the millennial passage in Revelation, is to minimize the importance of other than purely exegetical aspects. In most cases the determining factors for the theological education of a particular Church Father were the place of his ministry and the people with whom he associated. Through the labors of Papias and Polycarp the Johannine influence was felt most pervasively in Ephesus, Hierapolis and other cities of Asia Minor, whereas Origen and Clement of Alexandria held sway over the minds of bishops and catechumens in the Egyptian metropolis, using mainly the philosophical categories of Platonism to interpret the Bible. During the patristic period there existed a fruitful interchange between the Eastern and the Western branches of the Church. Irenaeus, for example, was born in Smyrna, a prosperous city in Asia Minor. According to his own testimony, he sat at the feet of Papias and Polycarp in his early years. In later life he became the Bishop of Lyons and exerted a great influence on the Western Church. Although he had left the Eastern Church physically, he never did so mentally or spiritually. His mind remained firmly set in the Hellenistic culture and apostolic tradition, in spite of his confession that, after having lived in Lyons for many years, his use of the Greek language had became inefficient through conversing in a local dialect. Jerome, who compiled a list of all the early Greek and Latin Church Fathers, included his name among the former and called him a Chiliast.

In the course of time the Latin Church grew more and more in prominence. Its ascendancy progressed in succeeding centuries as the main centers of Christendom shifted from the East to the West. Tertullian, Hippolytus, and Gaius are some of the main characters who shaped the theology of the Western Church in the third century. All of them played an important part in the chiliastic controversy. In the fourth century the discussion of the millennium was taken up by Tychonius and Augustine. In all fairness to Augustine's genius, Tychonius was probably the more original of the two. His hermeneutical rules and biblical commentaries exercised a tremendous influence, not only on Augustine but also on many other Christian expositors in later centuries. Yet it was Augustine, much more so than his Donatist contemporary, who set the tone of orthodox theology by writing the single most influential literary work, *De civitate dei*. This masterpiece of post-Nicene theology marks a decisive break in the chiliastic tradition, in that it established amillennialism as the authoritative position of the orthodox Church.

To see how the historical and exegetical components conspired to bring about the gradual development of millennial ideas, it will be necessary to look first at the concept of the Golden Age in Jewish apocalyptic literature. In a further step we will assess different modern interpretations of the millennial passage in Revelation 20 and offer an extended exegesis of its first ten verses. Then we will look at the different principles of biblical interpretation used by the Church Fathers. This will be followed by a study of Asiatic chiliasm, the millennial concept of Justin Martyr and that of the *Epistle of Barnabas*. In the two concluding chapters we will analyze the dramatic change in the chiliastic debate which occurred in the Eastern Church under the theological auspices of Origen and Dionysius of Alexandria and in the Western Church under that of Augustine.

Abbreviations

Books of the Old Testament:

Gn.	Genesis
Ex.	Exodus
Lv.	Leviticus
Nu.	Numbers
Dt.	Deuteronomy
Jdg.	Judges
1,2 Sa.	1,2 Samuel
Ps. (Pss.)	Psalm(s)
Is.	Isaiah
Je.	Jeremiah
Ezk.	Ezekiel
Dn.	Daniel
Ho.	Hosea
Am.	Amos
Jon.	Jonah
Mi.	Micah
Zc.	Zechariah

Books of the New Testament:

Mt.	Matthew
Mk.	Mark
Lk.	Luke
Jn.	John
Acts	Acts
Rom.	Romans
1,2 Cor.	1,2 Corinthians
Gal.	Galatians
Eph.	Ephesians
Col.	Colossians
1,2 Thes.	1,2 Thessalonians
1,2 Tim.	1,2 Timothy
Heb.	Hebrews
1,2 Pet.	1,2 Peter
Rev.	Revelation

OT Apocrypha and Pseudepigrapha:

Jub. The Book of Jubilees (Pseudepigrapha)
1, 2, 3 Macc. 1, 2, 3 Maccabees (Apocrypha)
4 Macc. 4 Maccabees (Pseudepigrapha)
Sib. The Sibylline Oracles (Pseudepigrapha)
Syr.Bar. Syriac Apocalypse of Baruch or 2 Baruch (Pseudepigrapha)

Classical and Hellenistic Writers:

Josephus Flavius Josephus (c. A.D. 37-97)
    Ant. Antiquitates Judaicae (Jewish Antiquities)

Philo Philo of Alexandria (c. 50 B.C. - A.D. 45)
    Ebr. De ebrietate

Plato Plato (c. 427-347 B.C.)
    Rep. Respublica (The Republic)

Early Christian Writers:

Augustine Aurelius Augustinus (A.D. 354-430)
    Conf. Confessiones (Confessions)
    De civ. De civitate dei
    De doct. De doctrina christiana (On Christian Learning)
    Quaest. in hept. Quaestionum in heptateuchum libri VII

Chrysostom Chrysostom (c. A.D. 347-407)
    Hom. on John Homily on the Gospel of John

Clem. Alex. Clement of Alexandria (c. A.D. 150-213)
    Exc. Theod. Excerpta ex Theodoto
    Strom. Stromateis

Commodian Commmodian (mid 3rd cent., possibly 5th cent.)
    Inst. Instructiones
    Carm. Ap. Carmen apologeticum

Euseb. Eusebius of Caesares (c. A.D. 260-c.340)

Hist. Eccl. or HE . . . . Historia ecclesiastica
(Ecclesiastical History)

Hippol. . . . . Hippolytus (c. A.D. 170-c.236)

Philos. . . . . Philosophumena

Ire. Irenaeus of Lyons (c. A.D. 140-202)
    Haer. . . . . Adversus haereses (Against the Heresies)

Jerome . . . . Jerome (c. A.D. 342-420)
    Com. Zach. . . Commentariorum in Zachariam prophetam
    Epist. . . . . Epistolae

Justin . . . . Justin Martyr (c. A.D. 100-c. 165)
    Apol. I, II . . . . Apology, I,II
    Dial. . . . . Dialogue with Trypho

Lactantius . . . . Lactantius (c. A.D. 240-c.320)
    Div. Inst. . . . . Divinae institutiones

Methodius . . . . Methodius of Olypmus (d. c. A.D. 311)
    De Resurr. . . . . De resurrectione (About the Resurrection)
    Conv. . . . . Convivium decem virginum
(The Banquet of the Ten Virgins)

Origen . . . . Origen (c. A.D. 185-c.254)
    Comm. on Mt. . . . . Commentary on Matthew
    Contra Cels. . . . . Contra Celsum (Against Celsus)
    De prin. . . De principiis or Peri archon (On the Principal Doctrines)
    Hex. . . . . Hexapla
    Hom. . . . . Homilies
    Schol. . . . . Scholia

Tert. Tertullian (c. A.D. 160-c.220)
    Adv. Marc. . . . . Adversus Marcionem (Against Marcion)
    Adv. Val. Adversus Valentinianos (Against the Valentinians)

Periodicals, Reference Works, and Serials:

ANF	Ante-Nicene Fathers
HNT	Handbuch zum Neuen Testament
HTR	Harvard Theological Review
JAOS	Journal of the American Oriental Society
JBL	Journal of Biblical Literature
JETS	Journal of Evangelicl Theological Society
JQR	Jewish Quarterly Review
JTC	Journal for Theology and Church
MGWJ	Monatsschrift für Geschichte und Wissenschaft des Judentums
NPNF	Nicene and Post-Nicene Fathers
PG	Patrologia Graeca
PL	Patrologia Latina
RAC	Reallexikon für Antike und Christentum
RQ	Römische Quartalschrift für christliche Altertumskunde und Kirchengeschichte
RSR	Recherches de science religieuse (RechSR)
SJT	Scottish Journal of Theology
ThQ	Theologische Quartalschrift (TQ)
TWNT	Theologisches Wörterbuch zum Alten Testament
ZNW	Zeitschrift für die neutestamentliche Wissenschaft
ZThK	Zeitschrift für Theologie und Kirche (ZTK)

Table of Contents

Endorsements III

Dedication VII

Acknowledgements IX

Foreword XI

Preface XIII

Abbreviations xviii

1. Jewish Apocalyptic 2

    1.1. Introduction 2
    1.2. Origin of Jewish Apocalyptic 6
        1.2.1. Extra-biblical Influence on Jewish Apocalyptic 6
        1.2.2. Biblical Influence on Jewish Apocalyptic 10
    1.3. Differences between Prophecy and Apocalyptic 12
    1.4. Canonicity of Jewish Apocalyptic 15
    1.5. Characteristics of Jewish Apocalyptic 19
    1.6. Historical Milieu of Jewish Apocalyptic 21
    1.7. Message of Jewish Apocalyptic 23
    1.8. Relationship between Revelation and Jewish Apocalyptic 24
    1.9. Conclusion 27

2. Millennialism of John 32

    2.1. Introduction 32
    2.2. Survey of Millennial Views 36
        2.2.1. Amillennialism 37
        2.2.2. Postmillennialism 42
        2.2.3. Premillennialism 47
            2.2.3.1. Historical Premillennialism 49
            2.2.3.2. Dispensational Premillennialism 53
    2.3. Revelation 20:1-10 59
        2.3.1. Binding of Satan 59

	2.3.2. Controversy between Premillennialism and Amillennialism	65
	2.3.3. Judgment and Resurrection	73
	2.3.4. First Resurrection	76
	2.3.5. Release of Satan and Final Rebellion	83
	2.3.6. Satan's Final Judgment	88

3. Principles of Biblical Interpretation in the Early Church — 92

3.1.	Introduction	92
3.2.	Patristic Exegesis	93
	3.2.1. Christological Interpretation	93
	3.2.2. Spirit-Enlightened Interpretation	98
	3.2.3. Allegorical Interpretation	100
	3.2.4. Literal Interpretation	102
3.3.	Patristic Formulation of Dogmas	105
3.4.	Conclusion	106

4. Asiatic Millennialism — 110

4.1.	Introduction	110
4.2.	Characteristics of Asiatic Millennialism	113
	4.2.1. Original Sources	115
	4.2.2. Influence of Jewish Apocalyptic	116
	4.2.2.1. Application of the Adamic Millennium	120
	4.2.2.2. Seventh Day of the Cosmic Week	122
	4.2.3. Chiliastic Interpretation of Old Testament Prophecy	123
	4.2.4. Restoration of the Earthly Jerusalem	125
	4.2.5. Sensual Aspects of Asiatic Millennialism	127
	4.2.6. Thousand Years	130
	4.2.7. Millennialism of the Montanists	132
4.3.	Conclusion	134

5. Chiliasm of Justin Martyr — 138

5.1.	Introduction	138
5.2.	Millennium	140
5.3.	Conclusion	145

6. Chiliasm of the Epistle of Barnabas ... 148

- 6.1. Introduction ... 148
- 6.2. Authorship ... 149
  - 6.2.1. Content ... 149
  - 6.2.2. Date ... 152
- 6.3. Millennium ... 153
  - 6.3.1. Cosmic Week ... 154
  - 6.3.2. Sabbath of Rest ... 155
  - 6.3.3. Eighth Day ... 155
- 6.4. Conclusion ... 157

7. Anti-Millennialism of Alexandria ... 160

- 7.1. Introduction ... 160
- 7.2. Origen ... 161
  - 7.2.1. Introduction ... 161
  - 7.2.2. Allegorical Interpretation ... 162
  - 7.2.3. Aversion against Millennialism ... 163
  - 7.2.4. First and Second Resurrection ... 164
  - 7.2.5. Second Coming ... 165
  - 7.2.6. Origen's Influence on the Church ... 166
- 7.3. Dionysius of Alexandria ... 167
  - 7.3.1. Introduction ... 167
  - 7.3.2. Chiliastic Dispute ... 167
    - 7.3.2.1. Origin ... 168
    - 7.3.2.2. Intent ... 169
- 7.4. Conclusion ... 170

8. Amillennialism of Augustine ... 174

- 8.1. Introduction ... 174
- 8.2. Millennium ... 177
  - 8.2.1. Overview ... 177
  - 8.2.2. Second Coming of Christ ... 178
  - 8.2.3. First Resurrection is Spiritual ... 179
  - 8.2.4. Thousand Years ... 180
  - 8.2.5. Binding of Satan ... 184
  - 8.2.6. Abyss ... 185
  - 8.2.7. Devil's Short Release ... 186

8.2.8. Church Authorities govern the Church.	187
8.2.9. Church represents the Kingdom of Christ.	188
8.3. Conclusion	189

9. Conclusion ... 192

9.1. Principles of Biblical Interpretation in the Early Church	192
9.2. Asiatic Millennialism	195
9.2.1. Categorization of Revelation	195
9.2.2. Jewish Apocalyptic	196
9.2.3. Apocalyptic Influence on Asiatic Millennialism	197
9.2.4. Similarity of Modern Premillennialism with Asiatic Millennialism	198
9.3. Millennialism of John	199
9.4. Millennialism of Justin Martyr	202
9.5. Millennialism of the Epistle of Barnabas	203
9.6. Anti-millennialism of the Alexandrians	204
9.7. Amillennialism of Augustine	206
9.7.1. Modern Amillennialism	208
9.7.2. Modern Postmillennialism	209
9.7.3. Modern Premillennialism	210

Bibliography ... 213

Index ... 223

Chapter 1
Jewish Apocalyptic

1.1. Introduction	2
1.2. Origin of Jewish Apocalyptic	6
1.2.1. Extra-biblical Influence on Jewish Apocalyptic	6
1.2.2. Biblical Influence on Jewish Apocalyptic	10
1.3. Differences between Prophecy and Apocalyptic	12
1.4. Canonicity of Jewish Apocalyptic	15
1.5. Characteristics of Jewish Apocalyptic	19
1.6. Historical Milieu of Jewish Apocalyptic	21
1.7. Message of Jewish Apocalyptic	23
1.8. Relationship between Revelation and Jewish Apocalyptic	24
1.9. Conclusion	27

1. Jewish Apocalyptic

1.1. Introduction

The belief in an earthly kingdom of limited duration separated from the present era of human history by God's supernatural intervention in fulfillment of his promises to the nation of Israel has been expressed in Jewish apocalyptic long before John wrote the book of Revelation.[1] It was seen as the prelude to the final consummation of the eternal kingdom of God. Scholars have suggested that the concept of a glorious Age on earth was the result of a compromise between two competing eschatological viewpoints of Judaism.[2] The earliest form of these two different positions comprised the idea of a restored Davidic kingdom ruled from its capitol Jerusalem. Governed on the basis of a theocracy, this kingdom would encompass the whole world. Its king, as the direct representative of God, would subject

---

1 It might be helpful to the following general discussion about the apocalyptic literature to look at the different rendering in the English language of the Greek word "ἀποκάλυψις" ("apokalupsis") and its cognate verb "ἀποκαλύπτω" ("apokalupto"): 1. a divine revelation of certain supernatural secrets frequently through visions, e.g. Ps. 97:2; Dn. 2:19, 22, 28; Is. 56:1; Rom. 16:25; Gal. 1:12; 2. in the eschatological sense of the disclosure of secrets belonging to the last days, e.g. Rom. 8:19; 1 Cor. 1:7; 2 Thes. 1:7; 2:8; 1 Pet. 1:7, 13; 4:13; 3. to reveal (disclose, bring to light) e.g. Mt. 10:26; Lk. 12:2; Jn. 12:38, Rom. 1:17, 18; Commonly, however, the emphasis of "ἀποκάλυψις", as it is used in both the LXX and the New Testament, lies on its particular meaning of a supernatural unveiling of divine mysteries, especially as it relates to the unveiling of hidden truths about the kingdom of God to his people (primary source: Bauer, Arndt, Gingrich, *A Greek-English Lexicon of the New Testament*, 2 ed., The University of Chicago Press, Chicago, 1958).

2 Cf. Arthur S. Peake, *The Revelation of John*, Holborn Publishing House, London, 1921, p. 357, "It [Satan's short release] is found in Jewish theology and probably originated from a combination of the prediction in the prophets of an earthly Messianic Kingdom with the later conception of a heavenly kingdom. The combination was effected by making the earthly kingdom come first and the heavenly succeed it." Otto Böcher, in *Das tausendjährige Reich*, p. 136, believes that the account of two resurrections in the Apocalypse of John and *Syriac Apocalypse of Baruch* (*Syr. Bar.*) can be explained on the basis of these two different eschatological viewpoints of Jewish apocalyptic.

all nations under his authority. Mount Zion would then be indeed the center of the earth.

> In the last days the mountain of the Lord's temple will be established as chief among the mountains; it will be raised above the hills, and people will stream to it. Many nations will come and say, "Come, let us go up to the mountain of the Lord, to the house of the God of Jacob" (Mi. 4:1-2a; cf. Is. 2:2-3).

At a later stage, however, this earlier form was transformed into a vision of a transcendent kingdom. It would comprise in its universal dimensions not only the earth as the sphere of God's absolute domain, but also the outer parts of the universe itself. The combined realm of a renewed heaven and earth was perceived as the only suitable dimension of God's kingdom. Typically no set time limits, as to its duration, appear in written form at that stage. The authors simply thought that it would last forever, regardless of the particular type of kingdom they favored.[3] Connected with this later view was the belief of a general resurrection which would be followed by a universal judgment.[4]

The most popular form, however, in which the kingdom of God was conceived, was a combination of these two earlier versions. A mediating position was adopted by appropriating elements of the two earlier views, probably caused by a gradual infusion of dualistic concepts into the eschatological understanding of Judaism in the 2nd century B.C.[5]

---

3 R. H. Charles, in *The Revelation of St. John*, T. & T. Clark, Edinburgh, 1920, II, p. 142, referring to the earlier views of the Messianic Kingdom said it in this way: "Before the year 100 B.C. it was generally believed in Judaism that the Messianic Kingdom would last *for ever* on the present earth. Sometimes the conception was universalistic in character, especially in the greater prophets of the O.T., as Jeremiah, the Second Isaiah, Jonah, Malachi; but in others, as in Ezekiel, Haggai, Zechariah, Joel, it was particularistic. The idea of the everlastingness of this kingdom on earth persisted, as we have above said, till about 100 B.C. For such it appears to be in *1 Enoch* lxxxiii.-xc., vi.-xxxvi" (ital. his).

4 Cf. *I Enoch* 22:2-13; 45-54.

5 Gerhard von Rad, in *Old Testament Theology*, II, London, 1965, p. 301, said, "The characteristic of apocalyptic theology is its eschatological

The cleavage between the present age and the age to come, in the mind of the Jewish apocalyptists, directly affected their teaching of the kingdom of God. They resorted to a dual concept of a preliminary earthly kingdom which is followed by an eternal kingdom (*4 Esdra* 7:28f.). Apparently, it became no longer possible for them to express a unified idea about God's universal rule.

In agreement with the earlier view, they envisioned a world-wide theocratic kingdom. God himself would transform the old order of things and create paradisal conditions on earth. The evidence of his blessings, both in material and spiritual aspects, would be visible everywhere.[6] Yet, most significantly, its duration would be limited to a certain number of years[7], in most cases to an interval of one thou-

---

dualism." Some of the dualistic concepts which influenced Judaism are the following: a supernatural dichotomy between God and Satan as two antagonistic powers; two distinct ages (the present one which is temporal and evil was seen under the control of Satan and the future one which is eternal and good under the immediate government of God); two worlds (the first was perceived as this present, imperfect world, followed by a perfect world which existed already from eternity past in heaven, cf. *2 Esdras* 7:30; *I Enoch* 45:4f.; 91:16f.; "new creation" *I Enoch* 72:1); the present suffering was contrasted with the future salvation; evil spirits were set against good spirits; God's people against the pagans; light against darkness; etc.

6 Apocalyptic literature is filled with detailed speculations about the blessings which the righteous will enjoy during the millennium. The particular accounts about the paradisal conditions on earth are reminiscent of passages like Gn. 1-3; Ezk. 36:35; and 47:1-12. The blessings are: abundant fruitfulness of the vegetation (*I Enoch* 10:18f.; *Syr.Bar.*, 29:5; cf. Joel 4:18; Zc. 8:12) and of mankind (*I Enoch* 10:17); the longevity of mankind (*Jub.* 23:27; *Syr.Bar.*, 49f.; 73:3) and the great wedding banquet (*I Enoch* 62:14; *TestIsaac* 8:11,20; 10:12; cf. Is. 25:6-8; 65:13f.; Rev. 19:9); see also Paul Billerbeck, "Vorzeichen und Berechnung der Tage des Messias", in (Herman L. Strack und) Paul Billerbeck, *Kommentar zum Neuen Testament aus Talmud und Midrasch*, IV 2, Munich, (1928) 1978, pp. 880-968; 1154-1156.

7 In Jewish eschatology there are many different suggestions about the exact time span of the "last days" (7000, 4000, 2000, 1000 – see the following footnote –, 600, 400, 60 or 40 years). The author of the *Apocalypse of Baruch* was more cautious in his proposal stating that the last phase of world history will end after some time. The four hundred year reign of the Messiah in *4 Ezra* 7:28 is based on dubious literary evidence. Other manuscripts state alternative numbers of years, e.g. 30, 300, or even

sand years.[8] The author of the *Secrets of Enoch* (32:2; 33:1-2), for example, believed that the history of the world will last for seven thousand years. The Messiah will set up his earthly kingdom during the last millennium. The natural environment will be changed as a result of God's blessings. At its completion it will lead into an eighth millennium which will be eternity itself.[9] R. H. Charles commented succinctly on Enoch's view by saying:

> As the world was made in six days, so its history will be accomplished in 6,000 years, and as the six days of creation were followed by one of rest, so the 6,000 years of the world's history would be followed a rest of 1,000 years. On its close would begin the eighth eternal day of blessedness when time should be no more.[10]

Enoch seemed to represent the thought of many Jews in the second century B.C.

In agreement with the later view, this kingdom was understood as being part of God's universal reign, transcen-

---

1000 years. Cf. Bruno Violet, *Die Apocalypse des Esra und des Baruch*, vol. II, 1924, p. 74.

8 The interval of one thousand years as the duration of the messianic kingdom appears frequently in late Jewish literature. The Testament of Isaac (prior to A.D. 70) promises the righteous to be participants at the millennial celebration (10:12) and banquet (8:11, 20). Rabbi Eliezer ben Hyrkanos (about A.D. 90) expected a messianic kingdom which, according to Ps 90:15, will last for one thousand years (*MTeh 90 § 17 [197a]*).

9 Sometimes, as in *4 Ezra*, the end of the millennium and the beginning of eternity would be marked by the death of the Messiah.

10 R. H. Charles ed., *The Apocrypha and Pseudepigrapha of the Old Testament*, II, Oxford University Press, New York, 1913, p. 430; cf. Peter Schäfer, „Die messianischen Hoffnungen des rabbinischen Judentums zwischen Naherwartung und religiösem Pragmatismus", in Simon Lauer und Clemens Thoma, *Zukunft in der Gegenwart, Wegweisungen in Judentum und Christentum*, Bern, 1976, pp. 114-116; Alfred Wikenhauser, „Herkunft der Idee des tausendjährigen Reiches in der Johannes-Apokalypse", *RQ* 45 (1937), pp. 4f.; Paul Billerbeck, „Vorzeichen und Berechnung der Tage des Messias", in Herman L. Strack, and Paul Billerbeck, *Kommentar zum Neuen Testament aus Talmud und Midrasch*, III, Munich, (1926) 1979, pp. 826f, 844f; ibid., IV 2, pp. 969-976, 989-994; Eduard Lohse, "Chilias Chilioi", *TWNT* IX (1973), p. 457.

dent, and eternal. Apocalyptic writers portrayed the culmination of history not in this-worldly terms, but in a new heaven and a new earth. They envisaged two ages, this age and the age to come.

The most definite expression of this mediating view found its way into the Apocalypse of John (chap. 20:1-10). Yet, even today, it is disputed how far the Seer John stood in the tradition of his Jewish predecessors.

Before we direct our attention to the millennialism of John in chapter 3 it might be profitable to spend some time on a more extended study of Jewish apocalyptic. In the course of that study it will be necessary to look at the message of the apocalypses, especially if contrasted with prophecy. Other areas of discussion will be the origin and canonicity of Jewish apocalyptic, its characteristics and historical milieu.

1.2. Origin of Jewish Apocalyptic

1.2.1. Extra-biblical Influence on Jewish Apocalyptic

A comparative study of the Jewish apocalyptic and the apocalyptic texts of other religions has furnished evidence which, after careful consideration, led to the conclusion that the apocalyptic phenomenon which has influenced orthodox Judaism for many centuries could not be the exclusive product of Jewish imagination. Thus the possible links between the Jewish apocalyptic and other religious traditions have been a point of discussion in academic circles for years. The plausibility of a source-critical hypothesis postulating that Jewish apocalyptic was influenced by, or even originated from, the eschatological conceptions of Hellenistic syncretism and Eastern mysticism[11] has been suggested by some scholars. Mythological speculations about a one thousand

---

11 A. T. Olmstead, "Intertestamental Studies", in *JAOS* 56 (1936), p. 245, expressed the opinion that the "background for Jewish apocalyptic is found ... in pagan sources." The revised *Hastings Dictionary of the Bible*, 2nd ed., likewise finds an amalgam of various sources including myth: "In the apocalypse we thus can see a union of the symbolism and myths of

year period can be found in Greek mysticism: Plato taught that the departed souls of human beings would go on a journey for one thousand years after the judgment of the righteous and the unrighteous.[12] Vergil spoke of a purification of souls for one thousand years.[13] Plutarch recorded a passage from the historian Theopompos of Chios (about 378 B.C.), who referred to a belief of Iranian magi in a "short" (one thousand year period?), but very happy time of repose for all human beings in Hades which would be preceded by a three thousand year reign of God and an equally long time of general warfare.[14] H. D. Betz asserts that the parallels between the ideas and expressions of Hellenistic syncretism and Jewish apocalyptic have been underestimated. He believes that the Hellenistic influence on Judaism originated the apocalyptic phenomenon.[15] Leon Morris counters this argument by stating that

> it is more than doubtful whether he [Betz] has really shaken Rowley's position ["apocalyptic is the child of prophecy."]. The parallels he adduces are often so inexact that we need not postulate syncretistic Hellenism as the necessary background to the world of apocalyptic. It may well have given apocalyptic some of its forms of expression, but it has yet to be shown that it was in any real sense determinative.[16]

Pointing to a literary affinity, scholars, such as G. Widengren and A. Hultgard[17], argued convincingly for

---

Babylonia with the religious faith of the Jews, under the influence of Hellenistic culture."

12 Plato, *Rep.*, 614b-615b; 621d.

13 Vergil, *Aen.*, 6,748.

14 Felix Jacoby, *Die Fragmente der griechischen Historiker*, II, Berlin, 1929, p. 547f., No. 115, Fragment 65; cf. *4 Ezra* 8:53

15 *Journal for Theology and the Church*, no.6, 1969, p. 155.

16 Morris, *Apocalyptic*, pp. 30, 31.

17 Cf. G. Widengren, "Leitende Ideen und Quellen der iranischen Apokalyptik", in *Apocalypticism*, pp. 77-162; A. Hultgard, "Forms and Origins of Iranian Apoclaypticism", *Apocalypticism*, pp. 387-411.

mutual dependence of different types of apocalyptic traditions. Iranian apocalyptic literature has often been mentioned as the source and foremost influence of a dualistic world view on Judaism.[18] An explanation based on the hypothesis that the Jewish apocalyptic was strongly dependent on Iranian dualism in rethinking its concepts about the kingdom of God seems to offer good results. Conzelmann carried this idea to an extreme in asserting that the origin of the apocalyptic must be primarily seen in the Iranian religion.[19] Although his proposition might be overstated, it contains a grain of truth as the more moderate views of Widengren and Hultgard suggest. In contrast Leon Morris is hesitant to endorse even a moderate view unreservedly. Although he concedes the idea of a possible influence of Iranian dualism on the apocalyptic doctrine of the two ages, he disclaims any such influence on the recurring apocalyptic idea of the near end of the present age. He concludes that an influence of non-Jewish sources on the apocalyptic has been indisputably shown by many scholars, but this does not mean necessarily that its characteristic ideas are obtained by any such non-Jewish source.[20]

Strong reservations, however, were voiced at the Colloquium at Uppsala (1979) concerning an influence of Egyptian apocalyptic[21] on its Jewish counterpart.[22] K. Rudolph

---

18 Cf. A. S. Peake, "The Roots of Hebrew Prophecy and Jewish Apocalyptic", *JRLB*, Jan.1923, pp. 233-255, reprinted in *Holborn Review*, 1924, n.s., v.15, pp. 62-76. That Persian conceptions pertaining to cosmogony, angelology, demonology and eschatology penetrated into Judaism without affecting its fundamental development is recognized by J. Scheftelowitz, *Die Altpersische Religion und das Judentum*, Giessen, 1920.

19 H. Conzelmann, *An Outline of the Theology of the New Testament*, Harper and Row, New York, 1969, p. 23: "The most important problem from the point of view of the history of religion is that of the origin of apocalyptic Persian influence is determinative."

20 Leon Morris, *Apocalyptic*, Eerdmans, Grand Rapids, 1972, p. 31.

21 C. C. McCown, "Hebrew and Egyptian Apocalyptic Literature", in *HTR* 18 (1925), pp. 357-411, assumed Egyptian origin.

22 Cf. J. Assmann, „Königsdogma und Heilserwartung, Politische und kultische Chaosbeschreibungen in ägyptischen Texten", *Apocalypticism*, pp. 345-377; H. Ringgren, "Akkadian Apocalypses", *Apocalypticism*, pp. 379-386.

said at that meeting: "The only genuine apocalypse, other than that of the Jewish-Christian apocalypse, occurs in the ancient East, in Iran, in the form of Zoroastrian expectations of the end times."[23]

F. M. Cross shares the same sentiments, but attributes the appearance and development of the apocalyptic to the spiritual ferment of syncretistic mythodology in Judaism itself. He disassociates himself, therefore, from the opinion of Rowley who sees prophecy as the mother of apocalyptic and postulates his own theory about the influence of ancient Canaanite mythology on Jewish apocalyptic. He says,

> With the recovery of the Canaanite mythic and epic poetry, certain judgments about the character of apocalyptic syncretism must be modified. It has become vividly clear that the primary source of mythic material informing Jewish apocalyptic was old Canaanite mythic lore. This, of course, is not to dispense with all resort to Iranian, Mesopotamian, or Greek borrowings in describing the evolution of apocalyptic. It does mean, however, that many apocalyptic traditions go back through earliest Israel to Canaanite sources so that more continuities with the old biblical community must be recognized rather than fewer.[24]

The essential weakness of Cross's idea, as Morris shows, must be seen in the unanswered question, why we have to wait so long for the appearance of the apocalyptic, if it originated in the ancient Canaanite myth? Morris continues to say that "there is clearly more to the story than old Canaan. It is better to see apocalyptic as gathering in from many sources, both old and new, but as being basically of Jewish origin."[25]

---

23 K. Rudolph, „Apokalyptik in der Diskussion", *Apocalypticism*, p. 780: „Die einzige echte Apokalypse neben der jüdisch-christlichen bietet im alten Orient der Iran in Gestalt der zoroastrischen Enderwartungen." (English trans. mine).

24 F. M. Cross, in *JTC*, no. 6, 1969, p. 165 (ital. his).

25 Leon Morris, *op. cit.*, p. 33.

Indeed, the influence of religious sources outside a purely Jewish environment must always be seen with those within. The assertion that the latter played a major role in the emergence of the apocalyptic possesses certainly a degree of truth commending itself to our consideration.

1.2.2. Biblical Influence on Jewish Apocalyptic

If the various sources which might have influenced the Jewish apocalyptic are taken in due account, it still remains indisputable that the most prevalent influence came from the Hebrew Bible. Wisdom literature[26] seems to be a source of inspiration for the formation and development of Jewish apocalyptic. Jewish liturgy has also been an influential factor.[27] Scholars are in general agreement, however, that the most prominent characteristic of the apocalyptic is its appropriation of prophetic themes[28], which are then further developed into something quite different from the original source of inspiration. D. S. Russell came to the same conclusion after an extended discussion of several prophetic passages in the Hebrew Bible. He stated that these prophecies

> cannot be called "apocalyptic" in the sense that the name can be applied to books like Daniel and its successors, but it can be said that they contain the "stuff" from which apocalyptic is made – the notion of divine

---

26 Cf. Gerhard von Rad, *op. cit.*, pp. 314-321; Gerhard von Rad, *Weisheit in Israel*, Neukirchen, 1970, pp. 337-363; G. Hölscher, *Die Weisheit der Mystiker: Apokalyptik*, pp. 204-213.

27 W. Harnisch, „Der Prophet als Widerpart und Zeuge der Offenbarung. Erwägungen zur Interdependenz von Form und Sache in IV. Buch Esra", *Apocalypticism*, pp. 461-493, esp. p. 485.

28 The writings of the prophets were naturally the place where the Jewish apocalyptic literature had its earliest beginnings. Prophetic passages which anticipated the apocalyptic literature can, for example, be found in Is. 24-27; 65f; Ezk. 38f; Joel; Zc. 9; 12-14; vgl. H. Gese, *Anfang und Ende der Apokalyptik*, p. 205,221: „Die Nachtgesichte des Sacharja sind die älteste uns bekannte Apokalypse." P. D. Hanson, *Alttestamentliche Apokalyptik in neuer Sicht*, pp. 440-470,461: „Sacharja 9 ist ein weiteres Beispiel früherer Apokalyptik."

transcendence, the development of angelology, fantastic symbolism, cosmic imagery, the use of foreign mythology, reinterpretation of prophecy, the visionary form of inspiration, a distinctly literary form cataclysm and judgment, the Day of the Lord, the destruction of the Gentiles, the Coming of the Golden Age, the messianic deliverer and the resurrection of the dead. When at last the historical conditions for growth were right, these seeds rapidly grew into full flower in the colourful and diverse literature of Jewish apocalyptic.[29]

Indeed, the symbolic imagery of the apocalyptic was foreshadowed in many expressions of the prophetic writings.

Robert H. Mounce confirmed the correctness of Rowley's judgment that the "apocalyptic is the child of prophecy".[30] He maintained also that the influence at work in shaping this class of literature can be traced back, not only to Jewish but also to Christian sources.[31] If one holds that the apocalyptic ideas have been a product of foreign influences, it must be stated likewise that apocalyptic is essentially a Jewish phenomenon.[32]

---

29 D. S. Russell, *The Method and the Message of Jewish Apocalyptic*, SCM Press LTD, London, 1964, p. 91.

30 H. H. Rowley, *The Relevance of the Apocalyptic*, Association Press, London, (1944) 1963, p. 15.

31 R. H. Mounce in *The Book of Revelation*, Eerdmans, 1977, p. 19, called the Jewish/Christian origin of the apocalyptic a "stubborn fact".

32 A strong proponent of this thesis, S. B. Frost, summarized his view as follows: "In general, prophecy shifted its eschatological interest from the outworking of history to the end of time itself, and re-emerged as apocalyptic" (*Old Testament Apocalyptic*, Epworth, London, 1952, p. 83). Leon Morris, in his critic of Frost, charges him with inconsistencies: "Actually Frost is not fully consistent on this point, for he sometimes sees myth as basic (Frost, *op. cit.*, p. 76: 'Apocalyptic is the result of the eschatologizing of Semitic myth, or to put it more truly, the result of Hebrew eschatology expressing itself in terms of semitic myth.' Cf. ibid. p. 39, pp. 247f.) and sometimes he sees un-Hebraic elements as when he refers to 'the task of Hebrew-Babylonian synthesizing' and goes on to say, 'although the apocalyptic school flourished so strongly at the beginning of the Christian era, it was nevertheless always conscious of its exotic and alien origin' (ibid., p. 86)" (Leon Morris, *Apocalyptic*, p. 28).

Undoubtedly the apocalyptic literature was written for, and readily received by, Jewish and Christian communities. Its authors could easily relate to the religious sentiments of their target audience as they had been members of the same communities. Yet they had no ambition to be classed among the prophets of old. Constituting a new class of writers they created their own type of literature. In due time distinctive features in genre and content made their way into the apocalyptic literature. The prophetic message seemed to become a thing of the past. Rowley has not only become known for his views about the prophetic origin of Jewish apocalyptic, but also for his assertion about its clear distinctiveness from the prophetic literature. He called the unique character of the apocalyptic "a hardly disputable fact".[33]

1.3. Differences between Prophecy and Apocalyptic

The impact of those diverse influences on Judaism, as a religious system, and the alterations which it precipitated, especially in regard to its eschatological beliefs, are thus generally seen as one of the causes which led to the decline of prophetic literature in favor of apocalyptic. Although apocalyptic ideas were not completely absent from the mind of the prophets, they played always a minor role in their overall prophetic presentation. The predominance of the apocalyptic elements in the later Jewish literature must be seen as a further development of the eschatological understanding of the Jews.[34] Beckwith, in general agreement with other scholars[35], described the process of this transformation as a

---

33 H. H. Rowley, *op. cit.*, p. 15.

34 C. C. Rowland called this view of apocalyptic into question. In his book, *The Open Heaven* (1982), he dismissed on the basis of insufficient evidence the function of Jewish apocalyptic as a description of the world's transcendent future. In his opinion it serves only as a revelatory act of God's concealed control of human history in bringing about its intended future purpose on earth.

35 Cf. Lücke, *Einleitung in die Offenbarung des Johannes*, I; Hilgenfeld, *Jüdische Apokalyptik*, Baldensperger, *Messian-Apok. Hoffung, etc.*, 3rd ed., pp. 172ff., Bousset, *Jüdisch Apokalyptic und Judenthum*, pp. 230ff.,

development in which a universal and transcendental outlook appears as the principle characteristic instead of the national and earthly. While the expectations of both prophecy and apocalyptic center in a coming messianic era, that is, in a final era in which the kingdom of God will be established, the former conceives this kingdom chiefly in political and earthly aspects, the latter in those that are non-political and supernatural. The main interest of the one is mundane; of the other supermundane.[36]

In distinguishing further the differences between these two classes of Jewish literature, he pointed out that

in apocalyptic the principle factors of the eschatological hope are the advent of the coming age, spiritually perfect in contrast with this present age, hopelessly corrupt; the universal judgment, not of Jew and Gentile as such, but of the righteous and the wicked, not of men only but also of angels and spirits; the resurrection of the dead; the everlasting destruction of the power of Satan and his hosts; the superhuman Messiah reigning with God in a renewed heaven and earth; eternal life in the presence of God and the Messiah for the righteous, and for the unrighteous unending punishment in Gehenna.[37]

The apocalyptic message itself could take on bizarre forms of thoroughly symbolic content. Its frequent use of the most graphic language to describe the calamitous occurrences of the end times is one of its strongest characteristics. That is exactly where the genre of the apocalyptic eschatology diverges most noticeably from the literary form of the

---

Volz, *Jüdische Eschatologie*, pp. 4ff., Drummond, *The Jewish Messiah*, pp. 3ff., Porter, "Messages of the Apocalyptic Writers", in *Hast. Enc. Bib.* and the *Jewish Enc.*.

36 Isbon T. Beckwith, *The Apocalypse of John*, Baker Book House, Grand Rapids, Michigan, 1967, pp. 166, 167.

37 Ibid.

prophetical writings. If the latter had taken up, among other themes, the climactic grand finale of world history merging into the eternal kingdom of God, the former was exclusively interested in the cataclysmic unravelling of those events. To portray the eschatological consummation of world history in the form of visionary revelation was the all-consuming concern of the apocalyptic writers. Yet there was an even more fundamental distinction between these two schools of Jewish thought.

History, as it was understood by the prophets, was leading up to a final consummation. These visionaries were grounded in the past, lived in the present, and looked forward to the future. Hence their message was not purely a prediction of future events, but a "trumpet call" to turn "the house of Jacob" from sin and rebellion (Is. 58:1) and to incite them to righteous living (Is. 33:15). More than once they had to pronounce the impending execution of God's severe judgment, because the Israelites were not willing to heed the call for repentance (Is. 65:2-7). As this judgment came, the prophets were confronted with the plight of national disintegration during the Assyrian and Babylonian captivity. Yet, they had not lost hope in a restored national identity, preceded by a renewed spiritual awakening, and the return to the land of their ancestors. Therefore, the consequences of God's judgment on an apostate Jewish nation, forcing it to carve out an existence in exile away from its own native country, did not diminish the prophets' faith in God's promises of calling the Gentile nations to account for their treacherous acts against the Israelites. This was, however, only part of their message. The prophets were pointing to another universal judgment and future deliverance of the Jews from their dispersion among all the nations to be accomplished by the Messiah himself (Je. 23:5-8). His intervention on behalf of the exiled Israelites would be on a much bigger scale. He would bring them back from the four corners of the earth to the Promised Land (Is. 11:10-12) and establish his glorious kingdom (Is. 65:8-25). If the prophets were speaking about the future, it was with this hope of salvation for the nation of Israel in mind. Thus, their prophecies were firmly rooted on the basis of a unique relationship with a covenant-keeping

God who would fulfill his promises in the future just as he had done in the past. The prophetic literature, therefore, stands out as a monument of divine faithfulness, turning the fate of the exiled Israelites and re-establishing them as a religious community in the land of Palestine under divine blessing and authority.

The apocalyptists departed from this tradition of the prophets. They left the sound foundation of historical perspective and developed an eschatological philosophy instead. They did not entirely lose the prophetic character of their message inherited from the Hebrew Bible, but modified its form and content under the impression of different historical conditions and the influence of other spiritual conceptualizations. D. S. Russell shared this view when he wrote, "that apocalyptic is not a substitute for prophecy but a readaptation and development of the same message for a new historical situation – prophecy in a new idiom."[38]

The apocalyptists divested themselves from the past to dwell exclusively on a future epoch when God will intervene into this world's affairs and bring this age to a final culmination and judgment.

If the apocalyptic was different from, and yet similar to, the prophetic books a decision had to be reached in regard to its inspiration and authority. Was it a message given by divine revelation and thus constituting another portion of God's word, as the apocalyptic writers insinuated? Or was it only part of a particular collection of religious literature, profitable to read, but not to be taken too seriously? Its canonical value lay in the air and needed to be addressed.

1.4. Canonicity of Jewish Apocalyptic

D. S. Russell, in *The Method and Message of Jewish Apocalyptic*, pp. 37f., lists seventeen apocalyptic books: *The Book of Daniel* (canonical); *I Enoch* 1-36, 37-71, 72-82, 83-90, 91-108 (a composite work, with the oldest part written c. 120 B.C.);

---

[38] D. S. Russell, *op. cit.*, p. 92.

The Book of Jubilees[39]; *The Sibylline Oracles*, Book III, IV & V; *The Testaments of the Twelve Patriarchs*[40] (probably first century A.D., though others date them earlier; the apocalyptic parts are in the Testaments attributed to Levi and Naphtali); *The Psalms of Solomon*; *The Assumption of Moses* (written about the beginning of the Christian era); *The Martyrdom of Isaiah*; *The Life of Adam and Eve*, or *The Apocalypse of Moses* (of uncertain date; contains little apocalyptic); *The Apocalypse of Abraham*; *The Testament of Abraham*; *II Enoch*, or *The Book of the Secrets of Enoch*; *II Esdra* (= *4 Ezra*) (the best specimen of a theological apocalypse); *II Baruch*, or *The Apocalypse of Baruch* (dating from the beginning of the second century A.D.; though written originally in Hebrew or Aramaic it is preserved only in Syriac); *III Baruch* (all of them non-canonical).

As far as canonicity is concerned, preference was given to prophetic writings rather than apocalyptic. However, the explanation for this phenomenon does not lie in the differences of genre. These differences could not have been taken as the major criterion for the determination of canonicity of a particular book. Otherwise the *Book of Daniel*, with its close affinity to the apocalyptic literature, would, if judged exclusively on grounds of its literary genre, not have been included in the Hebrew Bible. In the final analysis the canonicity of a book must have been determined on other grounds than its literary genre. Generally, however, most of the apocalyptic literature was regarded as non-canonical, though not devoid of practical value in the religious experience of the Jewish community. Its reassuring message was that God had not completely abandoned them in their misery, and thus he would surely meet their spiritual and emotional need in due time.

In this context it should be noted that not all modern scholars agree about the particular attitude towards apocalyptic literature found among the Pharisees. R. H. Charles believed that in pre-Christian times the apocalyptic and

---

39 Charlesworth does not list the *Book of Jubilees* as apocalyptic.

40 According to Charlesworth the *Testaments of the Twelve Patriarchs* are only partially apocalyptic.

pharisaic wing of Judaism were not essentially antagonistic. In the first century A.D., however, so he continued, the apocalyptic elements were absorbed almost completely by Christianity. In his eyes the destruction of the temple marked the final turning point in the struggle about the predominance of the different sectarian groups among the Jews. Pharisaism had won the day and prevailed in suppressing all other factions.[41] Charles C. Torrey, another proponent of this view, saw an affinity in thought among Pharisaism and apocalypticism.[42]

Other scholars, however, have expressed themselves as very much opposed to any such consideration. George F. Moore, for example, saw it as "a fallacy of method for the historian to make them [the apocalypses] a primary source for the eschatology of Judaism, much more to contaminate its theology with them".[43] He also asserted that the apocalypses were not only ignored in the Tannaite literature, but many of the subjects with which they deal were foreign to it.[44]

At the outset there does not seem to exist any real basis of reconciling these contrary views with each other. However, the solution to this problem might lie in the simple suggestion of W. D. Davies. He proposes that the different pharisaical rabbis may have held various opinions about apocalyptic in much the same way as modern Christians differ in their attitude to the Second Advent of Christ.[45] This statement reiterated what he had said earlier in his book, "To deny the difference of emphasis in Apocalyptic and Pharisaism would

---

[41] R. H. Charles (ed.), *The Apocrypha and Pseudepigrapha of the Old Testament*, II, Oxford University Press, New York, 1913, p. vii.

[42] "The Jewish apocalyptic writings were not the property of any sect or school. Their point of view was in general that of Palestinian orthodoxy, of the type of which the Pharisees were the best representatives" (Charles C. Torrey, *The Apocryphal Literature*, I, Yale University Press, New Haven, 1948, p. 673). W. D. Davies shares the same opinion. He adduces considerations which "at least invalidate any complete differentiation of Apocalyptic from Pharisaism" (W. D. Davies, *Christian Origins and Judaism*, London, 1962, p. 25).

[43] George F. Moore, *Judaism*, I, Harvard, 1958, p. 127.

[44] Ibid.

[45] W. D. Davies, *op. cit.*, p. 29.

be idle, but it is grievously erroneous to enlarge this difference into a cleavage."[46]

His opinion has much to commend itself to us. The argument that no congenial sentiments were exchanged between the pharisaic and the apocalyptic segments of Judaism seems to be an overstated simplification of the complex situation. In fact, in accord with Davies, it appears reasonable to assume that the Pharisees were divided on the issue of apocalyptic. Some of them certainly expressed strong antipathetic feelings towards apocalyptic writings, whereas others must have held them in high esteem. Yet we are left in the dark about the proportional importance of either one of those factions within Pharisaism. The scarcity of literary evidence, supporting one view or the other, does not allow us to reach any final conclusion on this subject. However, in light of later developments in Jewish orthodoxy, it seems justified to concur with the opinion of Leon Morris that, "while some apocalyptic concepts still remain in the later Rabbinic literature, there can be no doubt but that as a whole it is antagonistic to all that apocalyptic stands for."[47]

That the apocalyptic was, almost entirely, excluded from the canonical writings of the Hebrew Bible, should not delude us in assuming that the study of its influence on Judaism and Christianity is only marginally relevant. One needs to keep in mind that it enjoyed much popularity among the Jews for nearly three hundred years influencing strongly the subsequent emergence of Jewish mysticism, most notably in the cabalistic tradition. In all likelihood it was influential in the composition of Revelation and thus extending its ideas and genre into the Christian era. This consideration, however, leads us to ask what type of literature the Jewish apocalyptic actually represented?

---

46 Ibid., p. 29.

47 Leon Morris, *op. cit.*, p. 15.

1.5. Characteristics of Jewish Apocalyptic

As it appears on the outset, the question about the type of literature is not easily answered. The more one tries to understand the nature of Jewish apocalyptic, the more one realizes that numerous problems present themselves. Modern scholarship has not yet come to a consensus about the essence of apocalyptic as a religious phenomenon.[48] Although F. Lücke's[49] initial attempt to determine the relationship of apocalyptic literature to prophecy and eschatology has been followed by many more extensive studies, a satisfactory understanding about its nature and genre has not yet been forthcoming. Modern scholars try to come up with a definition about the nature of the apocalyptic, which is as comprehensive and descriptive as possible. At the same time they are keenly aware of the inadequacy of any such definition, because the different elements which comprise this class of literature are too manifold and complex. H. Stegemann's attempt is representative of some other, more or less elaborate, formulations.

> Apocalypses are literary works, which in regard to content are recognized by the fact that they identify what they portray as "heavenly revelation", by means of which the whole work centers in the aspect of the "heavenly revelation".[50]

---

48 H. D. Betz, „Zum Problem des religionsgeschichtlichen Verständnisses der Apokalyptik", *ZThK* 63 (1966), p. 392, described the dilemma succinctly: „Was Apokalyptik ist, ist umstritten." H. Stegemann, „Die Bedeutung der Qumranfunde für die Erforschung der Apokalyptik", *Apocalypticism*, pp. 495-530, 526, affirmed Betz's opinion some years later when he said: „... daß sich bei dem Apokalyptik-Kolloquium in Uppsala 1979 hinsichtlich einer Definition dessen, was Apokalyptik sei, eine Einigungsmöglichkeit nicht einmal im Ansatz abgezeichnet habe."

49 F. Lücke, *Versuch einer vollständigen Einleitung in die Offenbarung Johannis und in die gesammmte apokalytische Literatur*, 1832.

50 H. Stegemann, „Die Bedeutung der Qumranfunde für die Erforschung der Apokalyptik", *Apocalypticism*, p. 495: „Apokalypsen sind literarische Werke, die inhaltlich dadurch gekennzeichnet sind, daß sie das in ihnen Dargestellte als 'himmlisch geoffenbart' ausweisen, wobei das gesamte Werk – inbesondere auch in seinem literarischen Rahmen – auf

Thus, any definition has to be further qualified by a list of specific elements of apocalyptic literature. Recent suggestions of those elements are: more or less cyclical understanding of history, prophecy about the end times, pessimistic perspective of the world, dualism, images of doom and salvation, esoteric knowledge about supernatural events in correspondence with revelations about the future and extraordinary visions, recorded in written documents, bizarre imagery.[51]

Jewish apocalyptic is further characterized by accounts of visual or oral revelations, which, by depicting scenes of heavenly journeys or dialogues, frequently employ symbols, metaphors, and pictures. These visions were, in most cases, delivered by a heavenly messenger, like an angel, and received by the authors themselves, or, at times, by persons closely associated with them. The authors were writing often under the cloak of a pseudonym in seeking to appropriate the spiritual authority of a religious predecessor for their own works. The authorship of the apocalyptic writings was often attributed to those great men of Jewish history, who like Abraham, Moses and Ezra, were held in such high esteem that supposedly anything coming from their pens would be regarded as being of high quality and divine origin. The deliberate use of this method by the apocalyptists has been explained in numerous ways. It has been described as a justifiable procedure in communicating a new message from God in a time when prophecy had ceased to exist and a strict adherence to the legal code had become the norm of Jewish orthodoxy.[52] Some scholars see it as a means of protection which the apocalyptists utilized for themselves to prevent any possible reprisals from the civil authorities; others, that

---

diesen Aspekt des 'himmlischen Geoffenbarten' abgestellt ist." (English trans. mine).

51 Cf. K. Rudolph, *op. cit.*, pp. 771-789.

52 Cf. R. H. Charles, *Religious Development Between the Old and the New Testament*, pp. 38-46; S. B. Frost, *op. cit.*, pp. 11f., 166f.; D. S. Russell objected to this explanation and said that the view of the "autocracy" of the law "cannot find any substantiation in fact" (*op. cit.*, p. 52).

it grew out of a heightened interest in Jewish history. Probably all those factors played a role to a certain degree.

The uniqueness of a particular type of literature can often be traced back to the penetrating atmosphere of a special historical milieu. For three hundred years the Jewish nation experienced a continuous drama of oppression and warfare which produced a climate of religious fanaticism and mystical imagination. Thus the emergence of Jewish apocalyptic must be seen against the background of political oppression and religious persecution.

1.6. Historical Milieu of Jewish Apocalyptic

Several events of momentous significance in Jewish history churned up religious turmoil. As the Seleucid domain expanded southward the Jews lost once more their national autonomy. Palestine came under the authority of Antiochus III (223-187 B.C.) after his victory over the Egyptians in 198 B.C. As soon as Antiochus (Epiphanes) IV (175-163 B.C.), his son, succeeded to the throne of Syria (1 Macc. 1:10; 6:16), he tried to impose his Hellenistic culture and religion on the Jews. The Seleucid king forbade circumcision and authorized the destruction of all the scrolls of the Hebrew Bible. The Jews despised the imposition of a pagan culture, imbued in idol worship, on their own religious life, especially after Antiochus IV had committed the ultimate sacrilege by sacrificing a pig on the altar in Jerusalem. In 168 B.C. they began to revolt against their oppressors. After a few months of guerrilla warfare, the insurrection was led by the three remaining sons of the priest Mattathias who had started the revolt. These outrages developed into the Maccabean war in which the Syrian armies were repeatedly defeated by Judas Maccabeus. In 143 B.C. the Jews regained their political autonomy only to lose it again to the conquering Romans some decades later. As the temple and the city of Jerusalem were destroyed by the Roman emperor Titus in A.D. 70, the *Apocalypse of Baruch* and *Fourth Esdras* were written with the expressed purpose of consoling the despondent Jews at the moment of extreme national calamity. Thus, the element of hope, expressed in apocalyptic, became one of its most dominating features. It infused new strength into the national bloodstream of the Jews. At the moment of utter defeat, they were told to persevere and wait for a speedy deliverance to be accomplished, not by any human means, but by divine intervention. Despite its glaring irrationality, the Jews readily embraced the prospect of a sudden change of their desperate situation. Apocalyptic literature offered them an emotional panacea which enabled them to endure their existence. Their eager receptivity of anything which promised them inner relief and a bright future, possibly realized in their own life-time, showed, all too clearly, the suggestive power inherent in apocalyptic literature. Its potency to arouse mass-excitement, instead of being diminished, proved to become only stronger in the inevitable case of delayed fulfillment.

To a modern observer this seems to be more a case of collective escapism, into a dream world of national vengeance and exultation, than an expression of faith against all odds.[53] Although modern scholarship might be able to discover a hidden, possibly unconscious, motive behind this type of literature, amounting to nothing but a collective longing of the Jewish nation to see the prophetic promises being fulfilled in the most extravagant manner, there is no clear evidence in the literature itself which would give reason to suspect any ulterior motive on the side of its authors. The mere thought that apocalyptic literature originated only in the minds of their alleged authors, as the outgrowth of wishful thinking and a deep longing for the realization of God's final triumph over the powers of evil, would be very far from a Jewish mind. At least Julius Wellhausen, as a representative

---

53 The spiritual and political consequences of such hope inspiring literature must be seen and evaluated on the basis of its effects on later Jewish history. Although such an evaluation would exceed the bounds of this chapter, it would be interesting to research the possible influence of apocalyptic ideas on the political aspirations and subsequent tragedy of a Bar-Kochba in A.D. 132 and other pseudo-Messiahs who followed him (i.e. Abu Isa of Ispahan in the seventh, Zonarias of Syria in the eighth, and Saadya ben Joseph in the tenth or Sabatani Zevi in the seventeenth century).

of an older critical school, expressed his opinion in favor of this particular viewpoint.[54]

Far from being deluded demagogues the apocalyptists saw themselves as the messengers of God, charged with the responsibility to communicate his divine thoughts about the destiny of the Jewish nation. God's hidden plan of history was delineated in these apocalyptic writings, culminating in the impending destruction of the oppressive pagan empire and the redemption of the Jews from all their afflictions[55].

1.7. Message of Jewish Apocalyptic

Apocalyptic literature belongs to a type which was once the most popular form of expressing pious sentiments among Jewish writers. Today most scholars argue that the introduction of a heightened eschatology into Judaism was caused by the tendency among Jewish writers to delineate history as a gradually intensifying struggle between the forces of good and evil culminating in the climactic finale of God's ultimate victory and his subsequent universal dominion over all creation.

In general, the apocalyptic attempted to formulate symbolically the unfolding of eschatological events. If at the beginning of the second century B.C. apocalyptic writings had just come in vogue, they had become very popular in the Jewish literary market at the close of the first century A.D. Mirroring their spiritual sentiments, the Jews interpreted these visionary "revelations" as the descriptive progression of God's future intervention in human history on their behalf. More so, these visions portrayed graphically the substance of their nationalistic hope. Despite the present reality of tribulation and suffering, they would be delivered by a direct act of God. The Almighty would defend their cause, defeat their adversaries, and subsequently establish his everlasting kingdom. Yet, the visionary nature of the

---

54 Julius Wellhausen, „Zur apokalyptischen Literatur", *Apokalyptik*, pp. 58-66.

55 Cf. Dn. 7:2-27.

apocalyptic language and the symbolic descriptions of how the culmination point of history would be reached militated against any attempt of a literal interpretation. If prophetic writings possessed still certain concreteness, at least in their core message, pointing to a corresponding contemporary or future event, this quality was almost, but not completely, lost with the symbolic words and figures of speech of apocalyptic literature. Thus its figurative form of expression could assume, at times, rather dramatic features, often couched in vivid and colorful concepts of the most imaginative kind.

The apocalyptic tradition was perpetuated in its Christianized form in the book of Revelation. Its author must have been an expert on Jewish apocalyptic, as his use of apocalyptic imagery suggests. However, he also demonstrated the resourcefulness of his mind in that he composed a piece of literature which exhibited numerous examples of originality.

1.8. Relationship between Revelation and Jewish Apocalyptic

The Apocalypse of John is usually classified as part of apocalyptic literature. Yet, in light of what is known today about the apocalyptic literature, is this classification really justified?

In the past, scholars have vacillated between two extreme positions. At one time it was confidently affirmed that any possible dissimilarities did not affect the categorization of the Apocalypse as being genuinely apocalyptic. The proponents of this position have argued that the book's very name "Apocalypse" is indicating the nature of the book.[56] More so, the book of Revelation shares almost all the characteristics of that particular genre which makes the Jewish apocalyptic so unique. It was argued that only in minor details does Revelation differ from any other apocalyptic composition. These differences were accounted for by asserting that they had been the product of a creative mind, exer-

---

56 As indicated above, "apocalypse" is a derivation from the Greek word "ἀποκάλυψις", which occurs in the opening verse of Revelation.

cising a legitimate amount of freedom in composing an original piece of literature within the bounds of the apocalyptic genre.[57]

At other times, however, scholars have contended just as vehemently for a position which perceives the Apocalypse as a category of its own.[58] It is seen as related to, but not organically connected with, any other apocalyptic literature. Naturally not every scholar was completely satisfied with either of these positions. To take a fixed position at either end of the scholarly spectrum was not regarded as a fortunate development in this discussion. The expression of a moderate viewpoint, paying due attention to the strengths and weaknesses of the two opposing positions, was perceived as a necessity. It was argued that a one-sided answer would not be sufficient to account for all the unique characteristics of the Apocalypse. Finally a compromise was reached in equally emphasizing both the similarities and dissimilarities in the attempt to study the relationship between the Apocalypse and the Jewish apocalyptic as objectively as possible. In fact, most scholars today are convinced of the advantages of this mediating position, although, as they readily concede, it does not provide a fully satisfying answer to the problem of categorization. This debate among scholars indicates, moreover, that the Apocalypse of John is not as easily classifiable as it seems on the outset.

There are, however, enough similarities between the Apocalypse of John and its Jewish counterparts to group

---

57 Leon Morris, in *Apocalyptic*, alluded to this group of scholars by saying "we must give attention to the last book of the New Testament, for Revelation above all others is confidently hailed as a typical example of apocalyptic" (p. 91).

58 Jürgen Roloff, in *Die Offenbarung des Johannes*, preferred the "category of its own" solution. He wrote the following: „Aber ist die Offenbarung wirklich der Gattung der Apokalypsen zuzurechnen? Diese Frage, so überraschend sie zu nächst klingen mag, ist berechtigt. Es zeigt sich nämlich, daß sie im Rahmen der gesamten apokalyptischen Literatur des Judentums und frühen Christentums eine *Sonderstellung* einnimmt" (p. 13). "Nach alledem fällt es schwer, die Offenbarung der Gattung der Apokalypsen zuzurechnen. Auch wenn sich zahlreiche apokalyptische Stil- und Formelemente in ihr finden, wird man urteilen müssen, daß diese nicht eindeutig genug ausgeprägt sind, um die alleinige Grundlage für die Gattungsbestimmung des Buches liefern zu können" (p. 15).

them both together under one heading. Enough literary evidence can be marshalled to prove undoubtedly an existing affinity.

An account of similarities in respect to the millennium is certainly the most important consideration in light of our study objective. For this purpose a summary of the *Syriac Apocalypse of Baruch* might help convey the most basic ideas about the messianic kingdom on earth as perceived by the Jewish apocalyptists. Its message can be summarized as follows: At first a divine judgment occurs (*Syr.Bar.*, 24-28); followed by the appearance of the Messiah, but only for a short time (*Syr.Bar.*, 29); he will return to heaven again (*Syr. Bar.*, 30:1a); the righteous will come to life in a partial resurrection (*Syr.Bar.*, 30:1b-3); while the godless people who still remain will find their doom (*Syr.Bar.*, 30:4f.); Jerusalem will be rebuilt (*Syr.Bar.*, 32:2), but shortly afterwards destroyed once more (*Syr.Bar.*, 32:3a); finally it will be reconstructed, most gloriously, to exist for all eternity[59] (*Syr.Bar.*, 32:4); the righteous will participate in the world wide government of the Messiah, which is preceded by a general, universal resurrection and the subsequent judgment of the world (*Syr.Bar.*, 39:7-40:3); at last, salvation will be the lot of the pious, torment that of the wicked (*Syr.Bar.*, 50:2-52:7).[60]

---

[59] The belief that the New Jerusalem will descend from heaven to earth in the "days of the Messiah," as it is expressed in *4 Ezra*, occurs in the apocalyptic literature only sporadically. This stands in contrast with the vast amount of Christian literature describing this event. Often it appears in the form of an exposition of Revelation 20. Cf. R. H. Charles, *The Revelation of St. John*, vol. II, pp. 144-180. Usually the Jewish rabbis taught that the earthly Jerusalem will be rebuilt in unimaginable splendor. The temple will be the prominent building in the city. At a later period, however, it was believed that the temple will be superfluous in Jerusalem during the messianic era, because sin would not exist anymore.

[60] Other symbols which can be found in common between the Apocalypse of John and Jewish apocalyptic literature include the following: a woman, representing a people (chap. 12) and a city (chap. 17); horns, speaking of authority (5:6; 12:3; 13:1; 17:3; etc.); eyes, signifying understanding (1:14; 4:6; 5:6); trumpets, representing a superhuman or divine voice (1:10; 8:2; etc.); white robes, portraying the glory of the world to come (6:11; 7:9, 13, 14; 22:14); and crowns, indicating dominion (2:10; 3:11; 4:10; etc.); the symbolic use of colors (white = victory; purple = kingship; black = death), number (seven = fullness or perfection; twelve = the eschatological perfection of the people of God; four = the visible world),

The dissimilarities, however, are just as pronounced and numerous. A simple comparison of the respective texts would suffice to substantiate this view. The similarities exist basically in more general ideas about an earthly messianic kingdom, but the accounts differ in detail.

In general the Apocalypse stands apart from the other apocalyptic writings in a number of ways. First, it is not pseudonymous. We know that its author was John (Rev. 1:1, 4, 9; 22:8). He is not interested to pose as somebody else, as if his book needed the endorsement of an illustrious name to appear as a revelation from God.[61] Second, it contains no revelations of the mysteries of cosmogony, astrology, or the unfolding of ancient history since the beginning of the world. Third, it offers a specifically christological conception of history.

1.9. Conclusion

As the Old Testament period was coming to an end the specific feature of the religious life of the Jewish community underwent a noticeable change. The characteristic prophecy of the Old Testament became gradually less important until it gave way to a related element of apocalyptic, which, although not completely unknown to the Hebrew prophets, played a much less significant part in their writings than it did among later Jewish authors. Reacting against the atmosphere of a repressive domination by a Gentile nation, the general tone of the Jewish literature altered to exhibit increasingly cataclysmic features. Its tone reflected the anxiety and hope of the Jewish nation. Constantly forced to

---

horn symbolizing power, angels (mentioned sixty-seven times) and visions (fifty-four times) also link the Apocalypse with the apocalyptic tradition.

61 Leon Morris gave a good answer to the objection that John was the name of one of the greatest of Christ's disciples by saying, "that the author of this book makes no attempt to indicate that it is that John and not another that is in mind. He says nothing at all about being an apostle. While it is open to any student to argue or assume that the two are identical, the point is that our author makes no claim equivalent to those in the apocalyptic writings" (*Apocalyptic*, p. 93).

assert themselves against despotic powers and religious upheavals, the Palestinian Jews were exposed to the most turbulent convulsions of historical forces. These forces were of such magnitude that the ensuing changes left a lasting mark on their religious conceptualization about the ultimate destiny of the world and of themselves, as the chosen people of God.

The Jews were challenged by a set of historical-theological problems which, as George E. Ladd has shown, are mainly responsible for the formulation of apocalyptic literature. They can be summarized as follows: (1) the emergence of a "righteous remnant" who maintained loyalty to the law over against the prevailing mood of compromise; (2) the problem of evil in the sense that even when Israel was apparently keeping the law she was undergoing suffering and national abuse; and (3) the cessation of prophecy at the very time when the people needed a divine explanation for their historical plight.[62] The purpose of apocalyptic literature was intended to provide an answer to those vexing questions and pressing problems. Why were the righteous still living in a world of suffering, why was the promised Golden Age not yet in sight?

The apocalyptists pointed out that the troubles of the present age were transient, a passing mode of life which would be followed by a Golden Age on earth. Thus the apocalyptic was understood by the Jews as a promise of an imminent reality of deliverance, awaited anxiously for its historical actualization.

The conviction grew among them that the cataclysmic end of world history would come about in two stages. In the first act of this eschatological drama God would unleash his wrath on the Gentile nations as the due punishment for their treacherous treatment against his chosen people. In the second he would publicly vindicate the Jewish nation in the sight of all other nations by declaring it to be the most eminent among them all. The wrongs which have been afflicted on the Jews would be judged and rectified by God

---

62 George E. Ladd, "Apocalyptic, Apocalypse", in *Baker's Dictionary of Theology*, pp. 50-51.

himself. Hence the Jewish apocalyptic is both pessimistic and optimistic in its intention and purpose. It draws a true, but dark, picture of humankind in its impotence to avert the manifestation of injustice in its many forms, and its subjection to the sufferings injustice brings.[63] But the Jews are not left in despair about the final outcome of this struggle of light and darkness. God will not abandon his people to the destructive forces of evil. Righteousness will triumph at the end. Thus the bright light of hope is embedded in this promise of deliverance and redemption. God will directly intervene into the affairs of mankind in such a way that evil, in its many forms, will be rooted out in a catastrophic scenario in which righteousness and justice will ultimately prevail. Frequently, but not always, this deliverance is associated with the appearance of the Messiah who would inaugurate the visible manifestation of God's kingdom on earth.

After having looked at the concept of the Golden Age in Jewish apocalyptic we will continue our study with an assessment of different modern interpretations of the millennial passage in Revelation 20 and offer an extended exegesis of its first ten verses.

---

[63] Schmithals, in *The Apocalyptic Movement* (p. 21), writes, "The apocalyptist meets this present age with radical pessimism. The world is on a downward course and cannot be halted."

Chapter 2
Millennialism of John

2.1. Introduction ... 32
2.2. Survey of Millennial Views ... 36
   2.2.1. Amillennialism ... 37
   2.2.2. Postmillennialism ... 42
   2.2.3. Premillennialism ... 47
      2.2.3.1. Historical Premillennialism ... 49
      2.2.3.2. Dispensational Premillennialism ... 53
2.3. Revelation 20:1-10 ... 59
   2.3.1. Binding of Satan ... 59
   2.3.2. Controversy between Premillennialism and Amillennialism ... 65
   2.3.3. Judgment and Resurrection ... 73
   2.3.4. First Resurrection ... 76
   2.3.5. Release of Satan and Final Rebellion ... 83
   2.3.6. Satan's Final Judgment ... 88

2. Millennialism of John

2.1. Introduction

A purposeful plan underlies the literary fabric of Revelation. Its message can be divided up into seven visions.[1] From the first vision to the last, the book of Revelation develops into a well-rounded prophetic picture of the end times. If this book begins with a vision of the exalted Christ, a supernatural encounter which only John was entitled to experience, it is brought to a close by a vision of God living amongst his glorified saints in the New Jerusalem.

In the seven letters to the churches of Asia Minor, God is admonishing, comforting and judging his Church by emphasizing their distinctiveness from the world as the recipients of his divine promises. The most comforting message of Revelation is its assurance of God's sovereignty. His decrees and purposes will be fulfilled as outlined in his word. As the King of kings (Rev. 19:16; cf. 1:5b), he can exact his will over any power which braces itself against his authority.

In chapter 4 John commences his account of the things "which will take place later" (cf. Rev. 1:19). As Beckwith said, "the writer now passes to that future with the persons and forces working within it."[2] The vision which begins here lays the foundation of all those which will follow. Heaven is

---

[1] These seven visions can be grouped together as follows: 1. Inaugural Vision and Seven Letters to the Churches (chs. 1:9-3:22); 2. Heavenly Courtroom Vision and Seven Seals Vision (chs. 4:1-8:1); 3. Seven Trumpets Vision (including the Vision of the Angel, the Temple and the Two Witnesses (chs. 8:2-11:18); 4. Birth of the Male Child; the Fight with the Dragon; the Beast from the Sea and False Prophet (chap. 12:1-14, 20); 5. Seven Bowl Plagues (chs. 15:1-16, 21); 6. Vision of the Fall of Babylon (chs. 17:1-19:10); 7. Vision of the Final Victory and the New Jerusalem (chs. 19:11-22:5); There are numerous other possibilities of outlining the content of Revelation (cf. G. R. Beasley-Murray, *The Book of Revelation*, Eerdmans, Grand Rapids, Mich., 1974, p. 32; I.T. Beckwith, *The Apocalypse of John*, Baker Book House, Grand Rapids, 1967 (1919), pp. 255-295; R. H. Mounce, *The Book of Revelation*, Eerdmans, 1977, pp. 47, 48).

[2] I. T. Beckwith, *op. cit.*, p. 261.

revealed to John as a magnificent court. God is seen sitting on his throne surrounded by heavenly beings. His appearance is likened to the preciousness of jasper and carnelian. A rainbow, resembling an emerald, is encircling his throne (Rev. 4:3). As the creator of all things (Rev. 4:11), God is being worshipped day and night in all his splendor and glory (Rev. 4:8). Flashes of lightning, rumblings, and peals of thunder are proceeding from the throne (Rev. 4:5).

In chapter 5 the Lion of the tribe of Judah (Rev. 5:5) is seen standing in the center of the throne of God. He is also portrayed as the Root of David and the Lamb (Rev. 5:6). The one being thus described is unmistakably Jesus Christ himself. His presence inspires the four living creatures and the twenty-four elders to adore him. By his death he has purchased "men for God from every tribe and language and people and nation" (Rev. 5:9). The redeemed are made into a kingdom of priests and are entitled to reign on the earth (Rev. 5:10).

The opening of the first seal in chapter 6 marks the beginning of terrible judgments executed progressively on a guilty world. In another scene, an angel, coming up from the east, carries the seal of God in his hand (Rev. 7:2). He puts it on the forehead of the 144,000 servants of God. They are representatives of all the tribes of Israel (Rev. 7:4). After this John sees a great multitude from every nation standing before the throne and the Lamb. He is told by an elder that "these are they who have come out of the great tribulation; they have washed their robes and made them white in the blood of the Lamb" (Rev. 7:14).

The opening of the seventh seal in chapter 8 marks a decisive break in the narrative. A new series of visions is introduced, beginning with the seven trumpet judgments. They are preceded by half an hour of silence in heaven. Terrible judgments are executed on the earth following the sounding of the seven trumpets (Rev. 8:6-9:21).

The vision of the mighty angel with the little scroll lying in his hand opens up another chapter of this book. John is commissioned to prophesy again (Rev. 10:11). In chapter 11 he is asked to measure the altar, the temple, and the temple court with a measuring rod. He is prohibited, however, from measuring the outer court of the temple. An angel tells him that Jerusalem will be trampled down by the Gentiles for 42 months (Rev. 11:1ff.). During a three and a half year period two witnesses of God appear on the scene. Their prophetic ministry brings upon them the deadly wrath of the beast of the Abyss. After they have been put to death, they are refused burial and triumphantly exhibited to the inhabitants of the world. Only three and a half days later God raises them back to life again and they ascend to heaven (Rev. 11:7-12).

In chapter 12 John paints a bizarre picture of a woman in labor pains and an enormous red dragon. God snatches away the new-born child to heaven before it can be assaulted by the dragon. The woman flees to a secure place in the desert to await the end of 1260 days. The dragon, who is unable to harm her, persecutes the rest of her offspring. Hurled down to the earth by the angel Michael, Satan knows that his doom is approaching soon. With renewed energy he pursues his evil plans (Rev. 12:12c).

In that critical moment a beast is coming out of the sea (Rev. 13:1, 11). This creature is empowered by Satan to rule over the whole world (Rev. 13:4). Later it is joined by another beast coming out of the land. Bewildered by the irresistible power of the first beast and the miracles of the second, the inhabitants of the earth worship Satan and the beast.

The scene, however, changes drastically in the following chapter. John sees the Lamb and 144,000 of his saints standing on Mount Zion. God, in his mercy, offers one last chance for repentance. An angel proclaims the eternal gospel to all the people on earth (Rev. 14:6). As this universal proclamation of the gospel (Rev. 14:7) remains seemingly unheeded, at least by the greater part of mankind, another series of severe judgments follows. Seven bowls of God's wrath are poured out upon the earth and its population.

Ugly and painful sores break out on the people (Rev. 16:2). The rivers and the springs of water are turned into blood. At this moment of horror the angel who is in charge of the waters proclaims (Rev. 16:5, 6): "You are just in these judgments, you who are and who were, the Holy One, because you have so judged for they have shed the blood of your saints and prophets, and you have given them blood to drink as they deserve" (Rev. 16:5, 6).

A little later we see mankind, writhing in agony, scorched by the intense heat of the sun. In their sinfulness they still refuse to repent of their wicked deeds. Instead, they curse the God of heaven for their pains and sores (Rev. 16:10, 11; cf. 16:9; 9:21). These cataclysmic events seem to approach a final climax. John describes graphically the destruction of Babylon, the great prostitute (Rev. 14:8; 17; 18; 19:2). In his sovereignty God uses the powers of evil to judge the adulterous city that rules over the kings of the earth (Rev. 17:17, 18). In one hour Babylon has been reduced to smoking ruins. The stage is now free for Christ's Second Coming. He returns with his saints to earth in order to subdue the remaining powers of evil. The beast and the false prophet are captured and thrown into the lake of fire. Satan is bound and cast into the Abyss. This last event marks the beginning of the millennium, the glorious manifestation of God's kingdom on earth. The true King sits on the throne and governs the affairs of the world. The martyred saints are resurrected and reign with Christ for one thousand years (Rev. 20:4).

At the end of this epoch Satan is released from the Abyss once more and allowed to deceive the nations. In revolt against Christ's authority these rebellious nations march against Jerusalem only to meet their doom. Finally Satan is judged and thrown into the lake of fire (Rev. 20:10).

With the completion of the millennium, God will create a new heaven and a new earth. Death, sin and sickness will not exist anymore (Rev. 21:4). God will reside forever with his people in the New Jerusalem (Rev. 22:5). The book of Revelation closes with a benediction on God's people (Rev. 22:20b, 21): "The grace of the Lord Jesus be with God's people."

Before we can begin with interpreting Rev. 20:1-10, a preliminary study will have to be made about the different millennial views in general.

2.2. Survey of Millennial Views

The dispute about the correct interpretation of the first ten verses of Rev. 20 has been going on for a very long time. These verses constitute the core passage of the controversy raging about the precise nature of the millennium. The difficulties are compounded by the fact that certain truths, such as the temporary binding of Satan (20:2) and his final doom (20:10), do not appear in any other parallel passage of the Bible. At least in the New Testament there is no additional description of the millennium as the period of Christ's reign on earth with his resurrected saints.[3]

Conflicting interpretations have been put forward by amillenarians, postmillenarians, and premillenarians[4], using these verses as the basis for their arguments.[5] In order to understand the differences between each system of interpretation, it will be necessary to present a short survey on the particular variances of each.[6]

---

3 Although many scholars have argued on the basis of 1 Cor. 15:20-28 that Paul believed in a millennial reign of Christ between his Second Coming and the final consummation of the eternal kingdom, there is sufficient reason to doubt the validity of such an assumption; see Beckwith's extended discussion on this point, in *The Apocalypse of John*, pp. 98-100; the present writer is, however, not completely convinced of Beckwith's refutation of Pauline millennialism.

4 Premillennialism, again, is divided up into two different branches, namely historical and dispensational premillennialism.

5 Generally it can be stated that the three terms, amillennial, postmillennial, and premillennial, are to be thought of as describing the Second Coming of Christ. Literally, therefore, the word "amillennial" means that the Second Coming of Christ is to be without a millennium. The word "postmillennial" connotes that Christ will return *after* the millennium and finally, the word "premillennial" that he will return *before* the millennium.

6 Although the emphasis in the following survey will be put primarily on the difference between the various systems of interpretation, it should be noted that amillennialism and postmillennialism are less at variance with each other than with premillennialism, which, especially its dispensational branch, takes a different approach in interpreting the millennium. Amillennialists agree with postmillennialists on three points: (1) the millennium does not involve a visible reign of Christ from an earthly throne; (2) it is not thought of as being exactly a thousand years in duration; (3) the return of Christ is placed after the millennium. As will be

We will begin with a description of the amillennial system, proceed then to the postmillennial system, and complete this part of the study with the premillennial systems of interpretation.

2.2.1. Amillennialism

W. Hendriksen, in *More Than Conquerors*, devised a system of interpretation of Revelation which he termed "progressive parallelism".[7] A. A. Hoekema, in summarizing Hendriksen's lengthy exposition, describes this method of interpretation thus:

> According to this view, the book of Revelation consists of seven sections which run parallel to each other, each of which depicts the church and the world from the time of Christ's first coming to the time of his second.[8]

This system of interpretation, as Hoekema concedes, is not without its difficulties, but it seems the most satisfactory

---

shown later, historical premillennialism shares some similarities with amillennialism, as well. It should be noted, however, that there is also a particular group of amillennialists who do not believe in any millennium at all. Werner G. Kümmel expresses the view of this latter group in his book, *Heilsgeschehen und Geschichte*, Elwert Verlag, Marburg, 1965, pp. 162, 163, as follows: „Es ist aber ebenso unmöglich, eine apokalyptische Sonderanschauung wie die Erwartung eines tausendjährigen Messiasreiches vor dem Weltende, die Apk. 20 vertritt, als in engem sachlichem Zusammenhang mit der zentralen neutestamentlichen Verkündigung stehend nachzuweisen; diese Vorstellung ist vielmehr wirklich isoliert, steht zu der Ablehnung aller apokalyptischen Berechnung durch Jesus (Lk. 17,21) im Widerspruch und ermangelt darüber eines klaren heilsgeschichtlichen Gehaltes, so daß diese mythologische Einzelvorstellung als dem zentralen neutestmanentlichen Kerygma inadäquat durchaus einer kritischen Eliminierung unterworfen werden muß."

7 W. Hendriksen, *More Than Conquerors*, Baker Book House, Grand Rapids, 1939, pp. 11-64; cf. R. G. Clouse, *The Meaning of the Millennium. Four Views*, IVP, Downers Grove, Ill., 1977, p. 156.

8 R. G. Clouse, *op. cit.*, pp. 156-157; cf. A. A. Hoekema, *The Bible and the Future*, Paternoster, Exeter, 1978, p. 223.

method to him. He further explained the idea of progressive parallelism thus:

> Note that though these seven sections are parallel to each other, they also reveal a certain amount of eschatological progress. The last section, for example, takes us further into the future than the other sections. ... Hence this method of interpretation is called *progressive* parallelism.[9]

He rejects an exclusively futuristic interpretation of Revelation which would refer only to events that are to happen around or at the time of Christ's Second Coming. Furthermore, he does not believe that the events described in Rev. 20, necessarily follow in chronological order with that which is presented in chapter 19. If this would be the case, an interpreter of Revelation would be virtually compelled to assume that the thousand-year reign depicted in 20:4 must come after the return of Christ described in 19:11. However, Hoekema, as one of the foremost scholars of the reformed tradition[10], objects to that understanding and suggests the following:

---

9 Hoekema's remarks about progressive parallelism are of such vital importance to anyone who wants to understand the whole amillennial system that it is helpful to give a few examples of what he means: "Although the final judgment has already been announced in 1:7 and has been briefly described in 6:12-17, it is not set forth in full detail until we come to 20:11-15. Though the final joy of the redeemed in the life to come has been hinted at in 7:15-17, it is not until we reach chapter 21 that we find a detailed and elaborated description of the blessedness of life on the new earth (21:1-22:5)" (Ibid., p. 158; italics his). Cf. A. A. Hoekema, *op. cit.*, p. 226.

10 The reformed tradition was always strongly amillenarian in doctrine. This is not surprising considering the precedent which Calvin set in branding those who were interested in millennialism with such names as "ignorant" or "malicious". (John Calvin, *Institutes of the Christian Religion*, ed. J. T. McNeil, trans. F. L. Battles, Westminster Press, Philadelphia, 1960, III, 25, 996. Note also Heinrich Quistorp, *Calvin's Doctrine of the Last Things*, trans. H. Knight, John Knox Press, Richmond, Virginia, 1955).

If we see Revelation 20:1-6 as describing what takes place during the entire history of the church, beginning with the first coming of Christ, we will have an understanding of the millennium of Revelation 20 which is quite different from the one just mentioned.[11]

Implementing the interpretational system of progressive parallelism, he outlines the book of Revelation in seven sections. The first of these seven sections is found in chapters 1-3. It contains John's vision of the glorified Christ and the letters to the seven churches in Asia Minor. Hoekema believes that the key to interpret the entire book of Revelation is included in the following two observations about the first three chapters:

First, there are references to events, people and places of the time when the book of Revelation was written. Second, the principles, commendations and warnings contained in these letters have value for the church of all time.[12]

The second section in chapters 4-7 describes the vision of the seven seals. After the breaking of the seals by Christ various divine judgments on the world are poured out on the earth. Hoekema interprets this vision as the description of a persecuted and suffering church.[13]

The third section, found in chapters 8-11, depicts the seven trumpets of judgment. An avenged, protected and victorious church is the center of attention in these chapters.

The fourth section, chapters 12-14, introduces some of the other main figures in Revelation, the woman with her child, the persecuting dragon, and the two beasts. Hoekema, again, sees the primary message of these chapters as that of

---

11 R. G. Clouse, *op. cit.*, p. 157.

12 Ibid.; cf. A. A. Hoekema, *op. cit.*, pp. 223-226.

13 Ibid.

Satan's opposition to the church.[14] According to this scheme, Hoekema continues his interpretation of Revelation to the end of the book.[15]

Thus, having set the stage, he continues his description of the amillennial position by proceeding to interpret Revelation 20:1-6. As it is impossible to go into every detail of his intricate interpretation, we shall present only the most salient points of Hoekema's understanding of amillennialism[16] in a summary form, concentrating on the aspects most relevant to Rev. 20:1-6.

Chapters 20-22 of Revelation belong to the seventh section of the book. Thus they do not describe chronologically what follows the return of Christ in chapter 19, but recapitulate for the seventh time the progressive development of the church age. This leads Hoekema to assert that Revelation 20:1 relates again the events surrounding the beginning of the New Testament era. After a brief discussion of this idea, he comes to the obvious conclusion that "the

---

14 Ibid., p. 157-158.

15 The fifth section is found in chapters 15-16; the sixth in chs. 17-19; and the seventh in chs. 20-22.

16 Different scholars think that the term "amillennialism ", is not an accurate description of this view, because it suggests that amillennialists either do not believe in any millennium or that they simple ignore that first six verses of Revelation 20, which speak of a millennial reign. Neither of these two statements is true. However, it is true that amillennialists do not believe in a literal thousand-year earthly reign which will follow the return of Christ. Professor Jay E. Adams has suggested that the term "amillennialism" be replaced by the expression "realized millennialism" (*The Time Is at Hand*, Presbyterian and Reformed, 1970, pp. 7-11). The latter term describes the "amillennial" position more accurately than the usual term, since "amillennialists" believe that the millennium of Rev. 20 is not exclusively future but is now in process of realization (A. A. Hoekema, *op. cit.*, pp. 155-156). Hoekema, however, concedes that the expression "realized millennialism", is a rather clumsy one, replacing a simple prefix with a three-syllable word (ibid.). Cf. P. E. Hughes, *Interpreting Prophecy*, Eerdmans, Grand Rapids, 1976, pp. 97, 99-100: He believes that amillennialism does not relegate the thousand years of Revelation 20 to the nonexistent, but rather understands the number to have a symbolic value, interpreting "the millennium as virtually synonymous with the present age between the two comings of Christ, or, more precisely, between the coronation of the ascended Saviour and His return in glory".

thousand-year reign of Revelation 20:4-6 must occur *before* and *not after* the Second Coming of Christ".[17]

After reminding his readers repeatedly of the particular system of interpretation he uses, he begins with the exegesis of the passage. Following the observation that the book of Revelation is full of symbolic numbers, he objects to a literal interpretation of the number "one-thousand". Rather, this number must be understood as a long period of indeterminate length.[18] In a further step, he identifies this thousand-year period of indeterminate length, as the period which extends from Christ's first coming to just before his Second Coming.

Since the "lake of fire", the place of final punishment, is qualitatively different from the "Abyss", the latter is thought of as a figurative description of the way in which Satan's activities will be curbed during the thousand-year period.[19]

He then continues to interpret the binding of Satan, the occupants on the thrones[20], the two resurrections, and the reigning of Christ with his resurrected saints.[21]

---

17 Ibid., p. 160 (italics his); cf. A. A. Hoekema, *op. cit.*, p. 227.

18 Ibid., p. 161; His argument runs like this: "Since the number ten signifies completeness, and since a thousand is ten to the third power, we may think of the expression "a thousand years" as standing for a complete period, a very long period of indeterminate length." Cf. A. A. Hoekema, *op. cit.*, pp. 227-230.

19 Note Hoekema's use of words in describing the duration of the millennium. After he interpreted the number "one-thousand" as meaning a period of indeterminate length, he continues to refer to it only as "thousand-year period".

20 First he identifies these persons sitting on the thrones as the martyrs, who had suffered death because of their faithfulness to Christ (ibid., p. 166). Yet later he expands this group to include all Christians who had remained true to Christ and resisted anti-Christian powers [i.e. who did not worship the beast or his image (13:15)] (ibid., p. 167). Cf. A. A. Hoekema, *op. cit.*, p. 231.

21 Hoekema concludes his exegesis by asserting that the passage says nothing about an earthly reign of Christ over a primarily Jewish kingdom. Rather, it describes the reigning with Christ in heaven of the souls of believers who have died. They reign during the time between their death and Christ's Second Coming (ibid., pp. 161-172). For an expanded exposition of these verses, see also Hendriksen, *op. cit.*, pp. 221-229. Cf. A. A. Hoekema, *op. cit.*, pp. 232-235.

In these particular points amillennialism diverges farthest from any other system of interpretation, primarily from the premillennial system. Thus it might be advantageous to come back to these particular interpretations of amillennialism at a later stage of this chapter in order to analyze it against the background of premillennialism. Therefore I will proceed now to a representation of the postmillennial system of interpretation.

2.2.2. Postmillennialism

Postmillennialism[22] is best defined by Loraine Boettner as

> a view of the last things which holds that the kingdom of God is now being extended in the world through the preaching of the gospel and the saving work of the Holy Spirit in the hearts of individuals, that the world eventually is to be Christianized and that the return of Christ is to occur at the close of a long period of righteousness and peace commonly called the millennium.[23]

The Church Age is seen as the time when the gradual realization of the millennium is accomplished. This age of spiritual prosperity will be brought about by forces which are already active in the world. They will become progressively more visible as the end of the age draws near, reaching its climax at the return of Christ. Postmillennialists allow for

---

22 Complaining about the inadequacy of terminology, L. Boettner, in *The Meaning of the Millennium*, ed. R. G. Clouse, p. 120, states, "The use of prefixes *pre-* and *post-*, as attached to the word *millennium*, is to some extent unfortunate and misleading. For the distinction involves a great deal more than merely "before" or "after". The millennium expected by the premillennialist is quite a different thing from that expected by the postmillennialist. It is different not only in regard to the time and manner in which it will be set but primarily in regard to the nature of the kingdom and the manner in which Christ exercises his control."

23 Ibid., p. 117; cf. Loraine Boettner, *The Millennium*, Presbyterian and Reformed, Philadelphia, 1957, pp. 14-16, 18-22, 30, 35, 38-41, 47-48, 50-53, 58-59, 82-86, 98-101.

a "limited manifestation of evil" shortly before the Second Coming. They point to the passage in Rev. 20:7-10, which describes the loosing of Satan at the end of the millennium, as the basis of this assumption. However, they also assert that the church, as the primary object of Satan's assault, will be miraculously preserved by the direct intervention of God. The shortness of time allotted to Satan for the accomplishment of his evil purposes, so they say, plays a major role in Satan's abortive attempt to destroy the church.[24] Postmillennialists do not think that this concession of a brief resurgence of evil at the end of this age is inconsistent with their particular interpretation. Therefore they continue to look optimistically into the future with the expectation of strikingly improved living conditions on earth prior to Christ's Second Coming.

In keeping with a postmillennial interpretation J. Marcellus Kik asserts that the great tribulation of Matthew 24 and the apostasy of 2 Thes. 2 are events of the past.[25] Boettner agrees with Kik on these points. Otherwise it would be impossible for him to maintain a consistent interpretation of the millennium as the gradual transformation of this present age into, what he calls, "a Christianized age of the church".[26]

---

24 Cf. Loraine Boettner, *op. cit.*, pp. 67-70.

25 J. M. Kik, *Revelation Twenty*, Presbyterian and Reformed, Philadelphia, 1955, pp. 33-37. It might be objected that certain occurrences mentioned in Mt. 24 and 2 Thes. 2 have not yet come to pass. For instance, Mt. 24:24 speaks of false prophets who will perform great signs and miracles to deceive the elect. As far as I am concerned, these prophets have not yet lived. Again, in 2 Thes. 2:3, 4 Paul predicts the coming of the 'man of lawlessness.' As the characteristics of this figure are clearly outlined (e.g. 2 Thes. 2:4, 9 "working all kinds of counterfeit miracles" etc.), it is difficult to match them with any historical figure. These passages pose a greater problem to postmillennialists, than they generally admit. Simply to relegate to the past biblical passages which seem to portray a drastic deterioration of conditions on earth shortly before the coming of Christ is based on a defective hermeneutic. Cf. A. A. Hoekema's criticism of this interpretation. He says that the common postmillennial interpretation of the great tribulation and the apostasy of 2 Thes. 2 has no scriptural justification (*op. cit.*, p. 178).

26 Kik defines the expression of a "Christianized age of the church" not directly, but the meaning he attributes to it becomes clear during the

Both postmillennialists and amillennialists understand the millennium as an indefinite period of time exceeding, probably by a large margin, the mark of one-thousand years. They contest that the duration of the millennium cannot be expressed in any number of years, as no one knows the exact time span between the first and Second Coming of Christ.

The intensified witness of the Church will become the primary means of extending the kingdom of God on earth. The conversion of a vast majority of the world's inhabitants will transform the present age into a Glorious Age. As the Gospel message permeates gradually all areas of life, positive changes will be introduced into the social, political and economic structures of the world. As the latter immensely improve, paradisal conditions will be established on earth and the millennium will become a reality. Righteousness, justice, and peace will be enjoyed by a majority of the world's population. At that time Christian principles of belief and conduct will be the accepted standard for nations and individuals. Thus postmillennialism, as Boettner continues to say,

> places a strong emphasis on the universality of Christ's work of redemption ... Since it was the world, or the race, which fell in Adam, it was the world, or the race, which was the object of Christ's redemption. This does not mean that every individual will be saved but that the race, as a race, will be saved."[27]

As these statements could easily be construed to intimate a sinless society, Boettner, asserts that no postmillennialist propagates the emergence of a sinless society. Although he believes that the world at large will eventually enjoy millen-

---

course of his presentation of postmillennialism. He believes that this present age, which he calls the age of the church, will be radically changed by the influence of the Gospel. This change will manifest itself world-wide in the growing acceptance of Christian values as the moral basis of a standard way of life.

27 Ibid., p. 123.

nial blessings[28], he qualifies this understanding by saying that,

> this does not mean that there will be a time on this earth when every person will be a Christian or that all sin will be abolished. But it does mean that evil in all its many forms eventually will be reduced to negligible proportions, that Christian principles will be the rule, not the exception, and that Christ will return to a truly Christianized world.[29]

Reflecting on the present state of affairs, he concedes that the redemption of the whole world will be a tedious and slow progress of many centuries. That this process is beset by many disappointments and setbacks, does not mean, however, that its ultimate realization culminating in the millennium will not be accomplished.[30]

Obviously the principles of interpretation employed by postmillennialists are largely the same as those of amillennialists. Proponents of both views generally assert that the biblical authors used figurative language in conveying the symbolic nature of many portions of Scripture. Thus they do not object in principle to figurative interpretation and readily accept this method as suitable to accommodate the peculiarities of biblical language.[31] They also maintain that a literal approach of interpretation, as advocated by premillennialists, is inadequate to convey the true meaning of the figurative language of the Bible.[32]

---

28 In his opinion a state of righteousness does exist already now in relatively small and isolated groups, like some family circles and local churches etc.

29 R. G. Clouse, *op. cit.*, p. 118.

30 Boettner describes this process in these terms: "From the human point of view it often looks as though the forces of evil are about to gain the upper hand. Periods of spiritual advance and prosperity alternate with periods of spiritual decline and depression. But as one age succeeds another there is progress" (ibid., p. 125).

31 Ibid., p. 134.

32 Boettner argues against the practice of "premillennialists [who] often materialize and literalize prophecies to such an extent that they keep

As postmillennialists and amillennialists favor the same hermeneutical principles, it is not surprising that they hold many common interpretations about the millennium. A. A. Hoekema, in *The Bible and the Future*, observes that two eminent postmillennialists, L. Boettner and B. B. Warfield, have adopted the common amillennial interpretation of the first six verses of Revelation 20, especially in regard to the binding of Satan.[33] J. Marcellus Kik is also in complete agreement with them as far as the binding of Satan is concerned. Other postmillennialists, however, divert from this interpretation slightly. Norman Shepherd, for example, argues for a future binding of Satan.[34]

General agreement, however, exists among the exponents of postmillennialism, concerning the first resurrection

---

them on an earthly level and miss their true and deeper meaning" (ibid., p. 137). Boettner actually means that premillennialists interpret prophecies so literalistically that they keep them on a material level ('materialize', has different connotations; the verb 'literalize' does not exist in the English language). He then gives an example of Jews who, by interpreting Messianic prophecies literally, rejected and crucified the real Messiah as he came in the person of Jesus Christ. They thought that the Messiah would be a political ruler and fulfill their hopes of an earthly kingdom. Taking this example as a precedent, Boettner comes to the following conclusion. "The fearful consequences of literalistic interpretation as it related to the first coming should put us on guard against making the same mistake concerning the Second Coming" (ibid.). That the Jews interpreted the prophetic passages literally cannot be the reason why they crucified their Messiah. What would have happened if they had interpreted the passages about the suffering servant just as literally as the passages about the exalted king? The problem with the Jewish exegesis is not to be sought in its use of a literal hermeneutic, but in its selectiveness of what was deemed to constitute a messianic passage.

33 *Op. cit.*, p. 176; B. B. Warfield maintained that Rev. 20:1-6 describes the binding of Satan during the present church age and the reign of the souls of deceased believers with Christ in heaven during the present age (*The Millennium and the Apocalypse*, in *Biblical Doctrines*, Oxford University Press, New York, 1929, pp. 648-650). In his newest writings, Boettner changed his previous view on the subject, as expressed in his book *The Millennium*, pp. 65-66, to agree with Warfield's interpretation. Cf. R. G. Clouse, *op. cit.*, pp. 202-203.

34 N. Shepherd, "postmillennialism", in *The Zondervan Pictorial Encyclopedia of the Bible*, ed. M. C. Tenney, Zondervan, Grand Rapids, 1975, IV, pp. 822-823.

as referring to "regeneration".³⁵ Norman Shepherd believes that the phrase "the living and reigning with Christ" is describing the present life of believers on earth.³⁶

As A. A. Hoekema points out, however, there are at least two arguments which can be brought against this interpretation.

> First, to understand "the souls that reign with Christ" as referring to believers who are still living on earth conflicts with the earlier statement, "I saw the souls of those who had been beheaded" (v.4), and also with a later statement, "the rest of the dead did not come to life ..." (v.5). Second, how can living believers be said to reign with Christ for a thousand years, when each one lives not much longer than the normal life span of "threescore years and ten" – if that long?³⁷

Yet even more devastating to the postmillennial position is Hoekema's following remark: "Moreover, even on the basis of Kik's interpretation of the passage, what ground is there in these words for expecting a future millennial golden age?"³⁸

If postmillennialism has yet to demonstrate that its interpretation of the millennium is superior to any other alternative interpretation, its main contestant is premillennialism and not amillennialism. Hence it will be necessary to turn our attention to premillennialism now.

2.2.3. Premillennialism

All premillennial interpreters consider the Second Coming of Christ as an event which inaugurates his thousand-year reign on the earth. They hold various opinions, however, not

---

35 A. A. Hoekema, *op. cit.*, p. 176.

36 Ibid.; cf. N. Shepherd, "The Resurrections of Revelation 20", in *The Westminster Theological Journal* XXXVII, 1 (Fall, 1974), pp. 34-43.

37 Ibid., p. 179.

38 Ibid.

only in regard to the interpretation of preceding passages of the book of Revelation, but also in their understanding of the millennium itself.

There are essentially three different types of premillennialism. The first type has been generally termed "premillennialism of the historical school", the second, "historical premillennialism", and the third, "dispensational premillennialism". As the first of these types is held by a small minority, the present writer will describe it only in passing, whereas the second and third types will be presented in greater length.

Premillennialists of the historical school tend to interpret Revelation 6 through 19 as largely fulfilled in history but hold that chapter 20, and the following, are dealing with the future and are to be interpreted somewhat literally. An illustration of this form of premillennialism is expressed by E. H. Horne who believes that symbolism to a large extent ceases in chapter 20 and specific prophecy is given. Horne states:

> The symbolic language in which previous chapters have been written is here dropped, and certain predictions are made in plain words, though they contain allusions to the Dragon and the Beast, which are symbolic figures. The meaning of the Dragon is here not carefully explained, as "the old serpent, which is the Devil and Satan," that all of symbolism is removed: and the Beast is only indirectly referred to at all. The change in style is no doubt due to the change of subject; though the predictions found in this chapter relate to the consequences of the Second Advent, and that event will remove all need of concealment of things future.[39]

Horne maintained that from the viewpoint of John all prophecies recorded in Revelation would be fulfilled sometime in the future. He believed, also, that most of these prophecies laid out in the first 18 chapters had already been

---

39 Edward H. Horne, *The Meaning of the Apocalypse*, S. W. Partridge, London, 1916, pp. 283-284.

fulfilled, at least in most cases, during the time since Revelation was first written. In regard to the prediction of Christ's Second Coming and the establishment of a literal millennium, however, he persisted in asserting that these events have not yet occurred and will constitute the climactic finale of world history.

Historical and dispensational premillennialism must be distinguished from the historical school of premillennialism, especially in regard to the interpretation of the book of Revelation.

However, they share a common understanding about the millennium in broad terms. Therefore, we will proceed at this stage first to represent the historical, and then, the dispensational branch of premillennialism.

2.2.3.1. Historical Premillennialism

Historical premillennialism underscores the soteriological character of the millennium. Covenant theologians, if they do not champion amillennialism, are among those advocating this viewpoint. But there are also other scholars, such as George E. Ladd, who belong to the group of historical premillennialists, because they do not want to be classified as covenant or dispensational theologians.[40]

The millennium is considered by them as primarily an aspect of God's soteriological program, and the political character of the kingdom and the prominence of the nation Israel are subordinated.

Critics have pointed out that Historical premillennialism is more or less a mediating position trying to appropriate congenial elements from two incompatible positions, amillennialism and premillennialism, and molding them into its own system. Exponents of historical premillennialism, however, have contested this allegation by claiming that

---

40 George E. Ladd presents his interpretation of the millennium most extensively in his book *Jesus and the Kingdom*, Harper and Row, New York, 1964. Another source is his commentary on Revelation (see footnote no.41).

their position used to be the historical interpretation of the millennium by the apostolic church.[41]

The truth of the matter is, as I understand it, that historical premillennialism is indeed a system which tries to approximate amillennialism while maintaining a premillennial understanding of Christ's return. This contention can be substantiated by looking at some common features of historical premillennialism and amillennialism.

George E. Ladd asserts that the passage in Revelation 20:1-10 is the only place in the Bible which speaks of a millennium.[42] Hoekema, the amillennialist, agrees with him on this point. He also finds an affinity of interpretation in the following views: (1) That the church is the "spiritual Israel" in the New Testament[43]; (2) that the present spiritual reign of Christ is the dominant theme and fulfillment of Old Testament prophecy[44]; (3) that the kingdom of God is both now in the present as well as taking place in the future; (4) that the church is enjoying eschatological blessings already at the present time; (5) that the signs of the end times have been present from the time of Christ's first coming but will assume an intensified form before his Second Coming; and finally (6) that the Second Coming of Christ is not a two-phase

---

41 The argument regarding its historicity will be investigated later. At the moment it should suffice to quote H. A. Hoyt's objection to this claim. He says, "Reference to "historic" premillennialism suggests something that I do not believe is true. The fathers of the church from the second century on have not held this view, and this therefore does not establish its validity. Any fundamental validity that is truly historic is to be found in the New Testament - something that was espoused by the early church and persisted for several hundred years" (R. G. Clouse, *op. cit.*, p. 41).

42 But in another passage he speaks of 1 Cor. 15:23-26 in these words, "There is, however, one passage in Paul which may refer to an interim kingdom if not a millennium" (*Commentary on Revelation of John*, Eerdmans, Grand Rapids, 1972, p. 38).

43 "God does not have two separate peoples with distinct destinies (namely, Jews and Gentiles, or Israel and the church) but only one people" (A. A. Hoekema, *op. cit.*, p. 183).

44 R. G. Clouse, *op. cit.*, p. 55; Charles L. Feinberg, in *millennialism. The Two Major Views*, 3 ed., Moody Press, Chicago, (1936) 1980, p. 322, commented on this affinity of historical premillennialism to amillennialism by saying: "No wonder amillennialist Hoekema is elated over his easy ... victory."

occurrence but a single event.⁴⁵ It should be added that a synthesis of amillennialism and historical premillennialism is attempted by proponents of the latter view by finding some prophecies relating to the future kingdom as being fulfilled in the present age.

This does not change the fact, however, that historical premillennialism is still fundamentally different from amillennialism, most obviously in its understanding that Christ will set up an earthly kingdom *after* his return.

As the scriptural basis for historical premillennialism, George E. Ladd offers the following interpretation of Revelation 19 and 20. Revelation 19 describes the Second Coming of Christ. Because this chapter precedes chapter 20, Christ's return must happen prior to the events recorded in Revelation 20:1-10. The first three verses of this passage describe the binding of Satan during the millennium.⁴⁶ Revelation 20:4 depicts the reigning of risen believers with Christ on earth during the millennium. Ladd insists that the Greek word "ἔζησαν"; "ezēsan" (they lived, or came to life), found in verses 4 and 5, must mean raised from the dead in a physical way.⁴⁷ He finds in verse 4 a description of the physical resurrection of believers at the beginning of the millennium (later called "the first resurrection"), and in verse 5 a description of the physical resurrection of unbelievers at the end of the millennium.

This interpretation of Rev. 19 and 20 constitutes the basic understanding of premillennialism in general, over against any other millennial view. However, there are some differences between historical and dispensational premillennialism which are more subtle, but nonetheless of elementary importance.⁴⁸

---

45 Ibid.; Hoekema makes a sharp distinction between historical and dispensational premillennialism.

46 G. E. Ladd, *op. cit.*, pp. 262-263.

47 R. G. Clouse, *op. cit.*, pp. 35-38.

48 N. Hoyt sees the aversion against the dispensational view of the millennium not in the dispensational system of interpretation, but in its insistence on a literal interpretation of Scripture. He says, "I find it hard to understand why one system is labeled dispensational and others escape

The distinguishing mark of historical premillennialism which sets it apart from any other millennial understanding, especially from its dispensational counterpart, is its view about the chronological sequence of eschatological events. In particular its insistence upon the interpretation that the church will not be raptured until after the Great Tribulation. This interpretation presupposes the understanding that all believers will be resurrected at the first resurrection (20:5) simultaneously.

In contrast dispensational premillennialism places the rapture of the church at the beginning of the Great Tribulation which coincides with the resurrection of deceased believers and Old Testament saints.[49] The resurrection of the martyred believers, however, occurs not until after the Great Tribulation, thus constituting the final part of the first resurrection.[50]

---

that description. For the facts are these: Not one view of the millennium ... is without some arrangement of dispensations; it is impossible to interpret the Bible apart from some arrangement of dispensations; and most certainly the very mention of an eschatological millennium imposes another dispensation. But it is clear that Ladd [historical premillennialist] can find no place for any system of dispensations other than his own and that the chief difficulty for him lies in the emphasis upon literal interpretation of Scripture endorsed by those known as "dispensationalists" (R. G. Clouse, *op. cit.*, p. 42).

49 Theologians who use a dispensational system of interpretation try to harmonize different portions of Scripture with each other. This is especially true of dispensational premillennialists. Obviously the concept of a 'rapture' is not in Revelation as such, but is taken from 1 Thes. 4:17. Both eschatological concepts are combined in the attempt to explain the sequence of the events occurring just prior to, and after, the Second Coming of Christ. This approach of harmonizing the data of biblical eschatology has to be understood in order to appreciate the unique contribution of dispensational theology to the interpretation of the first resurrection.

50 J. D. Pentecost, in *Thing To Come*, Zondervan, Grand Rapids, (1958) 1977, p. 397, summarized the important aspects of a dispensational interpretation of the first resurrection thus: "This resurrection, usually called the first resurrection, but which might be called the resurrection unto life (John 5:29) with greater clarity inasmuch as this resurrection is made up of a number of component parts, is that part of the resurrection program in which the individuals are raised to eternal life. It included within it all who, at any time, are raised to eternal life. The destiny, not the

It will be necessary, therefore, to represent dispensational premillennialism as a whole system of interpretation, as this above statement needs some Biblical substantiation. This is because no Bible verse specifically indicates this first resurrection to be divided into two parts by the Great Tribulation. The perspective which will be gained by providing a wider framework of what the present writer thinks to be an equally satisfactory interpretation of the millennium will help to form a better understanding of the first resurrection as an integral part of the whole dispensational system.[51]

2.2.3.2. Dispensational Premillennialism

Dispensational premillennialism has become the most popular view of premillennialism in the twentieth century. John F. Walvoord, one of the leading authorities on dispensationalism, defines the basis, method, and content of this type of premillennialism. He states,

> [dispensational] premillennialism is founded principally on interpretation of the Old Testament. They [the Israelites] confidently anticipated the coming of a Savior and Deliverer, a Messiah who would be Prophet, Priest, and King. They expected that he would deliver them from their enemies and usher in a kingdom of righteousness, peace, and prosperity upon a redeemed earth. If interpreted literally, the Old Testament gives a clear picture of the prophetic expectation of Israel. The premillennial interpretation offers the only literal fulfillment for the hundreds of verses of prophetic testimony.[52]

---

time, determines to which part of the resurrection program any event is to be assigned."

51 Because the distinctive character of the millennial reign of Christ is maintained in contrast to the present age, this view is designated as the dispensational interpretation.

52 John F. Walvoord, *The Millennial Kingdom*, Findlay, Dunham, Ohio, 1959, p. 114.

Therefore, any attempt to represent dispensational premillennialism has to begin with an explanation of what is meant by a literal hermeneutic.[53] Bernard Ramm provides the following definition:

> The "literal" meaning of a word is the basic, customary, social designation of that word. The spiritual, or mystical meaning of a word or expression is one that arises after the literal designation and is dependent upon it for its existence. To interpret literally means nothing more or less than to interpret in terms of *normal, usual, designation.*[54]

If, for any reason, this method is abandoned by the interpreter, premillennialism itself will be endangered of its very existence. However, if it is strictly followed, no other system of interpretation will be able to assert itself against premillennialism in any of its three variations. Even amillennialists have recognized that this is the case. Floyd Hamilton frankly admits

> that a literal interpretation of the Old Testament prophecies gives us just such a picture of an earthly reign of the Messiah as the premillennialist pictures. That was the kind of a Messianic kingdom that the Jews of the

---

53 Cf. R. G. Clouse, *op. cit.*, pp. 18, 19. The terms "grammatical-historical" and "literal" hermeneutic are interchangeable.

54 Bernard Ramm, *Protestant Biblical Interpretation*, W. A. Wilde Co., Boston, 1950, p. 53. As has been shown, the opposite to a literal hermeneutic is a "spiritualized" hermeneutic, that is, a hermeneutic which finds, for example, Old Testament prophecies fulfilled in the Christian church. Thus amillennialists usually find a "spiritual" interpretation of the millennium. The millennium is not a literal reign of Christ on the earth; it is the reign of the martyrs after death in the intermediate state in heaven. However, there are differences of opinion among amillennialists (and postmillennialists) of just how to interpret the millennium spiritually, as has been partially demonstrated in the foregone sections. By its very nature a spiritualized approach lends itself to many diverse interpretations.

time of Christ were looking for, on the basis of a literal interpretation of the Old Testament.[55]

According to the futuristic interpretation of the book of Revelation, all material from 4:1 on is considered pure prophesy, still awaiting its fulfillment. This section is in contrast to what John saw in chapter 1, his vision of the glorified Christ described in the clause, "what you have seen" (Rev. 1:19), and in contrast to the revelation of chapters 2 and 3, messages to the seven churches designated as "what is now" (Rev. 1:19). Beginning in chapter 4, things to come are unfolded which have to do with the consummation of the age.

The concept that the book of Revelation beginning with 4:1 is pertaining to the future, from the standpoint of the twenty-first century, is a broad conclusion growing out of the lack of correspondence of these prophecies to anything that has been fulfilled. A normal interpretation of this section which understands these prophecies as literal events would require that they be viewed as futuristic. This concept is supported by the similarity of the expression in 1:19, "we take place later" to the clause in 4:1, "what must take place after this".

Scholars holding to this view consider the millennium as an aspect of God's theocratic program, a fulfillment of the promises given to David that his kingdom and throne would continue forever over the house of Israel.[56]

The millennium is interpreted as a period in which Christ will reign in Zion exercising his complete control over the nations. Arguments in support of this interpretation are based, as has been said above, on a literal under-

---

55 Floyd Hamilton, *The basis of Millennial Faith*, Eerdmans, Grand Rapids, Mich., 1942, p. 38. Oswald Allis, equally opposed to Premillennialism, agrees with Hamilton on this point by conceding that, "the Old Testament prophecies if literally interpreted cannot be regarded as having been fulfilled or as being capable of fulfillment in this present age" (*Prophecy and the Church*, Presbyterian and Reformed, Philadelphia, 1945, p. 238).

56 Advocates of this position include scholars like Lewis S. Chafer, Alva McClain, Charles L. Feinberg, Charles Ryrie, Wilbur Smith, Merrill Unger, C. I. Scofield, H. A. Ironside, and many others.

standing of many passages in the Old Testament which anticipate a kingdom on earth and prophesy a period of righteousness and peace with Christ.

Isaiah 2 parallels Micah 4:1-5 in describing the rule of Christ, with his capital in Jerusalem, in a period of universal peace. The prophecy relates to Judah and Jerusalem (v.1), and describes the nations as coming "to the house of the God of Jacob". "The law" is stated to come "out of Zion" and "the word of the Lord from Jerusalem" (2:3). Universal peace is described: "They shall beat their swords into plowshares, and their spear into pruning hooks; nation shall not lift up sword against nation, neither shall they learn war any more" (2:4). Such a period obviously is not being fulfilled in the present age and requires a future presence of the King of kings on the earth in Jerusalem.

Jeremiah speaks frequently of this glorious kingdom, as in Je. 23:5-8 where a descendant of David is declared to reign as a king. He "shall execute justice and righteousness in the land" at a time when "Judah will be saved, and Israel will dwell securely". (Je. 23:5, 6). The name of the king is "The Lord is our righteousness" (v.6). This kingdom period is preceded by the regathering of Israel "out of all the countries where he had driven them" (Je. 23:8). These promises have been taken to mean that Israel will be brought back to its original homeland, Palestine. Furthermore, the Jews will be supernaturally protected and spiritually revived by God.

Dispensational premillennialism is related to the major Biblical covenants of the Old Testament. The covenant of Abraham, introduced in Genesis 12:1-3, promises the perpetuity of the land title to his physical seed, a promise subsequently ratified by numerous Old Testament prophecies. The covenant with David (2 Sa. 7), which assures David's seed that his throne will be upheld forever, is seen as requiring a fulfillment on earth in keeping with the earthly character of the Davidic kingdom. A Davidic throne was never spiritual nor heavenly. David understood the covenant as being literal, and this interpretation is confirmed in the New Testament (Lk. 1:32, 33). Many Old Testament passages predict the revival of the rule of David, as does Amos 9:11-15, with a glorious period of a kingdom on earth being fulfilled. The new covenant, promised Israel in Jeremiah 31:31-34 (cf. also Is. 61:8, 9; Ezk. 37:21-28), predicts a future time of spiritual blessing in Israel when all will know the Lord, a purpose of God supported by the prediction that God will never cast off Israel (Je. 31:35-37).[57]

In complete agreement with Old Testament pronouncements which portray glorious conditions for the Jewish nation at the time when the Messiah will set up his kingdom, the New Testament describes the anticipation and fulfillment of these promises. In keeping with its universal character it also integrates Gentile believers among those who would be the recipients of millennial blessings.

Numerous confirmations of the Old Testament prophecies concerning the kingdom are found. The Virgin Mary by the angel Gabriel was led to believe concerning her Son, "the Lord God will give to him the throne of his father David, and he will reign over the house of Jacob for ever; and of his kingdom there will be no end" (Lk. 1:32, 33). It is inconceivable that if the intent of the Old Testament promise was to be a spiritual role of God in the heart of believers, that the common anticipation of Israel of an earthly kingdom should be confirmed to Mary on this occasion. Mary obviously understood the prediction literally.

In like manner, the mother of the sons of Zebedee, (Mt. 20:20-23), anticipated an earthly kingdom in which her two sons might reign with Christ, indicating the general belief in such an earthly kingdom. Christ did not contradict her view, but he did rebuke her ambition for her sons. Christ also predicted that in his kingdom the apostles would "eat and drink at my table in my kingdom, and sit on thrones judging the twelve tribes of Israel" (Lk. 22:30). The kingdom in view seems to be a future earthly kingdom. In Mt. 24:25 Christ outlined a sequence of events beginning with the future great tribulation (24:15-22), his glorious Second Coming to the earth (24:27-30), and the establishment of his throne on

---

[57] Although the New Testament also outlines a new covenant for Christians in the present age, no claim is made that the new covenant in the present age fulfills the particulars of the covenant with Israel. A literal interpretation of these covenant promises, accordingly, requires a future kingdom on earth with fulfillment to the descendants of Jacob.

earth (25:31). Here the earthly throne follows the great tribulation and the Second Coming in chronological sequence, which by any normal interpretation harmonizes only with a premillennial view.

On the occasion of the Ascension of Christ, the disciples asked the question, "Lord, will you at this time restore the kingdom to Israel?" (Acts 1:6). Christ did not rebuke them for misapprehension that such a restoration was in prospect, but stated only that it was impossible for them to know when it would occur.

Opponents of dispensational premillennialism strongly disagree with this interpretation of Old and New Testament prophecy regarding the kingdom of God. They are convinced that dispensationalists falsely insist on interpreting these prophecies as if they would be detailed predictions about a millennial reign on earth. One of these critics, A. A. Hoekema, states his case against dispensational premillennialism thus:

> When one peruses the chapter and section headings of the New Scofield Bible, one finds that many sections of the Old Testament are interpreted as describing the millennium. As a matter of fact, however, the Old Testament says nothing about such a millennial reign. Passages commonly interpreted as describing the millennium actually describe the new earth which is the culmination of God's redemptive work.[58]

Again, Hoekema charges dispensational theology with maintaining erroneously a fundamental, and abiding, distinction between Israel and the church. He criticizes dispensationalists for saying that Israel and the church must always be kept separate.[59] Then he continues to observe that contrary to such an arbitrary distinction, "... the New Testa-

---

58 A. A. Hoekema, *op. cit.*, p. 201; italics added.

59 Once more A. A. Hoekema is criticizing dispensationalism by saying: "The teaching that God has a separate purpose for Israel and the church is in error. ... We must first of all challenge the statement that when the Bible talks about Israel it never means the church, and that when it talks about the church it always intends to exclude Israel" (*op. cit.*, p. 196).

ment itself often interprets expressions relating to Israel in such a way as to apply them to the New Testament church, which includes both Jews and Gentiles."[60]

Despite the criticism, which seems to be justified, dispensational interpreters defend these hermeneutical principles as scriptural. Charles Ryrie, for instance, cites approvingly a statement attributed to Daniel Fuller: "The basic premise of Dispensationalism is two purposes of God expressed in the formation of two peoples who maintain their distinction throughout eternity."[61]

As a discussion on the validity of either position, the amillennial and dispensational, will be taken up at a later stage, it should suffice at the moment to note that the differences between these particular positions are at the center of the millennial controversy.

After having looked at the main interpretational views of Rev. 20, the reader might be somewhat confused about the subject at hand. It should be emphasized, however, that a careful exegesis of this passage is indeed possible. The plain sense of the words used by the Seer John will be examined and brought to bear on the controversial issues. Thus we will proceed to exegete the passage in Revelation 20:1-10.

2.3. Revelation 20:1-10

2.3.1. Binding of Satan

> And I saw an angel coming down out of heaven, having the key of the Abyss and holding in his hand a great chain. He seized the dragon, that ancient serpent, which is the Devil, or Satan, and bound him for a thousand years. He threw him into the Abyss, and locked and

---

Hoekema devotes a whole chapter to refute dispensational Premillennialism (pp. 194-222).

60 Ibid.

61 Charles Ryrie, *Dispensationalism Today*, Moody Press, Chicago, 1965, p. 45.

> sealed it over him, to keep him from deceiving the nations any more until the thousand years were ended. After that, he must be set free for a short time.
>
> Rev. 20:1-3

In Revelation the change from one phase in the prophetic program to another is often indicated by the appearance of an angel (cf. 7:2; 8:1; 10:1; 14:6, 8, 9, 15, 17, 18; 17:1; 18:1). Chapter 20 begins with the majestic vision of an angel coming down from heaven. The different operations of the angel are as follows: he subdues Satan, binds him for one thousand years, casts him into the bottomless pit, locks its entrance with the appropriate key, puts a seal on the door in order to prevent Satan from continuing his deceptive activities, and finally to release him after the completion of his one thousand year imprisonment. A detailed discussion of each point will be necessary, because every one of them has come under dispute by the different schools of interpretation.

This angel appears to be an agent of God exercising enormous power which, as some commentators have noted, could only be the prerogative of Christ himself. He is the only one capable of defeating Satan and overcoming his power. Therefore they simply identified the angel with Christ. The majority of those commentators interpreted Revelation from a historical viewpoint as it relates to the age of the church.[62]

They postulated that the millennium began at Jesus' crucifixion, or possibly at Easter. Some also argue for its commencement at an unspecified time during Jesus' earthly ministry. All agree, however, that Christ had broken the power of Satan and cast him already into the Abyss.

Yet, in light of the fact that further characteristics concerning the angel's identity are missing, it might be better to assume that it is an angelic being operating under the authority of Christ. Since the dragon had lost his power already at the fight with Michael and his angels and, expelled from the heavenly realm, was thrown to the earth (Rev. 12:9), it is certainly not unthinkable that Christ could dele-

---

62 Some commentators, steering away from the historical interpretation of the millennium, contend that the angel is the Holy Spirit. This has remained, however, a minority view.

gate his authority again to another, or even the same, angel in the binding of Satan.[63] In this case it is significant that there is no direct confrontation between Christ and Satan. An angel suffices to subdue Satan. This authority is clearly symbolized in the possession of a key, which the angel used to open and close the "Abyss", the bottomless pit (cf. 9:1, 2, 11), sometimes translated also as "the deep" at other places of Scripture (Lk. 8:31; Rom. 10:7). It functions, according to Rev. 9:1ff., as the habitat of demonic spirits.[64]

To some commentators it appears doubtful that an angel can lay hold of Satan because both are immaterial beings.[65] Such a conclusion, however, can only arise in the mind of an interpreter who presupposes that spirits, i.e. immaterial beings, cannot function in the same ways that physical beings can. But why should this be inconceivable? Any interpreter of Scripture should be familiar with other passages which attribute physical properties to immaterial beings.[66] The biblical authors agreed upon the adequacy of using such language in describing the phenomena at hand. Therefore it must be possible that both aspects, the material and the immaterial, may coexist in the unseen realm, even though their correlation with each other is in its entirety incomprehensible.

The Seer John perceived another important item, a great chain, in the hand of the angel. Again this might be a symbolic feature pointing to the authority of the angel over its adversary, the dragon, or, as G. R. Beasley-Murray believes, a symbol for the word of God, which reduces Satan

---

[63] A passage resembling Rev.20:1-3 closely is found in *1 Enoch* 10:4-6. Raphael, an angel, is charged by God to bind Azazel, an evil desert spirit (cf. Lv. 16:8,10, 26), hand and foot, to throw him into a dark hole in the desert and close it up with stones in order to prevent his escape.

[64] Cf. Dt. 30:12-14 in LXX. Notice the contrast between the star fallen from heaven (Rev. 9:1), who has the key of the abyss and our present angel. The former fell; the latter descended.

[65] The Greek word which is used here to indicate the seizing of Satan is not "πιάζω"; "piazo", to capture, arrest, as in the case of the beast and false prophet in 19:20, but "κρατέω"; "krateo" implying fast or forcible seizure.

[66] (E.g. Gn. 6:2; Jdg. 6:11ff.; Ho. 12:4; Mt. 3:16).

to impotence.[67] A symbolic interpretation, as it is exemplified here, is, in my opinion, certainly adequate in explaining the true meaning of this passage.

Personally, however, I am more inclined to agree with J. A. Seiss, who countered the objection of some commentators that the actual binding of a spiritual being like Satan with a chain is impossible.

> Some have asked, with an air of triumph, how can a chain of iron or brass bind a spirit, and that spirit an archangel? But the record does not say that it is a chain of iron, or brass, or steel, or any other material of earthly chains. It is a chain of divine make ... What [it is] made of, and how [it] serves to bind the freedom of spiritual natures, it is not for us to know or show; but they are not therefore any less real and literal chains.[68]

The main thing which has to be kept in mind by interpreting this passage is that the language which the Seer John often employs is the language of appearance. Whatever visual impression he had seen as the images of the heavenly vision passed through his mind, he subsequently tried to describe in the most appropriate language possible. Bearing the purpose of his narrative in mind, he was not interested in giving his readers plausible arguments why it is possible to bind a spiritual being with a physical chain, but in describing its simple function, namely the binding of Satan. If he would have seen any contradiction in terms in describing his vision, he was in a position whereby he could have used a different word for the object which he saw in the hand of the angel. What reason should the interpreter of Revelation have in interpreting the word "chain" in Rev. 20 in any other than in its natural sense? Or what argument could be brought forth

---

67 G. R. Beasley-Murray, *Revelation*, Eerdmans, Grand Rapids, 1974, p. 284.

68 J. A. Seiss, *The Apocalypse*, Kregel, Grand Rapids, (1900) 1987, p. 446.

in favor of a spiritualized interpretation of the whole binding process of Satan?[69]

The whole thrust of the passage is focused on the fact that Satan's freedom of action is totally taken away from him by the direct intervention of God. The chain, which the angel had in its hand, was part of the equipment to accomplish that end. It must have been of such quality that Satan would not merely be hindered, but completely incapacitated in his operations. The added emphasis on his incarceration in the Abyss, which possesses all the qualification of an inescapable prison for spiritual beings (cf. Lk. 8:31; 2 Pet. 2:4; Jude 1:6), except if opened from without (cf. Rev. 9:1, 2), compounds the strength of the argument that God wanted his adversary to be shut up in a place where he would not be able to carry out his former activities. No person living at that time will be able to excuse his sinful behavior with the words "the devil prompted me to sin". Could God have chosen more forceful words to describe Satan's impotence and inability to be in touch with the affairs on earth at the time of the millennium than in this passage?

In verse 2 we read further that Satan is subdued and bound by the angel for a time span of one thousand years. The angel casts him into the Abyss and immediately thereafter locks its entrance. A seal is fastened on its door to ascertain Satan's incarceration and to render his deceptive activity among the nations impossible. This fact underscores, even further, that during the millennium Satan's interference with the proceedings on earth will be utterly impossible.[70] Only

---

69 J. A. Seiss expressed his opinion of what he thought would constitute the most appropriate interpretation of this passage in these words: "Is this a literal transaction? Certainly it is. The battle is literal; the taking of the Beast and the False Prophet is literal; the slaying of the kings and their armies is literal; Satan is literal; and his binding must be equally literal. It will not resolve itself into anything else, and fit to the connections or the terms" (ibid.).

70 The Greek word "σφραγίζω" („sfragizo") can mean the sealing of a stone to prevent its being moved (Dn. 6:17; Josephus, *Ant.*, 10.258; cf. Mt. 27:66), and may apply to the closing of a building so that one cannot open it (*Bel and the Dragon* 11:14); Walter Bauer, *A Greek-English Lexicon of the New Testament etc.*, 2 ed., The University of Chicago Press, Chicago, 1958, p. 796.

after the completion of one thousand years, as the angel declares, will he be allowed to leave his confinement for a little while.

Inasmuch as the incarceration of Satan is part of the systematic plan of God to punish his ancient adversary, it is seen here more under the aspect of a protective custody – "that he should deceive the nations no more" (Rev. 20:3b).

The idea of punishment, as important as it is, is probably only of secondary consideration in the present scenario.[71] As has been noted above, the final punishment of Satan will be meted out to him in the lake of fire at a later stage.

The different names of Satan are designations of abhorrence and contempt. They are descriptive of its bearer's evil nature. As the dragon, he fiercely persecuted the church throughout the centuries. As the ancient serpent (cf. Rev. 12:9), he was the deceptive force behind the original Fall of Man.[72] In both cases he exhibited utter hatred for his former creator, God, against whom he had rebelled in an ominous act of self-aggrandizement and became Satan, the adversary. Yet he will not finally succeed in his deceptiveness and cunning, his devilish nature will bring him down from heaven to earth and from earth to the Abyss, the abode of all unclean and evil spirits. When he is shut up in this horrible place which had been opened beforehand to release its inhabitants – the text speaks of locusts which were given the power of scorpions to torment those people on earth who did not possess the mark of God on their forehead (Rev. 9:1ff.) –, Satan will await his inevitable doom. As formidable as his evil power has been and as much havoc as he has caused, one thing becomes very clear, his confinement in the Abyss reveals his degradation to the status of an immeasurably inferior creature, incapable of averting his imprison-

---

71 The same contrast of ideas between punitive aspect of God's judgment and its liberating consequences can be observed in passages like *1 Enoch* 10:18 and Is. 24:21, 22, representing the first and *Jubilees* 48:15 the second aspect.

72 John Sweet thinks that in calling Satan the ancient serpent the author refers to Gn. 3. This reference prepares for the removal of the curse and recovery of the tree of life which is the theme of the next chapters (*Revelation*, SCM Press Ltd, London, 1979, p. 288).

ment by God through the agency of a heavenly angel. The attempt to usurp the heavenly throne has not only spoiled his once radiating beauty and holiness, but has also caused him to become the object of God's personal and unrelenting judgment.

We gather from these verses, especially verse 3, that the nations were not completely destroyed at the Battle of Armageddon, but spared from annihilation inasmuch as they did not join the armies of the Beast. These nations will form the subjects of Christ's kingdom during the millennium. For one thousand years Satan will by no means be able to interfere with the affairs on earth. The prince of this world has lost his destructive influence over the nations. The kingdom of God is visibly ushered in and the peoples on earth are ruled by the only rightful king, Jesus Christ. Justice and righteousness will prevail, as it has been promised of old (cf. Is. 9:7; 11:3b-5; 16:5; Je. 9:24; Dn. 9:24).

2.3.2. Controversy between Premillennialism and Amillennialism

If we come to the conclusion that John could have hardly used stronger words in describing Satan's incarceration, we shall have to take our stance in a weighty problem with which the interpretation of Rev. 20:1-10 confronts us. I am speaking of the controversy between the amillennial and the premillennial position.[73] The tempest of heated debates is

---

73 A further evaluation of the postmillennial position is not necessary for the purpose of this section. Lewis S. Chafer, wrote in the preface of Charles Feinberg's book, *Millennium. The Two Major Views*, p. 9: "Of the three contentions – postmillennialism, amillennialism and premillennialism, or as the latter was known in the early centuries from the Greek designation, chiliasm – postmillennialism is dead. Whether the present insane, corrupt condition of the world killed the theory by the contradiction of its own developing character, or whether the more intensified study of prophetic truth in these latter times so magnified its inconsistencies that it died, future historians must determine. To say that postmillennialism is dead, is not to imply that it does not occupy a large place in historical theology, nor that its theories are not found in theological works ... But it is dead in the sense that it offers no living voice in its own defense when the millennial question is under discussion."

raging around the first ten verses of Rev. 20. This passage constitutes the core, if not the only[74], passage about the millennium in the New Testament. The adherents of both camps recognize the mutually exclusive character of their particular systems of interpretation. This simply means that a decision in favor of one system is simultaneously a decision against the interpretation of the other. The answer to the following question is the touchstone of the differences between both systems. Is the scene which is portrayed in Rev. 20:1-10 referring to a future millennium or is it descriptive of the conditions present during this age, the age of the Church? In keeping with the interpretation of this passage as pointing to the interadvent period, amillenarians, in concord with Augustine, have to maintain that Satan is bound during the present age.[75] Is it tenable to assert that at Christ's first coming Satan has been cast into the Abyss? Can we follow Augustine's lead, as some commentators do[76], to take Luke 10:18, Christ's description of Satan's fall from heaven, as referring to his imprisonment (Rev. 20:1-3)? Does this text in Luke sufficiently prove that the devil was bound by Christ at his first coming? Beyond doubt the passage in Luke 10:18

---

74 See, footnote no.3.

75 The necessity of maintaining the binding of Satan can be avoided by "demythologizing" Satan or by seeing Jesus' death as conquering Satan, at least in principle (see footnote 78). In my opinion these two approaches in interpreting this text are fraught with grave difficulties in bringing out its true meaning.

76 A. A. Hoekema is representing this group of commentators. He wrote, for example, in referring to Lk. 10:17-18 the following: "These words [Satan's fall from heaven], needless to say, must not be interpreted as suggesting Satan's literal descent from heaven at that moment. They must rather be understood to mean that Jesus saw in the works his disciples were doing an indication that Satan's kingdom had just been dealt a crushing blow - that, in fact, a certain binding of Satan, a certain restriction of his power, had just taken place. In this instance Satan's fall or binding is associated directly with the missionary activity of Jesus' disciples" (*The Bible and the Future*, Paternoster, Exeter, 1978, p. 229). Another commentator defending this viewpoint is P. E. Hughes. He makes Mt. 12:24-32; 28:18-19; Mk 3:22-30; Lk. 10:17-19; 11:21-22; Jn. 12:31-32; Col. 2:15; Heb. 2:14-15; and Rev. 12:1-9 all refer to the binding of Satan in Rev. 20:2-3 and concludes that, because Satan is already bound, "the millennium is not a future but a present reality" (*Interpreting Prophecy*, Eerdmans, Grand Rapids, 1976, pp. 113-116).

teaches that Satan fell from heaven. We do not have any problems with that assertion. To say, however, that he was also bound and thrown into the Abyss is reading something into this text which is not stated or even implied. A. A. Hoekema quotes Mt. 28:19: "Go therefore and make disciples of all nations" as a scriptural basis to prove that Satan is bound during the interadvent age in the sense that he cannot hinder the preaching of the gospel. His argument runs like this: As Christ gave the Great Commission to his disciples, he might have been asked by them how it could be possible to obey this commandment if Satan continues to deceive the nations the way he has in the past. The reassuring answer, says Hoekema, is given by John in Rev. 20:1-3. His answer, although paraphrased, might have been like this:

> During the gospel era which has now been ushered in, Satan will not be able to continue deceiving the nations the way he did in the past, for he has been bound. During this entire period, therefore, you, Christ's disciples, will be able to preach the gospel and make disciples of all nations.[77]

Thus he concludes that "Satan cannot prevent the spread of the gospel nor can he gather all the enemies of Christ together to attack the church".[78] It is true that Satan is not able to prevent the spread of the Gospel in general. This, however, does not mean that he is bound. It only shows that he is limited in his power of what he can do. The question still remains to be answered whether Satan, if bound, is able to do anything at all. C. Feinberg made the observation

---

77 A. A. Hoekema, *The Bible and The Future*, The Paternoster Press, Exeter, 1978, p. 228; cf. P. E. Hughes, *Interpreting Prophecy*, Eerdmans, Grand Rapids, 1976, p. 112: "But his [Satan's] binding in relation to the nations is nonetheless real as the Gospel multiplies its conquests throughout the world."

78 Ibid.; cf. C. L. Feinberg countered the second part of Hoekema's conclusion as follows: "How many enemies are needed to attack the church? Does Satan find he is bound only to a certain number and free as to the rest?" (*Millennialism: The Two Major Views*, 3 ed., Moody Press, Chicago, 1980, p. 331).

concerning the interpretational dilemma of the amillennial system that

> one cannot have Satan bound and loose at the same time; the logic of language will not permit it. In what sense is Satan, then, bound? In what way is he loose? To empty plain language of all meaning is self-defeating, confusing, and less than worthy of the tremendous theme under discussion.[79]

Contrary to the amillennial position the combined testimony of the New Testament pictures Satan as a very agile and active spirit during this present age. It almost seems as if he is more at work today than in previous centuries. Although this might be overstated, he is certainly not less active in our time than in by-gone ages. He is still deceiving the nations with an unrelenting desire to bring them down to utter ruin. If the assertion is true that he was bound at the coming of Christ, how could he enter Judas and prompt him to betray his master (Lk. 22:3)? Who, if not Satan, incited Ananias and Sapphira to lie against the Holy Spirit as they pretended falsely to have given all the money from the sale of their property to the church? Did the Apostle Peter not immediately uncover the diabolic origin behind this hypocritical act as he retorted sharply, "Ananias, how is it that Satan has so filled your heart" (Acts 5:3)? In the first epistle of Peter the author admonished Christians "to be self-controlled and alert, [because] their enemy, the devil, prowls around like a roaring lion looking for someone to devour" (1 Pet. 5:8b). The reality behind this figure of speech cannot be reconciled with the notion of a currently impotent, incarcerated devil. The statement in 1 Peter is plainly depicting Satan's active opposition against all followers of Christ. Rev. 12:12 speaks of Satan as being filled with fury after his expulsion from heaven, because he knows that his time is short. He makes war against some of the woman's offspring – those who obey God's commandments and hold to the testimony

---

[79] C. L. Feinberg, *millennialism. The Two Major Views*, 3 ed., Moody Press, Chicago, 1980, p. 331.

of Jesus (Rev. 12:17).[80] Several passages in other portions of Scripture bring out the same truth.[81] We conclude from these passages that Satan is very agile and active during the present age and he has not yet been thrown into the Abyss. This means that the binding of Satan has not been achieved and will have to wait until the Second Coming of Christ.

The opponents of a literal interpretation of Rev. 20:1-10 contend that this passage is found in a book permeated with visionary and symbolic language which, by its very nature, lends itself to a figurative interpretation. Nobody would disagree with the observation that the book of Revelation is largely an account of diverse visions, apocalyptic scenes, and cataclysmic events. Very early in the book we read that the Seer John was invited to see a vision of the heavenly throne room. "At once," so John testified, "I was in the Spirit, and there before me was a throne ..." (Rev. 4:2). It should be noted that John was in some kind of altered consciousness ("in the spirit"), as he was shown these visions of heavenly and earthly scenes which he was commanded to write down. Revelation is therefore a book which is by its very nature a prophetic account of visionary events following, more or

---

[80] The story of Job, however, reveals a fuller picture of the actual power structure in the heavenly realms. Satan's power might be terrifying and imposing, but it has to yield ultimately to the supremacy and sovereignty of God. A dualistic world view in which the good and evil powers are set at parity with each other is not taught in Scripture. The devil is always subservient to God, just as a creature is subordinate to its creator. Satan's pretentious autonomy has no substance in reality. His claim to possess a certain measure of authority over the nations is, however, a somber reality which should not be belittled by any means (Lk. 4:5, 6; cf. 1 Jn. 5:18-19; Lk. 22:31).

[81] In his own unique style the Apostle Paul reiterated the same truth in his epistles over and over again. In his letter to the Corinthian church he portrayed Satan as a formidable adversary who tries to prevent human beings from understanding and accepting the Gospel (2 Cor. 4:3-4). In another passage he warned the believers about Satan's evil intentions of masquerading himself as an angel of light. Paul was referring here to the activity of false teachers who, under the influence of Satan, would try to subvert the truth of the Gospel (2 Cor. 11:14). He was also convinced that any unregenerate person would follow Satan (Eph. 2:2) and be dominated by him to carry out his will (2 Tim. 2:26). Yet he was also aware of Satan's attempts to avert believers from achieving their ministry objectives (1 Thes. 2:18).

less, an apocalyptic genre.[82] The passage in Rev. 20 unmistakably exhibits the same characteristics. While the expression "one thousand years" appears in verses 4 and 5, the section which belonged to the visionary part of this passage, it is mentioned also in verse 6. In this last verse John changed his form from merely describing his visions to interpreting the whole scene. Only by a direct revelation from God could John have known the exact length of time of Satan's imprisonment and thus understand its significance and purpose. His interpretation was based on additional information about the meaning of the vision which John, by necessity, received from God in the form of propositional revelation.

Although it is possible to come up with a spiritualized interpretation of the millennium, it is better to interpret the whole scene in an ordinary fashion, exegeting the natural sense of the words. Such an interpretation will lead to a premillennial position which argues for a literal millennium and the binding of Satan following Christ's Second Coming.

Much opposition was levelled against the idea of a literal millennium lasting exactly one thousand years. Abraham Kuyper, for example, voiced his opinion in this point by stating[83]:

> In every other writing the construction of the first ten verses of chapter 20 would require a literal interpretation, but as in Revelation the idea "thousand" is never taken literally, and also here merely expresses the exceeding fullness of the divine action, the precise, literal and historical understanding cannot be imputed to God, and the exegete is duty bound to interpret what as Divine language comes to us according to the claim of the exegesis that is adaptable to it.[84]

---

82 See chapter 2 of this book for a more extended study on the genre of Revelation.

83 It should be noted, however, that he made a surprising concession in regard to a literal interpretation as well.

84 A. Kuyper, *The Revelation of St. John*, trans. by J. Hendrik De Vries, Eerdmans, Grand Rapids, 1935, p. 277; cf. R. C. H. Lenski, in his commentary *The Interpretation of St. John's Revelation*, Lutheran Book Concern, Columbus, OH., 1935, pp. 568-569, follows along similar lines in stating

Even Augustine, while rejecting many features of a literal millennium in the attempt to harmonize the text of Rev. 20 with his own preconceived ideas, championed the concept of a literal one thousand year period, although he was not emphatic about it.[85] His expressions betray a certain degree of ambiguity.

At the turn of the first millennium the interpreters of Scripture who had adopted the Augustinian view were challenged in their amillennial position. The end of the world had not yet come as Augustine had anticipated. His interpretation of the millennium, as the interadvent age of the church lasting exactly one thousand years, was obviously a misconception and needed to be reinterpreted. But instead of looking for the exegetical fault in the equation of the interadvent age with the millennium, they revised Augustine's millennialism to mean only the unspecified length of the interadvent age. Following this decisive moment the general abandonment of a literal interpretation produced a high degree of arbitrariness in the exegesis of Rev. 20. It added considerably to the confusion of how the millennium should be understood. The millennium began, as it was postulated, at Jesus' crucifixion or possibly at Easter. Some commentators also argued for its commencement at an unspecified time during Jesus' earthly ministry. All agreed, however, that Christ had broken the power of Satan and cast him already into the

---

that, "these 1,000 years thus extend from the incarnation and the enthronement of the Son (12:5) to Satan's final plunge in hell (20:10), which is the entire New Testament period."

85 Cf. Augustine, *The City of God, The Fathers of the Church*, trans. by G.G. Walsh and G. Monahan, Fathers of the Church, Inc., New York, 1952, chap. 20. Augustine was an advocate of the view, common in his day, that human history would be completed in 6,000 years. Unlike some early premillenarians who held the same point of view but believed that the millennium would be the seventh millennium of history, Augustine felt that the seventh millennium was the eternal state. As Augustine followed what is known as the septuagint chronology which began the sixth millennium several centuries before Christ, he considered that the final millennium was well along at the time of his writing. In order to accommodate his point of view to Revelation 20, he held that "the first resurrection" is a spiritual resurrection which occurs when a person is regenerated by faith in Christ, while the second resurrection described in Revelation 20 occurs at the time of the Second Advent.

Abyss. From then on Revelation was interpreted from a church historical viewpoint. The twelfth-century Calabrian Abbot Joachim of Fiore, for example, believed that the angel, who cast Satan into the Abyss, is the Holy Spirit.[86] Zwingli's successor in Zurich, Heinrich Bullinger (1504-1575), thought the term "angel" needed to be understood spiritually as the "*ordo apostolicus*".[87] By this the Swiss reformer meant the spread of the Gospel as it was preached by the Apostle Paul. While Joachim of Fiore believed the millennium to be the time of the Holy Spirit, Bullinger put his emphasis on the expansion of the church as the hallmark of this period. The latter presented three possible options for the starting point of the millennium: (1) the ascension of Christ, (2) the imprisonment of Paul in Rome, or (3) the destruction of Jerusalem in A.D. 70. All three events contributed to the further advance of the Gospel, which, in Bullinger's eyes, was identical with the binding of Satan. In the nineteenth century Albert Barnes suggested that the millennium would last 360,000 years ("where a day [in the millennium] would stand for a year").[88] In the early twentieth century Baldinger, representing the sentiments of many others[89], was still vocal in repudiating the prophetic nature of Revelation and the idea of a millennial kingdom of Christ. Thus betraying the postmillennial bias so typical of his time he wrote, "[w]e believe it [millennium] refers merely to a great period of time of unknown length, in which evil will be

---

86 Joachim of Floris, *Expositio in Apocalypsis*, comm. on Rev. 20:1, A.D. 1527.

87 Heinrich Bullinger, *In Apocalypsin contiones*, comm. on Rev. 20:1, A.D. 1559.

88 Albert Barnes, *Notes, Explanatory and Practical, on the Book of Revelation*, Harpers, New York, 1851, pp. 260-261. Although he mentioned also other possibilities of interpreting the phrase of "one thousand years", for example, referring to a long but indefinite period of time or even a literal interpretation of one thousand years, he decided against them in his own commentary.

89 J. P. Lange, in his *Commentary on the Holy Scriptures*, Vol. XXIV: Revelation, pp. 342-346 listed several other examples.

more and more restrained and the gospel increasingly triumphant."[90]

2.3.3. Judgment and Resurrection

> I saw thrones on which were seated those who had been given authority to judge. And I saw the souls of those who had been beheaded because of their testimony for Jesus and because of the word of God. They had not worshipped the beast or his image and had not received his mark on their foreheads or their hands. They came to life and reigned with Christ for a thousand years.
>
> Rev. 20:4

Several factors are involved which render the interpretation of verse 4 difficult. The greatest problem lies in the fact that the author does not give enough information about the identity of those sitting on the thrones. He contents himself with saying that he saw thrones in heaven which were occupied with "those who had been given authority to judge".

In chapter 4 the occupants of the twelve thrones are simply called the elders (v.4). As far as the identification of the subject in Rev. 20:4 is concerned, we are left in the dark.[91]

The believers in Asia Minor might have been able to form a clear understanding as to the identity of those being mentioned by John in this scene. It is more likely, however, that they were in the same predicament, as later interpreters, of being left with the unsatisfactory alternative to make intelligent guesses. Consequently, different interpretations have been suggested by commentators in the past. Some of them thought that those sitting on the thrones were Christ in the company of all his saints, both of the Old and New Testaments. They pointed to Rev. 22:5 as indicating the

---

90 Albert H. Baldinger, *Sermons on Revelation*, G.H. Doran Co., New York, 1924, pp. 240-41.

91 In the Greek the subject of this clause is a personal pronoun (3 per. plural = "they") appended at the end of the verb "sit".

co-regency of Christ and his saints. This scene is also reminiscent of the heavenly court scene in Dn. 7:9ff. In this passage the Ancient of Days gave authority, glory and sovereign power to "one like a son of man" (v.13, 14). It was suggested that the parallelism of this passage in Daniel to the text of Rev. 20:4 supports the idea that Christ himself could be equated with the Ancient of Days (cf. Rev. 1:12ff. – the attributes of the Ancient of Days are those of Christ) and his saints as his assessors on the thrones (cf. Dn. 7:9; 1 Cor. 6:2).

It is, however, more likely to see God, the Father, in the Ancient of Days and Christ in the "one like a son of man". Then those who sit on the thrones might be the twenty-four elders mentioned in Rev. 4:4 (cf. 4:10; 5:8). Although the number twenty-four raises a problem with equating the elders with the twelve apostles, it seems as if they are included in this body of elders. Christ's prediction about the future position of the apostles in the Messianic kingdom renders such an interpretation possible. According to this prediction, Christ will confer a kingdom on his apostles, that they may "sit on thrones, judging the twelve tribes of Israel" (Lk. 22:29-30; cf. Mt. 19:28).

A further inference, similar to the one above, could be drawn from this interpretation that it is actually the church of which the apostles are only the representatives which will participate in the divine judgment. A few other passages in Revelation seem to support this interpretation. In Rev. 3:21 the right to sit on Christ's throne, is offered to those who overcome the world. A chapter earlier Christ had already made a similar promise, "To him who overcomes and does my will to the end, I will give authority over the nations – he will rule them with an iron scepter; he will dash them to pieces like pottery, – just as I have received authority from my Father (Rev. 2:26-27)." Therefore the identity of those who sit on the thrones might be first of all the twelve apostles who, quite possibly, function as the representative of the church as a whole. They will be employed by God to judge the house of Israel (cf. Ezk. 20:33-38).

Generally it is noticeable that whenever thrones are mentioned in Revelation they are set up in heaven and appear in connection with judgment. If judgment is executed it proceeds from the throne of God and those situated around it. However, in our present passage we do not find any reference to God or the elders. Nor do we perceive any intention on John's part to describe a detailed vision of judgment at this juncture of his narrative.

John seems much more interested in directing special attention to "those who had been beheaded because of their testimony for Jesus and because of the word of God." In defiance to the rule of the antichrist they did not bow their knees in homage to the beast or his image. Neither did they allow themselves to be identified with him by accepting the mark of his name, the number 666 (cf. Rev. 13:15-18), on their foreheads or hands. Being fully aware that persecution and martyrdom would seal their fate on earth, "they did not love their lives so much as to shrink from death" (Rev. 12:11c). As a reward the crown of life would be given to them by God (cf. Rev. 2:10-11). Arrayed in white robes, these martyrs, "who had come out of the great tribulation" (Rev. 7:14b), were worshipping God in heaven. John saw them standing in front of the throne of God, serving him continuously in his temple. In return they will be the objects of God's special attention. "[H]e who sits on the throne will spread his tent over them. Never again will they hunger; never again will they thirst ... For the Lamb at the center of the throne will be their shepherd; he will lead them to springs of living water. And God will wipe away every tear from their eyes" (Rev. 7:15b-17; cf. 7:9ff.). At the beginning of the millennium they will be resurrected and reign with Christ for a thousand years.[92]

---

[92] The verb "lived" (Gr. "ἔζησαν") in Rev. 20:4 implies the idea of coming to life again, thus the martyrs were resurrected by Christ at the beginning of the millennium, before they reigned with him on earth (cf. John 5:29; 11:25). Amillenarians who see here only a reference to a spiritual resurrection or regeneration contend that the verb "lived" does not mean a bodily resurrection, but simply "to live". Indeed, the word itself does not carry the particular meaning of resurrection. If, however, the context is taken into account, this word assumes the specific meaning of a bodily resurrection. Verse 5 referring to the rest of the dead who did not come to life until the end of the millennium uses the same verb "to live", thus alluding to the general resurrection of the unsaved, which is certainly a bodily resurrection. In Rev. 1:18 this verb is again used of Christ's resurrection. He states, "I am the Living One; I was dead, and behold I am alive

2.3.4. First Resurrection

> The rest or the dead did not come to life until the thousand years were ended. This is the first resurrection. Blessed and holy are those who have part in the first resurrection. The second death has no power over them, but they will be priests of God and of Christ and will reign with him for a thousand years.
>
> Rev. 20:5-6

The verses 5-6 further reveal the fact that the resurrection of the unbelievers will not coincide with the resurrection of the martyred saints. God intended to make a clear distinction between these two resurrections by chronologically separating them from each other by a time span of one thousand years. John is primarily concerned in these two verses with the resurrection of the martyred saints, calling it the first resurrection.

The word for "resurrection" (Gr. "ἀνάστασις") which he used here occurs about forty times in the New Testament. In all but one incidence it describes a bodily resurrection.[93] Therefore it is highly probable that this word carries the same meaning in Rev. 20:5-6. Amillennialists, however, believe that "ἀνάστασις" means spiritual resurrection (why we will see later). The question we have to address first is whether or not this word can indeed assume another meaning than bodily resurrection, i.e. spiritual resurrection, as it is used in 20:5. In answering this question the immediate context has to be the most determining factor. Such a study provides no cogent reason for understanding the first resur-

---

for ever and ever" (cf. Rev. 2:8). By necessity the saints who will be charged with governmental and judicial responsibilities will be given a glorified body similar to the one of Christ. Such an existence presupposes a bodily resurrection.

93 The notable exception is Luke 2:34. The word "ἀνάστασις" refers to the rising (figuratively) of those who would accept Jesus Christ as Messiah, as opposed to the falling of those who would not. In all other instances (e.g. Mt. 9:18; Rom. 14:9; 2 Cor. 13:4; Rev. 2:8 etc.) it means bodily (physical) resurrection.

rection as a spiritual resurrection limited to the martyred saints and the resurrection of the unbelievers at the end of the millennium as a bodily resurrection. This holds even true, if the broader context of the Old and New Testaments is considered. There is just no other instance where "ἀνάστασις" could possibly mean spiritual resurrection. The only conceivable reason why someone would want to change the common understanding and usage of "ἀνάστασις" in Rev. 20:5, is to maintain a consistent amillennial interpretation. If the first resurrection is indeed a spiritual resurrection, Rev. 20:1-10 could possibly describe the intermediate age, which, in turn, is of such great importance to an amillennial interpretation of the millennium. If "ἀνάστασις", however, means a bodily resurrection, a premillennial position has to be adopted, for only such a position harmonizes with this interpretation. Is it possible that hermeneutical principles are made subservient to theological presuppositions, only if it comes to interpret the passage about the millennium?[94]

Caird offers a unique interpretation of "ἀνάστασις", which appears to be an attempt to harmonize certain aspects of amillennialism with premillennialism. In his commentary he clearly states in regard to the necessity of two resurrections that:

> John seems to want the best of both worlds. He believes that the ultimate destiny of the redeemed is in the heavenly city, but he also retains the earthly paradise, the

---

94 If the word "ἀνάστασις" can also mean spiritual resurrection, why should Christ's resurrection be understood solely as a bodily resurrection and not also as a spiritual resurrection or any other kind of "resurrection", like a "resurrection" in the minds of his disciples to uphold the myth of his messianic claims. Of course, one has to apply the hermeneutical rule that the context qualifies the meaning of a word, if it can assume several meanings. That the word "ἀνάστασις" means bodily resurrection, if it is used in describing Christ's resurrection is thus determined by the context, for example, in Acts 2:31: "... he spoke of the "ἀνάστασις" (resurrection) of Christ ... that he was not abandoned to the grave, nor did his body see decay." The same rule should be strictly applied to determine the validity of any alternative meaning of "ἀνάστασις", which is proposed by commentators, especially if a diversion from the usual meaning occurs only rarely and would affect the interpretation of a passage drastically.

millennium. He therefore requires not one but two resurrections.[95]

Then Caird continues to explain what is meant by these two resurrections. "The first resurrection restores the martyrs to life for their millennial reign, the second brings all the dead before the great white throne."[96] Corroborating his assertion of an earthly paradise, he argues that John was not compelled by tradition to postulate two separate resurrections. "If he has wished to take the martyrs straight to heaven, there was ample precedent of his doing so."[97] He followed, however, the example of the Old Testament prophets who saw a historical significance in life on earth, be it that of individuals or nations. Ultimately it is God's purpose for his creations which has to be worked out in history and must be vindicated in history. Caird sees this purpose in the anticipation of a "time on earth when it is true to say: 'the sovereignty of the world has passed to our God and to his Christ.'"[98] Furthermore he states, that "unless the world is moving to such a goal, Christ has won only a Pyrrhic victory which, whatever the theologians may claim, leaves the powers of evil in possession".[99]

His interpretation of the first resurrection, up to that point, has much to commend itself to us. However, Caird does not leave it at that, but takes the whole idea a step further by asking what John meant by resurrection. "Did he really expect the martyrs to return to their fleshly bodies and resume a physical existence?"[100] Not only is the formulation of this last question curious considering what he said in the foregoing, but so are his answers. It seems as if he would

---

95 G. B. Caird, *The Revelation of St. John The Divine*, Hendricksons, Peabody, Mass., 1987, p. 254.

96 Ibid.

97 Ibid.

98 Ibid.

99 Ibid.

100 Ibid.

repudiate almost all assertions made up till now. As far as the first resurrection is concerned, he states:

> All the evidence we have is against such a literal interpretation. For John does not believe that the martyrs have all this time been lying in the sleep of death, waiting for the rending of the tomb. They have already put off their mortal garment of flesh and received instead the white robe of immortality (vi.11), breath of life from God has already come into them, and a cloud has carried them up to heaven (xi, 11f.).[101]

Either "John wished to take the martyrs straight to heaven," which, according to Caird, he could, but did not do, or, as Caird also asserts, "a cloud has carried them up to heaven." Again, did God intend to fulfill his purpose for his creation on earth including the resurrected martyrs, as Caird positively asserts, or did they share a common mode of existence with Christ in heaven, which he also believes?[102] His last argument is based on the assumption that the resurrection of the martyrs is parallel to that of Christ. "If they returned to bodily life, then [Christ] too must have done the same; if he did not, then neither did they."[103] Caird thinks he did not, thus the martyrs will not either. Yet he goes on to say, that "Christ's resurrection had a double sequel, in heaven and on earth: for in heaven he sat down beside his Father on his throne (3:21), and on earth he began a new activity, unbounded by limits of time and space, walking among the seven lamps of the world-wide church, ..."[104]

This argumentation leads Caird to conclude that the martyrs will share Christ's *heavenly* throne after their resurrection. The millennial reign of the martyrs is similar in kind

---

101 Ibid.

102 Ibid., p. 255.

103 Ibid. One is tempted to ask the question, did not Christ return to a bodily life on earth after his resurrection, though in his glorified body, which, as Christ himself testified, was made out of flesh and bones (Lk. 24:39)? Did he not eat a piece of fish in his disciples' presence (Lk. 24:43)?

104 Ibid.

to the reign which Christ had exercised ever since his own resurrection. This can only mean then that Caird believes in a future earthly paradise which will be ruled by Christ and the "resurrected"[105] martyrs in heaven. Why, however, does he conclude this passage in his commentary by stating that the resurrection of Christ and of the martyrs means "that they have been 'let loose into the world'"?[106]

Henry Alford pointed out that a literal understanding of Rev. 20:5-6 is more consistent with hermeneutical principles than any attempt to spiritualize the content of this passage. He observed generally that a spiritualized interpretation tends to yield to the dictates of a theological system. This can lead to distortions of the real meaning of the text. He mentioned Rev. 20:4-6 as a point in case.

> If, in a passage where two resurrections are mentioned, where certain [souls came alive] at the first, and the rest of the [dead] only at the end of a specified period after that first, – if in such a passage the first resurrection may be understood to mean spiritual rising with Christ, while the second means literal rising from the grave; – then there is an end of all significance in language, and Scripture is wiped out as a definite testimony to anything. If the first resurrection is spiritual, then so is the second, which I suppose none will be hearty enough to maintain: but if the second is literal, then so is the first, which in common with the whole primitive Church and many of the best modern expositors, I do maintain, and receive as an article of faith and hope.[107]

Thus I favor the interpretation of "ἀνάστασις" to mean bodily resurrection. If this is true, we have to explain why this bodily resurrection is called the first resurrection. It is

---

[105] Is it a spiritual resurrection, similar to the understanding of amillennialists? Caird does not state specifically, if he means that. However, it is not a bodily resurrection either. Caird is explicit on this point.

[106] Ibid.

[107] Henry Alford, *The Greek New Testament*, IV, 1894, revised by Everett F. Harrison, Moody Press, Chicago, 1958, p. 732-33.

certainly not the first resurrection chronologically. Obviously, Christ was resurrected as the firstfruit from the dead, as the Apostle Paul described him in 1 Cor. 15:20. He was the first to be raised from the dead and to receive a resurrection body. In the Gospel of Matthew another resurrection event is recorded as follows: "And when Jesus had cried out again in a loud voice, he gave up his spirit ... The tombs broke open and the bodies of many holy people who had died were raised to life. They came out of the tombs, and after Jesus' resurrection they went into the holy city and appeared to many people" (Mt. 27:50, 52-53). The interpretation of this passage is certainly not without its difficulties. It might be explained as an authentic resurrection of a token number of Old Testament saints in fulfillment of the symbolic meaning of the feast of the firstfruits (cf. Lv. 23:10). Personally, however, I believe that this particular incident was not a resurrection in the proper sense of the word, but rather a resuscitation. These OT saints were not yet given a resurrection body and died again some time later. I do not doubt, however, that this event had a symbolic character in keeping with the reason mentioned above.

The first resurrection in Rev. 20:5 is, therefore, not the first resurrection in an absolute, but only in a relative sense, describing primarily an order of resurrections and only secondarily a chronological sequence. The first is different in character from the second resurrection, but it also precedes the second by a thousand year period. As it is, only deceased believers will be raised in the first resurrection at the beginning of the millennium. The second resurrection, the resurrection of the unbelievers, will occur shortly after the millennium.

Again amillennialists contend that this text does not support the interpretation of two distinct bodily resurrections separated from each other by an interval of one thousand years. They believe this to be impossible in light of passages such as Daniel 12:2 and John 5:28-29 which apparently describe just one general resurrection. Apart from Rev. 20:4-6, so their argument runs, there is no other passage which possibly indicates a separation between the bodily resurrections of believers and unbelievers. Jn. 5:28 even uses the word "hour" (Gr. "ὥρα"; "hora") to emphasize the singleness of the resurrection event. This argument, however, is more apparent than real. It is certainly possible to interpret the passages supposedly referring to a general resurrection as a pronouncement of the fact that there will be a resurrection of the righteous and the wicked. This does not necessarily mean that this will occur at one particular moment, even though the word "ὥρα"; "hora" is used.[108] The very fact that detailed information is given in Rev. 20:4-6 about two distinct resurrections separated by one thousand years qualifies any other, more general, statements about the resurrection.[109]

In verse 6 the Seer John is particularly thrilled about his observation of the blessed state and holy character of those who participate in the first resurrection. They are assured that the second death, the eternal punishment in the lake of fire (Rev. 20:14b), will have no power over them. As priests of God and of Christ, they will share in the privilege of reigning with Christ on earth during the millennium. It should be noted again that this privilege is not only shared by the glorified members of the Church, but by all resurrected saints, including those of the Old Testament dispensation. As priests of God and of Christ, all aspects of the religious life of the earth's population will fall under their supervision. It is certainly not overstated that the worship of God will be their primary concern.

As the millennium draws close to its end, a change of the conditions prevailing during this Glorious Age will be expected. This change will be orchestrated by God himself in allowing Satan to leave his involuntary imprisonment again. The results following his release will be seen in the next two verses.

---

[108] Some Bible renditions like the *NIV* translate "hora" not as an hour, but as time period. "... for *a time* is coming when all who are in their graves will hear his voice" (v.28).

[109] An obscure, or less detailed, passage should always be interpreted in the light of a clear, or more elaborate passage.

2.3.5. Release of Satan and Final Rebellion

> When the thousand years are over, Satan will be released from his prison and will go out to deceive the nations in the four corners of the earth – Gog and Magog – to gather them for battle. In number they are like the sand on the seashore. They marched across the breath of the earth and surrounded the camp of God's people, the city he loves. But fire came down from heaven and devoured them.
>
> Rev. 20:7-9

The word indicating the end of the millennium is derived from the Greek word "τελέω"; "teleo". It occurs twice, in 20:3 and 20:5, and carries the connotation of "brought to the goal or the end". Thus it is often rendered into English by the words "finished", "completed", or "ended". Thus it is made clear that the millennium is only a preliminary stage of the following eternal kingdom of God. The end of the millennium coincides with the release of Satan from his prison, the Abyss. Its sealed door will be opened again and its prisoner allowed to escape. If we have hoped that Satan's evil nature might have been changed during his long imprisonment, we shall be disappointed. It seems as if the time of his confinement in the Abyss has only made him more determined to return to his former cunning ways. At the same time, however, he appears to be keenly aware of the shortness of the time allotted to him for the final completion of his diabolic activities. Now, after all restraints have been taken away, he will lead the nations in rebellion against God.

The question which needs to be addressed is: Why will Satan be released from his confinement in the Abyss after the completion of the millennium?[110] Why is he allowed to work havoc on earth again, after he had been successfully incapacitated for one thousand years? Why did God allow such an insidious act against his own sovereignty again?

---

110 The Gr. word "δεῖ";"dei" (must) in Rev. 20:3 implies divine necessity.

Obviously there must be a good reason for it. Commentators have given different answers. A partial answer was provided by the German NT scholar, Adolf Schlatter, in his *Erläuterungen zum Neuen Testament*:

> The reason why his time has not yet come to an end, but the Abyss is opened for him again, is that the plight and salvation, of which John prophesied, does not yet encompass the entire human race.[111]

An English commentator, Robert Govett, gave a more comprehensive answer. The four sensible reasons he mentioned are the following: first, to demonstrate that man even under the most favorable circumstances will fall into sin if left to his own choice; second, to demonstrate the foreknowledge of God who foretells the acts of men as well as his own acts; third, to demonstrate the incurable wickedness of Satan; fourth, to justify eternal punishment, that is, to show the unchanged character of wicked people even under divine jurisdiction of a long period of time.[112]

The nations will be an easy prey for the devil. They will give in quickly to the temptations set before them. Instead of resisting the diabolic insinuations to fall away from Christ, under whose government they had enjoyed unprecedented prosperity and peace, they will join forces to overthrow his righteous reign. This treacherous act of rebellion will be but a final manifestation of the corrupt nature of human beings. Despite paradisal conditions, the human nature, if left to itself, will remain evil and only the provision of an opportunity will suffice to arouse its hostile disposition towards God.

---

111 Adolf Schlatter, *Erläuterungen zum Neuen Testament*, vol. III, 1938, p. 323: „Der Grund, weshalb seine Zeit noch nicht zu Ende ist, sondern der Abgrund sich wieder für ihn öffnet, besteht darin, daß die Not und Errettung, von der Johannes weissagt, noch nicht die ganze Menschheit umfaßt." (English trans. mine).

112 Robert Govett, *The Apocalypse Expounded by Scripture*, Thynne, London, 1920, pp. 506-508.

The nations are termed "Gog and Magog", which might be an allusion to the event described in Ezk. 38 and 39.[113] Thus John would have described the invasion of the Holy Land and the siege of Jerusalem by an army from the north as the fulfillment of Ezekiel's prediction. At first glance this interpretation seems to explain the situation at hand. G. B. Caird, however, believes that it is inadequate and too simple. He states,

> It is inadequate because there has already been one fulfillment of this prophecy in the banquet of the birds, and there was no need to introduce another, unless John had found in Ezekiel some truth of ultimate and abiding significance.[114]

After discussing in detail the meaning of Gog and Magog, as they appear in Ezekiel, adducing additional evidence from the Jewish apocalyptic, he draws the parallel to the events described in Revelation. Then he says,

> The myth of Gog enshrines a deep insight into the resilience of evil. The powers of evil have a defence in depth, which enables them constantly to summon reinforcement from beyond the frontiers of man's knowledge

---

113 G. R. Beasley-Murray sees in the expression "Gog and Magog" a reference to the "Gog of the land of Magog" in Ezekiel. First, he explains the sequence of Ezekiel's prophecy about the invasion of the Holy Land. After the Jews return from their exile among the nations they dwell in the peace of the messianic age under the new David (see especially 38:8). Gog, a prince of a northern country by the name of Magog (Ezk. 38:1; cf. 39:6), comes at the head of many people 'like a cloud' and attacks Jerusalem presumptuously. The Lord, however, will create confusion amongst the invaders, so that every man's sword is against his brother. Then Beasley-Murray draws the parallel with the reference of Gog in Revelation by stating: "As Ezekiel sees in God's invasion the fulfillment of earlier prophecies of Gentile attacks on Israel, so John sees in the hosts of Gog and Magog a symbol of the evil in the world of nations which resist the rule of God. For him, therefore, the attack of Gog comes not from one corner of the earth - the north - but from all four corners. In congruence with Schlatter, he expresses doubt about John's intention to point to the nations beyond the Roman empire which had been untouched by the rebellion under the Antichrist (*op. cit.*, p. 297).

114 G. B. Caird, *op. cit.*, p. 256.

and control. However far human society progresses, it can never, while this world lasts, reach the point where it is invulnerable to such attacks ... But even when progress issues in the millennium, men must remember that they still have no security except in God.[115]

If the context is taken into account, it is more likely, however, that the term "Gog and Magog" has two different meanings in both cases. The event which Ezekiel predicted is an intrusion of a military power into Palestine from the north. In Revelation the designation "Gog and Magog" is a collective term comprising all nations. Another difference is seen in the chronological sequence of the events. The "Gog and Magog" of Ezekiel attacks the Holy Land, as it appears, shortly before the beginning of the millennium, whereas "Gog and Magog" of Revelation will march into battle at its end. Again the army from the north in Ezekiel will be slain and buried on the mountains of Judah, while the forces gathered against the reign of Christ in Revelation are consumed by fire from heaven. The term "Gog and Magog" is here employed in a wider sense than in Ezekiel, differing both in time and detail.

The camp of the saints will be encircled by a great number of enemies, as countless as "the sand on the seashore", coming from all directions. Under the leadership of Satan they intend to destroy the capitol city of God's sovereign rule and its inhabitants. The word "camp" (Gr. "παρεμβολή"; "parembole")[116] meaning "the congregation of those engaged in battle" suggests that God's army is prepared for the ensuing battle. Yet, as the text further reveals, the saints do not need to ward off and fight the hostile armies themselves.

---

[115] Ibid., p. 257; further on he states that "this is, in fact, the mythical equivalent of the Pauline doctrine of justification by faith alone, which teaches that from start to finish man's salvation is the work of grace, and never at any time his own achievement" (ibid.).

[116] Caird sees a parallel meaning between the Greek word "παρεμβολή" in this verse, and Israel's wilderness home in the story of the Exodus. Thus he makes the interesting remark that "God's people are still, even in the golden age of the millennium, the church in the wilderness, the church in pilgrimage" (Caird, *op. cit.*, p. 257).

Rather it is God who will pour out his wrath upon his enemies single-handedly. The camp is also described as "the city he loves". R. H. Charles asserted that this verse is part of the description of the New Jerusalem. This understanding created a serious problem for him, in that the context militated against such an interpretation. As a remedy he proposed a drastic surgical operation of the text.[117] However, the process of reconstructing passages of the Bible to align them with a given interpretation is dangerous. Thus it is much better to understand this phrase, as most commentators do, to mean simply the present city of Jerusalem. The array of innumerable enemies and their attempt to besiege the beloved city is soon followed by divine judgment. God sends fire from heaven to consume his enemies. In the instance of a moment the last rebellion of mankind is squelched supernaturally. The attacking armies will lie slain before the doors of Jerusalem. This picture of destruction is reminiscent of the fate which had met Sodom and Gomorrah centuries earlier. Certainly the writer of 2 Peter was thinking of the relationship between these two events, as he described God's judgment on the ungodly: "If he condemned the cities of Sodom and Gomorrah by burning them to ashes, and made them an example of what is going to happen to the ungoldy ... if he this is so, then the Lord knows how to rescue godly men from trials and to hold the unrighteous for the day of judgment, while continuing their punishment" (2 Pet. 2:6,9).

With the utter destruction of his allied armies, Satan's final doom is sealed. His pretension of usurping the throne of God and commanding the worship of mankind for himself have turned out as nothing more than the vain ambi-

---

117 Charles's problem with the structure of the last chapters of Revelation arose from his interpretation of the phrase "the city he loves" to mean the New Jerusalem, because at that point John has not yet seen the holy city descend from heaven. His proposed solution is to remove the passages, Rev. 21:9-22:2 and Rev. 22:14, 15, 17, from the contexts in which they are placed and to insert them after Rev. 20:3 (R. H. Charles, *The Revelation of St. John*, T. & T. Clark, Edinburgh, 1920, Vol. II, pp. 144ff.). In all due respect of Charles's scholarship, I believe that this practice is fraught with more difficulties than it is meant to solve. Caird's comment should be heeded: "There is no need for surgery" (Caird, *op. cit.*, p. 257).

tions of a rebellious spirit. The tragedy which his rebellion brought on countless millions of people is, however, fathomless. God's triumph over the powers of darkness has reached its culmination point in the final judgment of Satan.

2.3.6. Satan's Final Judgment

> And the devil, who deceived them, was thrown into the lake of burning sulphur, where the beast and the false prophet had been thrown. They will be tormented day and night for ever and ever.
>
> Rev. 20:10

Step by step God has executed his verdict on the powers of evil in rendering their deceptive influence upon the peoples of the earth inoperative and in punishing them positively for their wickedness. The Beast and the false prophet, the other evil characters in the eschatological drama, had been thrown into the lake of fire at the beginning of the millennium. Now their master, the originator of all wickedness and rebellion, will be compelled to join his former dupes at this place of torment.[118]

The Greek language could not possibly be more emphatic in describing the duration and severity of eternal punishment than by using the phrases "day and night" and "for ever and ever" (literally "to the ages of ages"). The punishment allotted to Satan, the beast, and the false prophet will be a consciously-experienced torment for all eternity. The Bible does not mention any indication of a possible redemption of fallen angels. Rather the opposite is often asserted in the respective texts. As Jesus, for example, healed

---

[118] In *1 Enoch* 18:12-16; 19:1-2; 21:1-6, the author described a scene of a burning abyss in which the evil angels are punished for ten thousand years until the final judgment day. The contrast between the abyss and the lake of fire is not so clearly drawn in these passages as in Revelation. The Abyss in Revelation is different from the lake of fire inasmuch as it is a prison for Satan and his demons whereas the latter is a place of active punishment.

two demon-possessed men in the region of the Gardarenes, the evil spirits were afraid he would throw them into the Abyss and torture them before the appointed time (Mt. 8:29b; cf. Mk 5:1ff.; Lk. 8:26ff.). Thus they must have been aware of their final condemnation and punishment.

The lake of fire, the second death, as it is called in verses 6 (also in v.14), will be populated by all those who did not accept God's salvation in Christ during their life time. Death for them will not mean the complete annihilation of their existence, but they will spend eternity in a state of agony and pain (cf. Mt. 13:42; 25:41, 46 etc.).

After having presented some modern views of the millennial passage in Revelation 20 and interpreted its first ten verses, in an attempt to present the millennialism of the Seer John, we will turn now to a study of the different principles of biblical interpretation used by the Church Fathers.

Chapter 3
Principles of Biblical Interpretation in the Early Church

3.1. Introduction 92
3.2. Patristic Exegesis 93
    3.2.1. Christological Interpretation 93
    3.2.2. Spirit-Enlightened Interpretation 98
    3.2.3. Allegorical Interpretation 100
    3.2.4. Literal Interpretation 102
3.3. Patristic Formulation of Dogmas 105
3.4. Conclusion 106

3. Principles of Biblical Interpretation in the Early Church

3.1. Introduction

In the course of Christian history many different methods have been employed to interpret the books of the Bible. These methods have evolved gradually as the community of believers was confronted with the need of making the biblical message understandable and applicable to the situation of their own day and age. Being the recipients of documents so highly esteemed as the Scriptures, they accepted the challenge to discover the spiritual treasures contained in these documents and to communicate them to their immediate audience. Simply to read them was not enough to meet that need. They recognized the modifying influence of different time periods and cultural settings on their own cognitive processes. Moreover, they became aware of the necessity to distinguish between those records in the Bible which were temporary, spoken specifically to a particular situation, and those which were eternal, delivered permanently to a universal audience. In this context they recognized the necessity to understand how God had manifested himself in concrete situations as the God of history. God's actions, if not overruled by his sovereignty, were variable and dependable on external factors. They were fixed to a particular situation, a specific time and a certain person or group of persons, but they pointed to the underlying principles of his holy character and made them perceivable to the human mind; and only the latter could provide the key to the knowledge of God. In understanding them, God's being was recognizable; and only the knowledge of his being made his action intelligible. Thus the task of correctly interpreting the Scriptures became paramount to the Church Fathers. They needed the hermeneutical tools in order to fulfill their obligation successfully. Their creativity in devising and developing a methodology of interpretation which met the apparent need will be seen throughout the following pages. However, before we begin with a detailed description of the different hermeneutical principles in the patristic literature, it will be helpful to shortly outline the flow of thought in this chapter.

The Church Fathers unanimously agreed upon one unifying element of Scripture in both the Hebrew Bible and the New Testament. Thus, we will ask ourselves first, what it was and how the Church Fathers did implement it? Secondly, we will look at the role the early Church ascribed to the Holy Spirit in the exposition of Scripture? Was it only seen as mediatorial, as the inspiring power behind the human authors of Scripture, or did it encompass broader hermeneutical significance as the illuminating factor in the process of interpretation? Thirdly, it will be interesting to see how the influence of different traditional methods of interpretation affected the hermeneutical principles of theological schools in cities like Alexandria and Antioch. In this context the competing systems of allegorical and historical exegesis will be looked at more closely. Lastly, the function of the ecumenical councils in providing a basis for an authoritative formulation of Christian dogmas will concern us in view of its influence on the development of hermeneutical principles in the early Church.

3.2. Patristic Exegesis

3.2.1. Christological Interpretation

In order to make the meaning of the books of the Hebrew Bible and New Testament understandable the Church began to look for teachers who were able to instruct the larger Church body in the truths of the Christian faith. The apostles and others, in imitating the example of the Lord, had instructed young believers in various churches. These believers were often gifted individuals who were soon to occupy leading positions in the Church. At a later time the most prominent among them were respectfully and with much affection called Church Fathers. Irenaeus, in his fight against the Gnostics, stressed the importance of ordained Church leaders who were reliable interpreters. He called them presbyters. In his opinion they had received their ecclesiastical authority through an uninterrupted line of continuity from the Apostles to their disciples. In order to be recognized by the Church, as such, they had to exhibit the evidence of their authority in their life and doctrine with the "charism of truth".[1] Thus he maintained that only within the Church, as the consequence and concomitant of apostolic succession, the function of sound scriptural interpretation could be rightly executed by authorized persons. The Church Fathers alone perpetuated the true apostolic tradition, not just any tradition. An interpretation based on this foundation was the true gnosis.[2]

The Church Fathers produce various commentaries and other devotional literature for the better understanding and dissemination of the Christian faith. In an age when inspired writings were not universally accessible to every believer their service in expounding spiritual truths was invaluable to the Church.

The hermeneutical question, however, posed a more, or at least equally, serious problem to them than the canonical. There was no unified approach to interpret the Scriptures. The Church Fathers had to devise a system of principles in order to interpret correctly the understanding of the biblical message. The principles which they developed were usually based on traditional exegetical methods found at various places. The Alexandrians, especially, utilized the concepts of Platonic philosophy to construe a well-defined system of hermeneutical principles. The Antiochenes were keen on methods which emphasized the literal sense of the documents. Their orientation tended toward a historical and typological interpretation. They strove after a hermeneutical methodology which was as closely in line with the practice of their apostolic predecessors as possible. Yet unconsciously, perhaps, they did not exclusively depend on the principles of apostolic interpretation, but incorporated into their exegesis hermeneutical elements of Rabbinic Judaism which they partially developed into their own schemes.

---

[1] Irenaeus, *Haer.* 4.26.2; 1.10.1-2.

[2] Ibid., 4.33.8.

Naturally any methodology of interpretation which came in vogue among the Church Fathers was based on theological presuppositions. This was just as true in the first centuries as it is today. The early Church realized that certain dynamic elements were at work in the exegetical process. As different interpretational principles were brought to bear on the biblical text, they influenced and altered the theological framework underlying them. Thus the interrelatedness between biblical text, theology, and interpretation became clear to them. Not always was the desire for a different hermeneutical approach accompanied by an improved theology nor did a defective theology bring forth a better hermeneutic. Robert Grant emphasized the same point when he said,

> When Gnostics insisted that the real God was quite different from, and even opposed to, the God of the Old Testament, they could hardly understand the revelation of the God whom Jesus called Father. When Alexandrian theologians laid tremendous emphasis upon the impassibility of God, they had to allegorize away the passages in the Old and New Testament alike, in which it is quite clear that God is not impassible. A faulty theology used a faulty method of exegesis as its instrument.[3]

A deeper knowledge of the Scriptures was needed to create a refined theological system which in its turn generated a more accurate hermeneutical methodology. With the help of better interpretational tools the Church Fathers could widen their understanding of God's word. In modern times this phenomenon has been termed a hermeneutical circle.

Let us go back now to the point where the early Church Fathers started on their hermeneutical quest. The most fundamental principle of biblical exegesis was the binding unity between the Hebrew Bible and the New Testament. In

---

[3] R. Grant and D. Tracy, *A Short History of the Interpretation of the Bible*, SCM Press, London, 1984, p. 4.

studying the prophetic books of the Hebrew Bible in the light of the Gospels it became abundantly clear to them that the events surrounding the life of Jesus Christ, his death, and resurrection were typologically foreshadowed long ago and had found their fulfilment. Thus the unity of Scriptures was perceived of as existing in two essential, complementary parts: the promises in the Hebrew Bible and their fulfilment in the New Testament. Was not the most basic message of the New Testament that the fullness of God's revelation had reached its pivotal point in the coming of his Son Jesus Christ? The predictions of the Hebrew Bible had looked forward to his appearance. Now that he had come, no further fulfilment was to be expected. The suffering Servant of God, so vividly portrayed by prophets like Isaiah (e.g. 50:6; 52:14; 53:1-10) had brought them anew into an existential encounter with the God. This God of the Hebrew Bible could only be comprehended as he was revealed in his Son, Jesus Christ, the central person of the New Testament. The provisional form of Judaism was brought to completion in the revelation of Jesus Christ. For example, it was fundamental to Origin's theology that in the substitutionary atonement of Christ the cultic sacrifices prescribed in the Pentateuch were fulfilled.[4] He used the metaphor of a symphony[5] to describe the essential oneness of both Testaments. Tertullian represented the Hebrew Bible symbolically as the seed of which the New Testament is its fruit.[6] They were both convinced that while the form in which the divine revelation might appear is subject to change, its essential meaning remains the same.[7] Commenting on this phenomenon Augustine could only reiterate what had been said before him; the New Testament is latent in the Old and the Old Testament is patent in the New.[8] Reading the Old Testament from the vantage point of the New was thus made imperative for a correct understand-

---

4 Origen, *Hom. on Lv.* 1, 4-6.

5 Origen, *Hom. on John* 5:8.

6 Tertullian, *Adv. Marc.* 4,11.

7 Ibid., 4,39; Origen, *Comm. on Mt.* 14,4.

8 Augustine, *Quaest. in hept.* 2 qu. 73; cf. Augustine, *De civ.* 20,4.

ing of both.[9] Thus every line of patristic thinking converged to the center of the Scriptures, Jesus Christ, the Messiah. This can be seen already in the typology of the *Epistle of Barnabas* (c. A.D. 135) which pictured the true temple and the true Sabbath in the person and work of Christ[10] or, as Irenaeus affirmed, in the higher righteousness of Christ being foreshadowed, but not realized in the law.[11] In *Adversus Haereses* 4.26 he argued further that in the event of Christ's coming the Christians possessed a key to unlock all the mysteries of God's eternal administration ("οἰκονομία"). These hidden truths of the Hebrew Bible must be brought to light. Yet without recognizing Christ as the underlying principle, the Jews were devoid of the right explanation. Chrysostom voiced the opinion that the deeper meaning of the Hebrew Bible can only be elucidated by looking at its Christ-centered purpose.[12] Augustine argued along the same line of thought. He stated that the disciples had been instructed by Christ about the fulfilment of all the prophecies of the Hebrew Bible in his person.[13]

Irenaeus envisioned also a universal biblical history and communicated these ideas in his writings to the early Church. Christ's first advent was "in the last times", but its significance extended to all generations. Therefore the Hebrew Bible did not only predict typologically his first coming, but also the dispensation of the Church and his glorious Second Coming.[14] He was probably the first Christian exegete who developed the concept of progressive revelation.[15] He saw no discrepancy between this idea and the assertion that the same God revealed himself both in the Hebrew Bible and the New Testament. Obscure passages in the Hebrew Bible, often written in the symbolic language of

---

9 Augustine, *De civ.* 20,4.

10 *Epistle of Barnabas* 15-16.

11 Irenaeus, *op. cit.* 4.12-13.

12 Chrysostom, *Hom. on John* 11.

13 Augustine, *Jews* 7.

14 Irenaeus, *op. cit.* 4.22; 4.33.1.

15 Ibid., 3.12.14; 4.13.

the prophets, could be interpreted according to the truths revealed in the New Testament.[16] This explains why the Church Fathers were so eager to exploit the apparent supremacy of Christianity over any other form of religion, especially Judaism. They knew that, in the process of finding its own identity, the Church had to distance itself from the wrong concept of being only a Jewish sect. They argued that the Christian Church superseded the Jewish synagogue by the providential intervention of God himself. As a consequence the Scriptures of the Hebrew Bible were now seen as the possession of the Church. Justin Martyr asserted in the presence of the Jew, Trypho, that the Christians would have a better claim on the Scriptures of the Hebrew Bible than the Jews because the latter read it without comprehending its meaning.[17] He based the Christians' exclusive claim on the Hebrew Bible on the fact that many prophetic passages were, even to the very minute detail, fulfilled in Christ. Trypho in his polite, but resolute, rejection of Justin's attempt to link the Hebrew Bible with the New Testament via fulfilled prophecy must have made an impression on the Christian apologete. Justin might have asked himself, why his Jewish friend did not see the apparent connections between the two parts of Scripture? Was there something, if it was missing, which prevented other people, Jews and Gentiles alike, from recognizing the unity of the Scriptures on the basis of a christological exegesis? Indeed this was the case.

3.2.2. Spirit-Enlightened Interpretation

The Church Fathers realized soon that they could not assume that everybody was agreeing with them on a unified meaning of Scripture. The Jews, certainly, did not share their enthusiasm about a christological interpretation of OT passages. Isaiah 53 was for them a prediction about the suffering people of Israel, not a prophecy about the vicarious death of Jesus Christ as the true Servant of the Lord. The

---

16 Ibid., 1.10.1.

17 Justin Martyr, *Dial.* 29.

New Testament was rejected by them in its entirety, because it formed the basis of the Christian faith, not their own. They did not want to accept the messianic claims of Jesus Christ as they were recorded in the Gospels. In their eyes the promises of the Hebrew Bible concerning the coming of the Messiah had not yet been fulfilled.

The unbelieving pagans were even less interested in the New Testament. The person of Christ was nothing more to them than an obscure Jewish man who had died a criminal's death. They could not understand why this Jesus of Nazareth, who failed so tragically in whatever his mission was, had such an irresistible attraction to the Christians. Although at times they might have even acknowledged him as an outstanding teacher of high moral standards, yet they did not feel obligated to worship him as the Son of God, the risen Lord of the universe.

These adverse reactions of both the Jews and the Gentiles were reason enough to conclude that, in order to understand the Scriptures, more was needed than the human mind was capable of comprehending. The Church Fathers discovered that a spiritual, and thus to them a correct, understanding of Scripture was a special gift of God to every believer. Only the Holy Spirit could illuminate the mind of even the most ordinary Christian to enable him in the task of interpreting the Bible. According to Clement of Alexandria, both the influence of the Holy Spirit[18] and an open mind[19] were essentially important for any Christian interpreter. Chrysostom emphasized that only a believer by exercising his faith could hear the voice of the Spirit and perceive spiritual realities.[20] Justin must have had a similar idea in his mind as he told Trypho that Christians are persuaded [by the Holy Spirit] whenever they read the Scriptures.[21] Augustine was convinced of the Holy Spirit's role in enabling the interpreter to receive a spiritual understanding of the Scrip-

---

18 Clement of Alexandria, *Strom.* 7, 29.

19 Ibid., 7,16,93ff.

20 Chrysostom, *Hom. on John* 1.

21 Justin Martyr, *op. cit.* 29.

tures.[22] In commenting on 2 Cor. 3:6, "the letter kills, but the Spirit gives life", he asserted that the Spirit is only found when a person approaches the Bible with piety and prayer, reason and intellect.[23] He frankly admitted that the profound mysteries of the Bible humble the interpreter in reminding him of his preliminary knowledge in spiritual matters. But he maintained also that the way of salvation can be known to anyone who has found the Holy Spirit.[24]

Augustine was destined to become one of the most influential Latin Church Fathers. In his advocacy of the allegorical method, although cautioning his contemporaries about its abusive potential, he opened the doors for its penetration into the Western Church to leave its indelible stamp on Latin Christianity.

3.2.3. Allegorical Interpretation

The Church Fathers' predilection for the allegorical method of interpretation can be seen already at an early date in the *Epistle of Barnabas*. In the attempt to allegorize even the most mundane facts, its author interpreted the number of Abraham's servants who routed the army of five kings, namely 318, as pointing to Christ and his crucifixion.[25] With the ascendancy of the Catechumen School of Alexandria the allegorical interpretation of Scripture received its strongest impetus which contributed to its wide-spread use among the Church Fathers. Its influence exceeded far beyond the boundaries of Egypt and left a lasting mark on the history of biblical exegesis. All Church Fathers, to a greater or lesser degree, employed the principles of a spiritualizing interpretation. Following the example of Philo, Origen saw various reasons for the allegorical interpretation of Scripture. First, many passages of the Scriptures could only be understood in

---

22 Augustine, *Conf.* 5,14.
23 Augustine, *De doct.* 2,42.
24 Augustine, *Letters* 137,1,3.
25 *Epistle of Barnabas* 9.

a spiritual sense.[26] Second, the New Testament authors seemed to have applied allegorical principles in their interpretation of quotations from the Hebrew Bible. Third, God differentiated between ordinary Christians and more intellectually inclined biblical scholars in elucidating spiritual truth differently to these two groups of believers. In regard to the first group he accommodated himself to their intellectual limitations, in that they were only able to understand the plain meaning of Scripture, the historical sense, as Origen called it. If a believer was empowered, through his higher intellect, not only to recognize the historical, but also the typological and devotional sense, he belonged to the second group. Origen derived the categories for his three senses of Scripture from an analogy with the body, soul, and spirit of a human being.[27] Furthermore he argued that the allegorical exegesis is best suited to bring out the spiritual meaning of Scripture, because of the spiritual nature of its actual author, the Holy Spirit. Origen adhered to these allegorical principles assiduously in his own writings. The voluminous amount of literature which bears his name points persuasively to the breadth of his imagination and the vastness of his intellect. Many succeeding generations of Church teachers followed in his footsteps and imitated his style of interpretation. Jerome, who became a strong opponent of Origen in his later years, still paid him homage in accepting the threefold understanding of Scripture.[28] Augustine developed Origen's allegorical method further into four different senses and changed the terminology slightly. The first sense of Scripture he called the historical, the second and third aetiological and analogical and the last figurative sense.[29] Augustine recognized the grave danger of allegorizing the Bible without the restrictions of any safeguarding principles. Biblical truth could too easily be subjected to arbitrary speculation, if the interpreter's imaginative power set the only

---

26 Origen, *De prin.* 4,3,1.

27 Ibid., 4,2,4.

28 Jerome, *Epist.* 120.

29 Augustine, *De. doct.* 3, 27, 38 etc.

limitation. Therefore, in his attempt to guard the interpretation of Scripture from the onslaught of unbridled fantasy, he argued for a controlled use of the allegorical method on the basis of two hermeneutical rules. A spiritualized interpretation is only acceptable if it corresponds to both the clear meaning of another biblical passage and the Christian principles of love and faith.[30] If these hermeneutical rules were to protect Scripture from a proliferation of interpretations based on the spiritualizing approach, they were not completely successful in achieving their objective. The trend to allegorize vast portions of the Bible became momentous as Augustine's fourfold classification developed into the well-known historical, allegorical, moral, and anagogical senses of later times. Augustine himself became famous for his own allegorical interpretations. Yet not all Church Fathers approved of the legitimacy of spiritualization, even if it was guarded against possible abuses by restricting rules. The value of a literal interpretation was emphasized by the Antiochene school of theology.

3.2.4. Literal Interpretation

The Church Fathers agreed upon the inspiration of the Bible by the Holy Spirit, the unity of both Testaments, and the centrality of Jesus Christ. The assumption that the patristic exegesis was irredeemably diversified cannot be upheld on the basis of historical evidence to the contrary. The great majority of Church Fathers were unified in their basic understanding of Scripture. Not in the broad principles, however, but in the hermeneutical methodology did the Church Fathers part company. The allegorical school of interpretation and the school which favored the literal interpretation of Scripture came into conflict with each other. The Alexandrians preferred the first, as has been shown above. The Antiochenes, on the other side, were more inclined to emphasize the historical elements of the Bible. Hence they became known for their literal approach of

---

30 R. Grant and D. Tracy, *op. cit.*, p. 111.

interpreting Scripture. In contending that a biblical expositor had to take the historical form, in which the Bible presented itself, and its literary styles at face value, they rejected any attempt to superimpose a hidden spiritual meaning on the text to the detriment of the literal sense. This brought them naturally into sharp contrast with the Alexandrians who were masters in spiritualizing Scripture. The Antiochenes felt constrained to keep a faithful representation of the actual wording of the biblical writings, whereas their opponents exercised greater liberties as they ventured to penetrate into the deeper spiritual meaning of the same documents. These different hermeneutical approaches had underlying causes which reflected the cultural atmosphere of both the Syrian and the Egyptian Church. Greek philosophy, especially Platonism, was as much responsible for a preferential treatment of the allegorical approach by the Alexandrian as an exegetical system of Jewish origin was for the Antiochenes. Thus the Antiochene School, represented by theologians like Theodoret, Theodore of Mopsuestia, and Diodore of Tarsus, opposed the abuses of an exposition of Scripture which substituted the natural sense of words for their supposedly spiritual significance. Yet not only in their insistence upon a literal interpretation did they presented a challenge to the Alexandrian, they also developed an alternative method of spiritualized interpretation. This shows that they were not altogether opposed to the idea of a spiritual message standing behind the literal meaning of at least certain portions of Scripture. Therefore they recognized and propagated the legitimacy of a typological exegesis, but rejected, in opposition to the Alexandrian, any broadening of its principles into the arbitrary sphere of allegory. The interpretation of Old Testament types as representing spiritual realities in the New Testament was perceived by them as a form of prophecy.[31] The Antiochenes were rather reserved in calling anything a type[32], unless Christ or the apostles themselves had set the precedence. At this juncture they departed from Christian exegetes like Melito of Sardis (late

---

31 Severion, *Creation* 4,2.

32 Diodore, *Psalms*, Pref.

second century), who in his *Paschal Homily* interpreted the exodus of the Israelites from Egypt as an analogue to Christ's death and resurrection. They also distanced themselves from earlier writings such as the *Epistle of Barnabas* which made no attempt to hide their preference, not only for the use of allegorical interpretations, as has been shown above, but also for a profuse typology. The Antiochenes saw examples for legitimate types in the brazen serpent which Moses had lifted up on a pole (Nu. 21:8, 9; Jn. 3:14, 15) and the story of Jonah as he had spent three days and three nights in the belly of a sea-monster (Jon. 1:17; Mt. 12:40).[33] Both historical episodes were authentic types only because Christ attributed them to himself as picturing his death, burial and resurrection. In commenting on different portions of the Hebrew Bible, especially the poetic and prophetic books, they exercised great diligence in determining first the historical background of the text, before they expounded its natural meaning. If they proceeded to interpret its spiritual significance, they did so on the basis of direct quotations in the New Testament or on the broader understanding of the Christian faith.

The Alexandrians did not subscribe to such a limited view of typological interpretation. They were not inhibited by the scruples of the Antiochenes. Their own allegorical concept gave them room to include and spiritualize far more passages of the Hebrew Bible and New Testament. In general, they did not concern themselves as much with typology anyway. For them the spiritual meaning of Scripture was perceived on an altogether different level of conceptualization. They did not distinguish in practice between the theoretical distinction of a typological and devotional sense. The real distinction, rather, was between the historical and the spiritual sense, or in other words, the literal and the allegorical sense. Typology was almost completely absorbed by the more dominant devotional (or spiritual) sense. Not even Origen, who had postulated a typological sense, followed it strictly. If the Alexandrians interpreted biblical passages according to its historical sense, they did so because they

---

33 Theodore, *John*, Pref.

recognized and respected the literal meaning of Scripture as a valid but inferior sense. In order to unlock a deeper spiritual reality, however, they employed the allegorical method almost indiscriminately, because it enabled them to penetrate further into the hidden truth of God's word. It invariably led them to appreciate the unity between the Hebrew Bible and the New Testament which was based more on their imaginative interpretation than on a true biblical Christology. Yet even here, the concurrence, although weak, with the concept of an organic unity between the Testaments was strengthening the cause of the orthodox Church against the assaults of heretical groups. However, a better solution which the early Christians devised to combat any dissenting tendency was an effort to systematize the dogmas of their faith.

3.3. Patristic Formulation of Dogmas

Heresies and schisms threatened the orthodoxy and unity of the Christian community. The Church Fathers were challenged to present the Church with a systemized formulation of orthodox teaching which, if tried, would stand the test of scriptural truth and apostolic tradition against falsehood and dissenting sentiments. As the Church Fathers were beginning to formulate theological dogmas the Church came gradually into possession of a powerful tool against its doctrinal opponents. The Church carried the responsibility to guard itself against interpretations which did not concur with the orthodox dogmas. This could only be achieved on a unified front.

Considering the ecclesiastical conditions of the second and third century, was the Church too idealistic in thinking that a hermeneutical consensus could be accomplished in spite of different approaches in the exegesis of the Scriptures at the main episcopal sees? The rivalry between Antioch and Alexandria, in particular, has led historians to conclude that the Church Fathers could not consent to a unified hermeneutical approach and thus the basis of unity had to be found somewhere else. Yet where should it be found other than on doctrinal grounds? There is no question in doubting that various interpretational models had been employed in the quest of finding the correct meaning of Scripture. How much this fact affected the Church negatively will remain disputable. It might have been only a reflection of a minor dilemma in the Church, presenting it with the additional challenge of not only refuting variances of a commonly accepted interpretation from a competing or opposing understanding, but also harmonizing differences within the agreed interpretation. Ultimately the solution to counteract dissenting tendencies was found in the convocation of ecumenical councils. The first in a long succession of similar councils was held in Nicaea in 325, summoned by the emperor Constantine himself. The bishops and laymen who were present at these councils were responsible for the formulation of the dogmas of the Christian faith.

3.4. Conclusion

The interpretation of the Scriptures in the early church was governed by principles which gradually developed as the Church Fathers reflected upon the message of God's revelation to them in the context of their particular historical, sociological, and theological situation. The Church Fathers were perceptive and, in most cases, well-educated individuals who exegeted the Scripture skillfully. Generally it can be said that they were guided in their biblical expositions by different traditional hermeneutical models. These models were either of Jewish or Hellenistic background and presented themselves with equal value to the Christian interpreter. The Jewish models were usually characterized by more literalistic features in contrast to the allegorical tendencies of Hellenistic hermeneutics. In particular details, however, the demarcation line was not strictly drawn as both literal and allegorical interpretations had found their way into Jewish and Hellenistic literature and, from there, into the Holy Scriptures. Typology, for example, as a mediating position between extreme literalism and allegorical fancy was employed in various forms to interpret the Hebrew Bible in the light of the New Testament by all Church Fathers. Most important, however, was the consensus on the christological exegesis as the binding element of both Testaments. Moreover, the spirit-guided interpretation of Scripture was seen as essential by any Christian exegete. Hermeneutical differences still existed among the Church Fathers in the questions of detail and continued to concern, and at times severely to plague, the Church, but if one looks at the patristic literature in a broader scope, the unifying principles of interpretation were far more predominant. The general success of ecumenical councils can be traced back to a common understanding of biblical doctrine and hermeneutical principles, even though dissenting voices inside the orthodox Church, but more so in the schismatic and sectarian movements, remained a reality.

The appearance of different chiliastic views in the patristic literature, for example, was a direct result of applying a variety of hermeneutical principles to the exegesis of the millennial passage in Revelation. A simple comparison between the Asiatic millenarianism and the Alexandrian anti-chiliasm would suffice to clearly illustrate this point. The underlying current of a unique interpretational model can also be observed in Augustine's amillennialism. Thus the chiliastic controversy was more a debate about differences of hermeneutics than of doctrine.

Chapter 4
Asiatic Millennialism

4.1. Introduction 110
4.2. Characteristics of Asiatic Millennialism 113
   4.2.1. Original Sources 115
   4.2.2. Influence of Jewish Apocalyptic 116
      4.2.2.1. Application of the Adamic Millennium 120
      4.2.2.2. Seventh Day of the Cosmic Week 122
   4.2.3. Chiliastic Interpretation of Old Testament Prophecy . . . 123
   4.2.4. Restoration of the Earthly Jerusalem 125
   4.2.5. Sensual Aspects of Asiatic Millennialism 127
   4.2.6. Thousand Years 130
   4.2.7. Millennialism of the Montanists 132
4.3. Conclusion 134

4. Asiatic Millennialism

4.1. Introduction

Papias (A.D.60-130)[1], the bishop of Hierapolis, a contemporary of Polycarp, represented a chiliastic tradition which had its antecedents in Palestine. His dependence on the oral teaching of the apostles and elders in regard to the millennium has been pointed out by both Irenaeus and Eusebius.[2] In his *Ecclesiastical History*, Eusebius gives us the fullest account of Papias' original sources, especially with reference to the elders, who were primarily responsible for the dissemination of millenarianism.[3]

In spite of his anti-millenarian bias, which surfaces not only in slighting comments about Papias' intelligence[4], but also in regard to the whole subject of chiliasm itself, Eusebius preserved valuable information on Asiatic chiliasm. He informs us also that Papias referred to unwritten sources to substantiate his millennialism. Papias,

> adduce[d] other accounts, as though they came to him from unwritten tradition, and some strange parables and teachings of the Saviour, and some other more mythical accounts. Among them he says that there will be a millennium after the resurrection of the dead, when the kingdom of Christ will be set up in material form on this earth.[5]

---

1 Papias might have died as late as A.D.155.

2 Both Eusebius, (*Hist. Eccl.*, III.39.2-5), and Irenaeus (*Haer.* V. 33:3-4) speak of Papias' acquaintance with the Apostle John.

3 Ibid., III.39.3.

4 Ibid., III.39.12-13: "I suppose that he [Papias] got these notions by a perverse reading of the apostolic accounts, not realizing that they had spoken mystically and symbolically. For he was a man of very little intelligence as is clear from his books."

5 Ibid., III.39.11-12.

Eusebius once deplorably remarked, that it was Papias who was responsible for disseminating chiliastic ideas.

> [was] responsible for the fact that so many Christian writers after him held the same opinion [about the millennium], relying on his antiquity, for instance Irenaeus and whoever else appears to have held the same views.[6]

Irenaeus (c.130 - c.202) was the bishop of Lyon at the end of the second century. Although he was born in Asia Minor, he spent most of his life in the West, and became one of the most renowned and learned of the early fathers. At times he functioned as an intermediary to solve the friction between the Eastern and the Western Church. In a letter to Florinus he wrote that in his youth he had listened to Polycarp, who had personal acquaintance with John and with the other apostles. Later he became known as an author and ecclesiastical administrator, working for the expansion of the Church in southern France.

The impact of his literary works can be appreciated only as the time and circumstance in which he lived are considered. The triumphal advance of Gnosticism into the world of the first and second century and the influence it commanded over broad sections of the Church gave great concern to Irenaeus. He realized that the Christian faith stood in danger of being inundated by a subversive undercurrent of pagan religiosity and needed to be defended against it. Facing up to the challenge he placed himself at the forefront of the ecclesiastical controversies of the time and became the champion of orthodoxy. As one of the first patristic writers, he attacked Gnosticism by demonstrating that its congruity with pagan mythology and philosophy was in direct opposition to the teaching of both the Old and the New Testaments.

His substantial writings include the monumental work, *Adversus Haereses*, consisting of five individual books, which could be described as the best Christian polemic against Gnosticism in the ante-Nicene age. Although the emphasis

---

6 Ibid., III.39.13.

of the first four books is placed on an exact examination and refutation of heretical doctrines, the fifth book accents a positive declaration of the Christian faith.[7] In contrast to the continuously changing and paradoxical speculations of the heretics Irenaeus set forth the consistency and harmony of the Christian faith. Basing his arguments primarily on the doctrines of the church, he succeeded in reversing the previous trend towards an acceptance of Gnostic speculations in the Church.[8]

The book *Adversus Haereses* is also one of the most important sources of millennial expositions in the ante-Nicene literature. In its pages Irenaeus advocates his own adherence to Asiatic chiliasm. After alluding to Papias' fourth book on *The Oracles of the Lord* he indicates a close affinity of his views with those of Papias. Indeed, it is an echoing of the same concepts, derived from the same sources, and even phrased, at times, in the same way.

It should be noted, however, that Irenaeus did not only use quotations from Papias and the Elders, but cited other sources as well. As John Lawson, in *The Biblical Theology of Saint Irenaeus*[9], pointed out, it was the application of a literal hermeneutic in interpreting eschatological texts which, more than anything else, contributed to the formulation of Irenaeus' millennialism:

> The sheet-anchor of all [exegesis] is the assertion, so utterly contrary to his general expository usage when other parts of the Bible are in review, that apocalyptical Scripture must not be interpreted in an allegorical or symbolical manner. It is fundamental that a literal interpretation is alone legitimate (V.35.1-2,ii.151,153). S. Irenaeus is thus firmly attached to the hope of a terrestrial Millennial Kingdom.

---

7 Irenaeus, *Haer.* book 5, Preface, in *ANF*, vol.1, p. 526.

8 Ibid.

9 John Lawson, *The Biblical Theology of Saint Irenaeus*, Epworth Press, London, p. 279, 1948.

In order to gain a better understanding of Asiatic chiliasm we will, therefore, concentrate our attention on the evaluation of millennial passages found in *Adversus Haereses*. At times we will also include some passages from Papias and other Church Fathers in our discussion.

4.2. Characteristics of Asiatic Millennialism

At first Irenaeus illustrates how the righteous must first receive the inheritance which God promised to the fathers; they rise again after the renewal of this creation at the Second Coming of Christ (lit. "the appearance of God"). All this will take place before the final judgment.[10]

Irenaeus refers to a number of Old Testament passages in order to illustrate further how God's promises given to the Patriarchs will be fulfilled. When speaking of the earthly millennial kingdom, he also tries to adduce scriptural evidence from the New Testament. He says, for example, of Romans 8:19-21: "The creation itself also shall be delivered from the bondage of corruption ... It is fitting, therefore, that the creation itself, being restored to its primeval condition, should without restraint be under the dominion of the righteous."[11] After quoting Christ's statement about his refusal to drink wine until the day when he will drink it anew in his Father's kingdom (Mt. 26:29), Irenaeus immediately adds the following comment: "He [Christ] cannot by any means be understood as drinking of the fruit of the vine when established with his disciples in a super-celestial place; nor, again, can those who drink it be devoid of flesh."[12] He is thus implying that this promise must be fulfilled during the earthly millennium.

---

10 Irenaeus, *op. cit.*, V, 32:1.

11 Ibid.: "... the creation itself also shall be delivered from the bondage of corruption ... It is fitting, therefore, that the creation itself, being restored to its primeval condition, should without restraint be under the dominion of the righteous."

12 Ibid., V, 33:1: "He [Christ] cannot by any means be understood as drinking of the fruit of the vine when established with his disciples in a super-celestial place; nor, again, can those who drink it be devoid of flesh."

Irenaeus assumes also that the hundredfold blessings which are promised to the disciples (Mk. 10:30) find their application in the times of the kingdom, again another description of the millennium:

> What are the hundredfold rewards of this world, the feasts to which the poor are invited, the banquets given as a reward? These are to take place in the times of the kingdom, that is upon the seventh day, which has been sanctificed, in which God rested from all his works, the true sabbath of the righteous, in which they shall not be engaged in any earthly occupation, but shall have a table at hand, prepared for them by God, supplying them with all sorts of dishes.[13]

In this context Irenaeus points to the testimony of Papias and the Elders regarding the fabulous growth of vegetation.

Considering the importance of the elders[14] we have to ask which sources they utilized for the formation of their millennial views. If Papias' testimony is taken at face value, we are informed that the decisive authority of Asiatic chiliasm is John, from whom the elders claimed to have obtained their information. Moreover, John, as again stated by Papias, ascribed the origin of millenarianism to Christ.[15]

Yet, looking at these statements objectively, it has to be conceded that they are more mysterious than elucidating in providing an answer to the question stated above. Obviously,

---

13 Ibid., V, 33:2: "What are the hundredfold rewards of this world, the feasts to which the poor are invited, the banquets given as a reward? These are to take place in the times of the kingdom, that is upon the seventh day, which has been sanctified, in which God rested from all his works, the true sabbath of the righteous, in which they shall not be engaged in any earthly occupation, but shall have a table at hand, prepared for them by God, supplying them with all sorts of dishes."

14 Papias' reference to the elders as quoted by Irenaeus, *op. cit.*, V.33:3ff: "I commit to writing those things which I have formerly learned from the elders, and committed to memory. The elders who had seen St. John, the disciple of our Lord, taught concerning those times and said, 'The days shall come when the vine shall bring forth abundantly ...'"; cf. Eusebius, *op. cit.*, III.39.4.

15 Eusebius, *op. cit.*, III.39.2-5; Irenaeus, *op. cit.*, V. 33:3-4.

there is no evidence in the New Testament that would substantiate the ascription of these views to the teaching of Christ. A negation of such a claim, even if it is attested by Papias and Irenaeus, does not necessarily mean to reject the possibility of an early conception of these views in the early Christian community at the end of the first century A.D. This accounts for the respect in which they were held by a man of the stature of Irenaeus. Yet, a closer examination of the pertinent literature leads us to consider another possible source of Asiatic chiliasm.

4.2.1. Original Sources

It has been suggested that the origin of Asiatic chiliasm, as it has been orally transmitted by the elders, must be found primarily in Jewish apocalyptic. The prodigious growth of vegetation at the time of the messianic kingdom which finds an exact parallel in the descriptions of the millennium by the Asiatic Church Fathers is portrayed, for example, in *I Enoch* 10:19. The same theme of unprecedented fecundity is also found in *II Baruch* 29:5-8, written at the close of the first or beginning of the second century.[16] The passage in the 29th chapter of *II Baruch* appears almost verbatim in the writings of both Papias and Irenaeus, without, however, mentioning the original source. As it became the most famous and widely used passage describing the millennium, it will be necessary to look at it more closely. It is cited, for example, in Irenaeus, *Adversus Haereses*, V, 33:3ff in the following words:

> The days will come in which vines shall grow each having ten thousand branches, and in each branch ten thousand twigs, and in each twig ten thousand shoots, and in each one of the shoots ten thousand clusters, and on every grape when pressed will give five and twenty measures of wine. And when any one of the saints will

---

16 Cf. *II Baruch* 73, 6; *Esdras* 6:20-28.

lay hold of a cluster, another shall cry out: 'I am a better cluster, take me; bless the Lord through me.'[17]

Irenaeus combines this passage with the blessing of Isaac and interprets it as referring to the time of the messianic kingdom when the righteous, after the first resurrection, will rule on earth. For, so he says, the blessing of Isaac will be a time when creation, having been made new and released from the captivity of sin, will bring forth an abundance of all kinds of food. This abundance will simply come from the dew of heaven and the fertility of the earth.[18] Irenaeus relates further that the animals in those days, obtaining their food solely from the produce of the earth, will live in peaceful harmony with each other and mankind.

If, indeed, Jewish apocalyptic is the main source of Asiatic chiliasm, it remains to be asked, how it came to occupy this place of distinction in the patristic literature of Asia Minor. What prompted the Asiatic Church Fathers to cast their ballot in favor of Jewish apocalyptic instead of using more prominently the prophetic passages of the Old Testament? In the following subsection we will try to find an answer to this and other related questions.

4.2.2. Influence of Jewish Apocalyptic

It is interesting to observe that both Irenaeus and Papias must have seen an advantage in combining parallel concepts of Jewish apocalyptic with those of Revelation, rather than the latter with the corresponding prophetic passages. Furthermore, the exuberant fertility of the trees in Revelation is not so much part of the millennium as it is of the

---

17 "The days will come in which vines shall grow each having ten thousand branches, and in each branch ten thousand shoots, and in each one of the shoots ten thousand clusters, and on every grape when pressed will give five and twenty measures of wine. And when any one of the saints will lay hold of a cluster, another shall cry out: 'I am a better cluster, take me; bless the Lord through me.'"

18 Irenaeus, *op. cit.*, V, 33:3ff.

eternal world after the restoration of creation.[19] These facts underline clearly that Asiatic chiliasm was more indiscriminate in its selection of sources than any other form of millenarianism. It could just as easily apply to the millennium certain prophecies of the Old Testament which properly relate to the future world as apocalyptic speculations about the paradisal conditions of messianic times.

Although quoting a longer passage from Isaiah, Papias might have felt more comfortable in choosing an apocalyptic description of the messianic times for the portrayal of the fabulous fecundity during the millennium. It is impossible to determine if he thought that Hebrew prophecy was referring more to the eternal state than to the conditions on the earth before its general renewal. Likewise the question will never be satisfactorily answered why he did not quote more profusely from other Hebrew prophets, like Amos or Micah, who had expressed similar ideas about the messianic times (e.g. Am. 9:13; Mi. 4:1-8), instead of relying on Jewish apocalyptic. It seems, however, that Papias, in his choice of texts, wanted to indicate the this-worldly character of the millennium. For the purpose of our discussion it might be the best solution to propose such a possibility. In any case his preferential treatment of Jewish apocalyptic, by correlating its description of the messianic times to the Christian millennium, set a precedent which became increasingly the accepted approach in the millennial tradition of the Christian community of Asia Minor.

It will be noted that later Church Fathers, especially Commodian and Lactantius, advocated millennial conceptions which were even closer to those of Jewish apocalyptic. They referred directly to the prophecies of Isaiah, but presented rather the inflated concepts of Jewish apocalyptic. Commodian, for example, maintained that the institution of marriage will not disappear during the millennium.[20] Lactantius, on his part, stated that after the resurrection the Son of the Most High

---

19 Cf. *Visio Pauli*, 21-22.

20 Commodian, *Inst.*, II, 3; cf. H. Bietenhard, "The Millennial Hope in the Early Church", *SJT*, VI, 1953, pp. 24-25.

... will be engaged among men a thousand years, and will rule them with most just command ... Then they who shall be alive in their bodies shall not die, but during those thousand years shall produce an infinite multitude ...but they who shall be raised from the dead shall preside over the living as judges ... but the sun will become seven times brighter than it now is; and the earth will open its fruitfulness, and bring forth most abundant fruits of its own accord.[21]

The Asiatic Church Fathers had obviously no qualms in using passages from Jewish apocalyptic. Yet, in their representation of the millennium, they ascribed to these passages a purely Christian origin, as if they were sayings of Christ himself or his apostles. In reality they simply appropriated the fanciful descriptions of the messianic kingdom of the Jews for their own interpretation of the millennium which, as it turned out, was not much different from the original apocalyptic source. They embraced, for example, the Jewish idea that the righteous, even after their resurrection, will have to eat food. Otherwise, so they argued, would there be any need for the abundance of vegetation? Referring to Papias, another millenarian, Maximus the Confessor, particularly stresses this point: "In his fourth volume Papias spoke of the pleasure of food at the time of the resurrection."[22] The *Ascension of Isaiah* contains a corollary concept in that those who will participate at the first resurrection are given only partially glorified bodies which will still be subjected to some earthly limitations (i.e. the necessity of eating). It is only at the second resurrection, after the conclusion of the millennium, that the human body will be completely transfigured. In this context it is interesting to note that both the Asiatic Church Fathers and the Jewish apocalyptics concur

---

21 Lactantius, *Div.Inst.* VII, 24, in William Fletcher, trans., *The Works of Lactantius*, vol.1, T. & T. Clark, Edinburgh, 1871, p. 478-480. Augustine, at last, repulsed by the carnal elements of these later chiliastic interpretations, rejected his earlier views, which were akin to Asiatic millenarianism, thus marking a turning point in the chiliastic controversy about the interpretation of Revelation 20.

22 Maximus, *Schol.in Eccl.Hier.*, 7.

in their views that the body, even though resurrected, will remain corruptible for the duration of the messianic times. Irenaeus, for example, seems to understand the millennium as a time in which the righteous would be required to prepare their bodies for a future glorification in heaven, a conception which he expresses in these words: "Man will truly rise, and be truly trained for incorruption, and grow and become strong during the times of the kingdom, in order that he may be capable of receiving the glory of God."[23]

In the third century this view reappears in a modified and further developed form in the writings of Methodius of Olympus, who, besides Irenaeus, continued the chiliastic tradition of Asia Minor. At one time he expressed his millennial convictions thus

> ... as the Jews, after the repose of the Feast of Tabernacles, arrived at the Promised Land, so I too, following Jesus who has passed into the heavens, shall attain to Heaven, no longer living in tabernacles, or rather my own tabernacle no longer remaining as it was, but being transformed after the millennium from a human and corruptible form into angelic greatness and beauty.[24]

He understood the time when the Jews wandered in the desert and lived in tabernacles as a type of what he had earlier called "the thousand years of rest" and "the resurrection". The "tabernacles" represent the bodies of those who, although being resurrected, are still exposed to the decaying influence of their earthly environment. Incorruptibility, as such, will be granted to them only after they have entered into the eternal state. However, for the duration of the millennium, they enjoy a unique longevity of a thousand years, namely that of Adam in Paradise.

---

23 Irenaeus, *op. cit.*, V, 35:2: "Man will truly rise, and be truly trained for incorruption, and grow and become strong during the times of the kingdom, in order that he may be capable of receiving the glory of God."

24 Methodius, *Conv.*, IX, 5.

4.2.2.1. Application of the Adamic Millennium

Unlike Commodian and Lactantius, we do not find any reference to the continuance of procreation during the millennium in either the writings of Irenaeus or Montanus. The same could be said about the extant fragments of the Elders and Papias. Obviously this is only natural, if, indeed, the early Asiatic chiliasts applied the Adamic millennium to the messianic times of Jewish apocalyptic. The logic behind this omission becomes clear, inasmuch as it agrees with the conception of the Adamic millennium, which, although covering an entire thousand year period, counts only as a single generation, hence, not allowing for the birth of children.

Methodius of Olympus again takes up the same idea in opposition to the materialistic conceptions of Commodian and Lactantius:

> For now, at this very moment, the earth still yields its fruits, the waters are gathered, together, the light is still severed from darkness and the allotted number of men is not yet complete ... But when the times have reached their goal, and God ceases to work on this creation, in the seventh month, on the great day of the Resurrection, the Feast of our Tabernacles shall be proclaimed by the Lord ... Then, in the seventh thousand of years, the fruits of the earth shall all come to an end, men shall no longer beget nor be begotten, and God shall rest from the creation of the world.[25]

If we disregard for the moment Methodius' reference to the seventh millennium and its concomitant idea of the seventh day, this passage provides some evidence for the predominant view in Asiatic circles that procreation would cease during the millennium. Likewise, Methodius opposes the chiliastic idea of an unprecedented fertility of the earth.

That the *Sibylline Oracles*, an early source of millennial thought, do agree, to such an extraordinary degree, with this

---

25 Methodius, *Conv.* IX,1.

conception of Methodius, is more than accidental. The passage describing the final culmination of world history reads: "Then thy race shall cease to be as it was before; none shall cut the deep furrow with the rounded plough; there shall be neither vine-branch nor ear of corn, but all alike shall eat of the manna from heaven with their white teeth."[26] Yet, in aligning himself with this view, Methodius leaves behind one of the most characteristic features of Asiatic chiliasm. His chiliasm simply shows the nature of a later development in millennial thought constituting a reaction against the literal interpretation of prophetic and apocalyptic passages in Scripture. He must have hoped that, by allegorizing these passages, he would save the positive elements of Asiatic chiliasm without endangering its essential nature. It is also conceivable that he was advancing a different tradition of chiliasm which, although organically disconnected with that of Papias, interpreted the repose of the seventh day typologically. Irenaeus would not have conceded to this deficient form of chiliasm, although he might also have been influenced by this tradition, which was later carried to its logical conclusion by Lactantius.

It is, however, clear that Methodius, in the passage quoted above, directs his criticism primarily against the materialistic disposition of the Jews who "believe that the Law and the Prophets have explained everything in a material manner, and who only aspire to the good things of this world."[27]

Another of Methodius' conceptions occurs here as well, namely, the rest of creation. Furthermore, it will be observed that this passage seems to be speaking of the earthly millennium and not of the new world. Although the concept of rest is the same as the one found in I Thessalonians and the *Ascension of Isaiah*, Methodius relates it, in its unpolished form, to the theme of the cosmic week and the seventh day.

---

26 *Sibylline Oracles* VII, 145-149.

27 Methodius, *Conv.* IX,1. Jerome levelled the same charges against the Jews regarding their materialistic disposition of the messianic times (*Com. Zach.* III,14.).

Therefore, we have to proceed now to briefly discuss the concept of the seventh day.

4.2.2.2. Seventh Day of the Cosmic Week

Apart from Irenaeus, it was primarily Methodius who alluded to the millennium as the seventh day, an idea which is usually seen as part of the speculations of the cosmic week. M. Werner, in his book, *Die Entstehung des christlichen Dogmas*, pp. 83-84,[28] assumes that the origins of millenarianism can be traced exclusively to these speculations. As this view has not been held widely in academic circles, it must be seen as a minority opinion on the matter at hand. Some scholars have rejected it outright as a viable factor in Asiatic chiliasm or, at least, classified it as highly debatable.[29] It is argued that the Johannine theology, which was so prevalent in the Asiatic Church, was influenced by an apocalyptic tradition which did not divide world history into seven millennia. In *I Enoch* and *Jubilees* another, quite different, concept of world chronology can be found which is not altogether compatible with the idea of the seven millennia. The latter idea, like that of the seven heavens, was obviously conceived in Hellenistic Judaism.[30] It is, therefore, hardly surprising that the earliest occurrence of this idea appears in Alexandrian theology.[31] It is easy to see how, at a later time, this concept provided a basis for expecting the end of world history in the year A.D. 1000, the seventh and last millennium having been inaugurated by the first coming of Christ. Obviously, the change in millennial concepts did not occur

---

28 M. Werner, *Die Entstehung des christlichen Dogmas*, Leipzig, 1941.

29 Cf. Jean Daniélou, *A History of Early Christian Doctrine*, Darton, Longman & Todd, London, 1964, vol.1, p. 396.

30 The messianic idea of the seventh millennium is found among the Samaritans and elsewhere, but does not form any significant part of Asiatic millenarianism; cf. Walter Bauer, "Chiliasm", *RAC* II (1954), 1075.

31 See e.g. the *Epistle of Barnabas* chap. 15; the theme of the seven millennia will be discussed in this thesis in the chapter on the *Epistle of Barnabas*.

all at once. In its initial stages it was only a minor diversion of the original Asiatic chiliasm. As time passed on, however, it took on a form of quite different proportions.

Having thus demonstrated the preeminent position of Jewish apocalyptic in Asiatic chiliasm, over against the Hellenistic concept of the seven millennia, we now turn to the chiliastic interpretation of prophetic passages in the Old Testament.

4.2.3. Chiliastic Interpretation of Old Testament Prophecy

Irenaeus' treatise on the millennium also includes a discussion on Old Testament prophecy.[32] It seems as if Isaiah 65:20-25 attracted the greatest attention among many other similar passages.[33] Indeed, this text forms the scriptural basis, besides Rev. 20:1-10, on which Asiatic chiliasm built its chiliastic doctrine. Unlike Justin Martyr, however, Irenaeus does not show any particular interest in the verse, "As the days of the tree of life shall be the days of my people," which the translators of the LXX added to the original Hebrew passage of Isaiah 65.[34] Although it should be noted that, at an earlier occasion, he had referred to the days of the tree of life as lasting a thousand years.[35] His attention is, however, captured by Isaiah's description of the reconciliation of the animals. Irenaeus assumes that the animals, by returning to their primeval conditions of paradise, will be reverting to a former vegetarian diet. This, so he implies, presupposes the existence of an abundance of food. After referring to Isaiah 65:25: "The lion shall eat straw like the

---

[32] Cf. Is. 13:9 in V.35.1; 25:8 (LXX) in V.12.1; 26:19 in V.15.1 and in V.34.1; 30:25-26 in V.34.2; 32:1 in V.34.4; 54:11-14 in V.34.4; 65:17-18 in V.35.2; 65:18-22 in V.34.4; and 66:22 in V.36.1. Irenaeus interpreted these prophetic passages in light of the Second Coming of Christ and the establishment of the millennial kingdom on earth.

[33] The importance of this passage can be seen in the fact that Irenaeus quotes it twice; cf. 65:17-18 in V.35.2; 65:18-22 in V.34.4.

[34] Irenaeus, *op. cit.*, V, 34:4.

[35] Ibid., V, 23:2.

ox."[36] Irenaeus makes the interesting remark that "this indicates the large size and rich quality of the fruits. For if that animal, the lion, feeds upon straw, of what quality must the wheat itself be whose straws shall serve as suitable food for lions?"[37] Irenaeus does not hesitate to concede that the prophecy of the reconciliation of the animals can be applied to the union of the nations in the Church. He admits that an exegesis of this prophecy in terms of the period of the Church is legitimate in so far as it does not lead to the obliteration of more literal interpretations. This might only be an echo of what the writer of 2 Peter meant by quoting (3:8) the classic millennial text of the Old Testament: "With the Lord one day is as a thousand years" (Ps. 90:4). By applying this verse exclusively to the period between the Incarnation and the final catastrophe, he seems to be one of the few New Testament writers who relates the millennial reign to the times of the Church. If this is so, Irenaeus recognizes the validity of interpreting millennial passages allegorically, although acknowledging that this approach is limited in explaining the full meaning of the passage.[38]

His real aversion, however, is not directed towards the ecclesiological interpretation of prophecy, as such, but primarily towards the perversions of Gnosticism. Prophecy loses its meaning, if its historical message is transferred to the eternal sphere of the "Pleroma" and thus emptied of any real significance in the concrete world. By speaking of Jerusalem as our mother, Irenaeus contends, that Paul was not thinking of a wandering "Aeon", or of any other power which was separated from the "Pleroma".[39] His primary purpose of writing *Adversus Haereses* was not to defend Asiatic chiliasm, which he nevertheless affirms as scriptural, but to contest the heretic exegesis of Gnosticism.

---

36 "... and the lion will eat straw like the ox, ..."

37 Ibid., V.33.4: "This indicates the large size and rich quality of the fruits. For if that animal, the lion, feeds upon straw, of what quality must the wheat itself be whose straws shall serve as suitable food for lions?" See also V.34.1,4.

38 Ibid., V, 33:4; 35:1; cf. also Justin, *Dial.*, 81,1ff.

39 Ibid., V, 35:2.

There is, however, still another idea which betrays the influence of Asiatic chiliasm on Irenaeus' mind. Again, it is a passage in his book, *Adversus Haereses*, where he mentions those who are still alive at the beginning of the millennium and who will continue to live on the earth: "All these and other words were unquestionably spoken in reference to the resurrection of the just, which takes place after the coming of the Antichrist, ... and to those whom the Lord shall find in the flesh, awaiting him from heaven, and who have suffered tribulation."[40]

In this respect, millenarianism betrays, once again, its antecedents in the original messianic expectation of the Jews. These expectations were built on a promised intervention of God on behalf of his people by triumphing over their enemies and delivering them from persecution. In his triumph God even includes those righteous who have already fallen asleep. They will be resurrected, or rather, resuscitated, to a better life on earth awaiting their transference to the heavenly Jerusalem.

In this context one intriguing question needs to be addressed in regard to the introduction of another feature into Asiatic chiliasm, namely the restoration of the earthly Jerusalem. This feature poses a problem, because it does not form any part of the account in Revelation 20. Obviously, the last two chapters of Revelation mention only a heavenly Jerusalem descending from heaven after the new creation.[41]

4.2.4. Restoration of the Earthly Jerusalem

Irenaeus speaks about the restoration of Jerusalem as one of the main occurrences during the millennium, which he sees mentioned in prophecies like Is. 54:11 and 65:18.[42] Again, it

---

40 Ibid., V, 35:1: "All these and other words were unquestionably spoken in reference to the resurrection of the just, which takes place after the coming of the Antichrist ... and to those whom the Lord shall find in the flesh, awaiting him from heaven, and who have suffered tribulation."

41 Cf. Rev. 21:1, 2, 10; 22:1-5.

42 Cf. Is. 54:11-14 in V.34.4; 65:17-18 in V.35.2; 65:18-22 in V.34.4.

is the latter of these two passages to which Irenaeus pays special attention by saying that "such things cannot be understood of the heavenly world, for it is written: God will show to the whole earth that is under heaven thy glory. But they will take place in the times of the kingdom, after the earth has been renewed by the Lord and Jerusalem rebuilt after the pattern of the Jerusalem above."[43] Irenaeus, therefore, does not deny the existence of a heavenly Jerusalem. He sees it, moreover, as a model for the restoration of the earthly Jerusalem during the millennium. On the basis of Rev. 21:2, he reiterates the same point by saying, that, in this verse, the Apostle John is referring to the heavenly Jerusalem, which, although belonging to the new creation, served as a prototype for the earthly Jerusalem.[44] Hence, Irenaeus maintains that there are two different Jerusalems, one on earth, the other in heaven. That he understands the latter to be part of the new creation, coming down to a renewed earth, after the general judgment, is consistent with his interpretation of Revelation in general. The restored earthly Jerusalem, however, is a theme which he, again, appropriated from Jewish apocalyptic.

The apocalyptic influence on Asiatic chiliasm can be best observed in the connection of a restored Jerusalem with a renewal of the Temple sacrifices.[45] As the Temple worship necessitated such a restoration, it became an inseparable element in Jewish expectation of the messianic times. The reappearance of these features in Asiatic chiliasm provides the right framework to put the chiliastic views of Irenaeus, and others, in their proper setting. It clearly shows to what

---

[43] Ibid., V, 35:2: "... such things cannot be understood of the heavenly world, for it is written: God will show to the whole earth that is under heaven his glory. But they will take place in the times of the kingdom, after the earth has been renewed by the Lord and Jerusalem rebuilt after the pattern of the Jerusalem above."

[44] Ibid.: "It is after these things have taken place on the earth that John, the Apostle of the Lord, says that the new Jerusalem from above shall descend ... Of that Jerusalem the image is the city which was on the earth before (her descent), and in which the righteous were trained for incorruption."

[45] Cf. Commodian, *Carm.Ap.*, 941-946.

length Jewish messianism impacted the formulation of millennial concepts inside the Christian communities of Asia Minor.

That Marcion criticized those who expected the reestablishment of a Jewish state in Palestine during the millennium, was certainly not coincidental, considering his aversion to Jewish elements in Christianity in general. He could not gloss over the fact that the Asiatic Church Fathers attempted to hide Jewish apocalyptic concepts of the messianic times behind a thinly veneered form of Christian millenarianism. His criticism must not have been a bone of contention between him and Tertullian, our informant on Marcion, because the Montanists, to whom Tertullian belonged, anticipated the appearance of the New Jerusalem in Phrygia, not in Palestine.[46] Tertullian was obviously more opposed to Marcion's general anti-millenarian stance than to this particular point. Yet Marcion's criticism of Asiatic chiliasm carries still some weight considering the fact that he lived in Asia Minor himself.

However, it remains doubtful whether the chiliastic views of Papias and others, were so grossly material, as it has been generally made out to be by later critics. It seems appropriate to note that these critics stated their objections against Asiatic chiliasm in stronger terms than against any other Christian doctrine emanating from the East. But why and how did they present their case against a chiliasm which had been a generally accepted doctrine of the early Church?

4.2.5. Sensual Aspects of Asiatic Millennialism

In retrospect it is true that Asiatic chiliasm allowed itself to be influenced more by the material, and, in some cases, sensual descriptions of the messianic times in Jewish apocalyptic literature, than by the restrained language of Revelation. By connecting the extraordinary fruitfulness of nature with that of men, Jewish apocalyptic literature appeared to admit sexual licence which was supposedly sanctioned,

---

46 Tertullian, *Adv. Marc.*, III, 24.

according to some later opponents of Asiatic chiliasm, by both Papias and Irenaeus as well as later Church Fathers.

However, it is more than questionable if Papias or Irenaeus did indeed adopt, along with the exuberance of vegetation, the exaggerated sensual components of Jewish apocalyptic. To assume that the Asiatic Church Fathers applied uncritically any apocalyptic idea to the interpretation of Revelation 20 is certainly an exaggerated and unbalanced view. They did not, like the writer of *I Enoch*, expect the righteous to live until they had begotten a thousand children.[47] It is better to suppose that they were rather selective in what they considered to be valuable material for the description of the millennium. They did not exclusively depend on Jewish apocalyptic in formulating their chiliastic concepts. Papias, for instance, associates the idea of the fabulous fecundity of nature with that of the reconciliation of the animal world. It is undoubtedly true that he drew his inspirations, at least partially, from the traditional views of the messianic kingdom, as described by Isaiah.[48] Irenaeus himself made a similar observation in commenting on Papias.[49] Even *II Baruch* 29:5-8, the closest apocalyptic parallel to Papias' representation of the millennium, describes only the fruitfulness of the earth and not the reconciliation of the animal world.[50]

Eusebius' reference to Papias' alleged misinterretations[51], is understandable, if one keeps in mind that Eusebius was also opposed to the "sensual" character of millenarianism in general. Influenced, as he was, by the dualism of Alexandrian theology, he could not reconcile these carnal ideas of a material millennium with his idealistic sentiments.

That Dionysius of Alexandria could only attack Asiatic chiliasm by referring to the heretic Cerinthus, who inter-

---

47 *I Enoch* 10:17.

48 Cf. Is. 11:6-9; 65:25.

49 Irenaeus, *op. cit.*, V, 33:4.

50 The same could be said about *Sib.*, VII, 146-149.

51 See footnote no.4.

preted the millennium as a time of sensual pleasures, might be taken as evidence that the Asiatic Church Fathers were much more restrained in their use of graphic language in describing the millennium.[52] Dionysus also added the detail that Cerinthus believed in the restoration of animal sacrifices[53], a feature which neither appears in the writings of Papias nor in those of Irenaeus.

Caius of Rome, although objecting to the same distorted form of chiliasm, was able to equate it merely with nuptial festivals, once again, as he indicates, an idea of Cerinthus.[54] That Cerinthus was never included among the Asiatic Church Fathers must have eluded his attention. In fact, he was generally regarded as an adherent of Gnosticism and opposed, as such, by the Apostle John and the Asiatic Church Fathers.[55] Hence, his chiliastic views should be seen as a heterodox version of Asiatic chiliasm, although bearing similarities with the latter. The evidence which is provided by Irenaeus and Eusebius does not seem to support the supposition of some scholars who see in Cerinthus a true representative of Asiatic chiliasm.[56]

Irenaeus, in his refutation of Gnosticism, does not mention the chiliastic views of Cerinthus. This omission is often taken as evidence for his approval of Cerinthus' views on this point. However, as this constitutes an argument from silence, it cannot be positively substantiated. Therefore, we should not put too much emphasis on a possible congruence

---

52 Eusebius, *op. cit.*, III.28.3-4. It might be argued that Eusebius exaggerated this materialist aspect in his account of Cerinthus, specifically regarding his representation of Dionysus' views on Cerinthus' chiliasm. Yet there can be no doubt that it did form part of the general position of Cerinthus.

53 Ibid., III, 28:5.

54 Ibid., III.28.1-2. "He says that after the resurrection the Kingdom of Christ will be on earth, and that the flesh, dwelling at Jerusalem, will once more serve lusts and pleasures. And, enemy that he is of God's Scriptures, he asserts that there will be a period of a thousand years to be spent in nuptial feasting."

55 Ibid., III.3.4.

56 Walter Bauer regards Cerinthus' chiliastic views as derived from of the Asiatic millenarianism („Chiliasmus", *RAC* II (1954), col. 1076).

between the millenarianism of Cerinthus and Irenaeus. The significance of analyzing Cerinthus' millenarianism must be seen in that it provides some further insights into the diversity of millennial views current in Asia Minor at the end of the first century A.D. By virtue of the fact that later Church Fathers have adopted certain aspects of a sensual millennium, reminiscent of his descriptions, we will do well not to dismiss Cerinthus' millenarianism too quickly. The restoration of animal sacrifice, for example, reappears in the millenarianism of Apollinarius in the fourth century. Moreover, we gain additional information about a form of chiliasm, similar to that of the Asiatic Church Fathers, which might assist us in determining certain archaic origins of its themes. In this respect we are confronted with the most characteristic tenet of Asiatic chiliasm, namely its literal interpretation of the expression in Rev. 20, "χίλια ἔτη" ("chilia ete") as a one thousand year period.

4.2.6. Thousand Years

As we have examined Asiatic chiliasm, it becomes obvious that it was echoing Jewish anticipations of the messianic times. It might be asked, whether the parallel ideas about the fertility of the earth and the reconciliation of the animals can be extended to the concept of a "one thousand year" period.[57] Indeed, one of the characteristics of the messianic times was a phenomenal longevity, as a study of prophetic passages easily reveals. Therefore, Isaiah 65:20-22, relating the reconciliation of the animals, reads: "Neither shall there be any more a child that dies untimely, or an old man who shall not complete his time; For the youth shall be a hundred years old ..." Again, similar concepts are expressed in Jewish apocalyptic literature. *I Enoch* 10:17, for example, combines the theme of longevity with that of an extraordinary fecundity as a characteristic of messianic times. Moreover, according to the *Book of Jubilees*, God intended to grant to each human being a life-span of a thousand years in paradise, but because

---

57 Cf. *Visio Pauli* 21-22.

sin came into the world, Adam "lacked seventy years from one thousand years, for a thousand years are like one day in the testimony of heaven (Ps. 90:4) and therefore it was written concerning the tree of knowledge, 'In the day you eat from it you will die'. Therefore he did not conplete the years of this day because he died in it."[58] The significance of interpreting Gn. 2:17 in light of Ps. 90:4, as the writer of *Jubilees* wanted it to be understood, is that Adam indeed dies on the same day on which he sinned, but, as in this context, a day is equivalent with a thousand years, Adam dies shortly before he reached the age of a thousand years.

That this tradition of *Jubilees* was known in the Asiatic Church has been indicated by Irenaeus. He comments on Gn. 2:17 as follows:

> The Lord, therefore, recapitulating in himself this day, underwent his sufferings on the day preceding the Sabbath, that is, the sixth day of the creation, the day on which man was created ... Some, again, link the death of Adam with the period of a thousand years; for since, they say, 'A day with the Lord is as a thousand years (2 Pet. 3:8)', he did not exceed the thousand years, but died within them, thus fulfilling the sentence passed on his transgression.[59]

Irenaeus therefore testifies to an older Asiatic tradition, congruous with that of *Jubilees*, in which the life-span in Paradise was deemed a thousand years.[60]

Yet, until now we have barely touched on another spiritual movement which popularized chiliastic concepts in Asia Minor at the same time. This movement, generally known as Montanism, played an important part in the whole scenario of eschatological debate in the early Church, with-

---

58 *The Book of Jubilees*, IV, 29-30 in James H. Charlesworth, (ed.), *The Old Testament Pseudepigrapha. Apocalyptic Literature and Testaments*, Doubleday & Co., Garden City, New York, 1983, p. 430, 431.

59 Irenaeus, *op. cit.* V, 23:2.

60 Cf. also *Clementine Recognitions*, IV, 9.

out which we would be left with an incomplete picture of Asiatic chiliasm.

4.2.7. Millennialism of the Montanists

The conversion experience of Montanus marked the beginning of a spiritual movement which should subsequently challenge the orthodoxy of the Christian Church. In turning to Christ, Montanus adopted an attitude of uncompromising intolerance to the allurements of the world. He despised its sinfulness and looked at its amusements only with righteous indignation. He spent most of his life in Phrygia, a country in which its population cherished a rich spiritual heritage. For not too long ago their most prominent city, Hierapolis, was the center from which the radiating influence of Papias spread throughout the province of Asia Minor and beyond. If Papias, as we have seen, was one of the main propagators of millenarianism in the early church, it does not surprise us that his Phrygian compatriots were peculiarly predisposed to accept, not only the notions of a millennial kingdom, but whatever else would be able to inspire their imaginations. Thus their eccentricities savored strong feelings of ethnic superiority. Their own racial prejudice became almost proverbial and bore peculiar fruits in their literature. This national favoritism could even transfer fictiously geographical realities from one place to another. The location of Mount Ararat, for example, was placed inside the boundaries of Phrygia.

Montanism appears to have been a separatist movement which became soon known for its fervent eschatological expectation. That its theological outlook was similar to that of the Asiatic Church Fathers is obvious, especially in its high esteem of the Paraclete. Kurt Aland, in "Der Montanismus und die kleinasiatische Theologie"[61], indicates that the affinity of Montanism with the Johannine circle in Asia provides evidence for the origin of archaic doctrines, which

---

61 Kurt Aland, „Der Montanismus und die kleinasiatische Theologie", *ZNW* XLIV (1955), pp. 113-114.

are parallel to those of Papias and Cerinthus, with whose writings Montanus was certainly familiar.

In many respects, related to the millenarianism of Montanus, we have to rely on Tertullian as our best source of information. In *Adv. Marc.*, III, 24 he declares:

> We confess that a kingdom is promised to us upon the earth, before (entry into) heaven and in a different state of existence; but after the resurrection, and for a period of a thousand years in the divinely-built city of Jerusalem, a kingdom come down from heaven. ... And the word of the new prophecy [= Montanism] which is part of our faith bears witness to this Jerusalem, telling us even that there will be a vision of the city as a sign before its actual coming.[62]

It is amazing how well Tertullian was acquainted with Asiatic chiliasm, although he lived in North Africa for most of his life. In this brief summary he mentions the main chiliastic conceptions current in Asia Minor: the restored city of Jerusalem, a "one thousand year" period of divine reign on earth beginning with the resurrection and concluding with the inauguration of eternity, and the idea that the bodies of the resurrected will be in a different state than that in heaven. As this idea seems more implied in the statement above, he rephrased it again in clearer terms:

> This is the manner of the heavenly kingdom: within the space of its thousand years is comprised the resurrection of the saints, who arise either earlier or later according to their deserts: after which, when the destruction of the world and the fire of judgement have been set in motion, we shall be changed in a moment

---

62 "We confess that a kingdom is promised to us upon the earth, before (entry into) heaven and in a different state of existence; but after the resurrection, and for a period of a thousand years in the divinely-built city of Jerusalem, a kingdom come down from heaven. ... And the word of the new prophecy [= Montanism] which is part of our faith bears witness to this Jerusalem, telling us even that there will be a vision of the city as a sign before its actual coming."

into angelic substance, by virtue of that supervesture of incorruption, and be translated into that heavenly kingdom.[63]

If these concepts bring to mind passages from the *Ascension of Isaiah* and are reminiscent of the writings of Methodius of Olympus[64], it is only a sign of Tertullian's familiarity with the chiliastic doctrine of Montanism modelled after the millenarianism of the Asiatic Church Fathers which again was heavily influenced by Jewish apocalyptic. Beyond a doubt, one of the most intriguing aspects of Tertullian's portrayal of the millennium is the importance given to the restoration of the earthly Jerusalem. In accordance with Montanus, he derives this idea directly from the description of the New Jerusalem in the book of Revelation, but obviously disregards its heavenly aspects. By contrast, Papias does not seem to have attributed the same significance to the New Jerusalem, as described in Revelation. It is more likely that he reinterpreted the apocalyptic tradition of the new Paradise in order to arrive at the same concept. This concept connects the millenarianism of Montanus with that of Cerinthus, and anticipates the theories of Apollinarius.

4.3. Conclusion

The Asiatic Christian community, the circle in which the Revelation of John was written, and for which Eusebius is our main informant, is regarded as the stronghold of early millenarianism. The accession of Papias to the bishop's seat in Hierapolis was one of the most significant events in regard to the development of chiliasm in Asia Minor. He became an

---

63 Tertullian, *Adv. Marc.*, III, 24: "This is the manner of the heavenly kingdom: within the space of its thousand years is comprised the resurrection of the saints, who arise either earlier or later according to their deserts: after which, when the destruction of the world and the fire of judgement have been set in motion, we shall be changed in a moment into angelic substance, by virtue of that supervesture of incorruption, and be translated into that heavenly kingdom."

64 Cf. *De resurr.* 25.

early representative of that tradition which was strongly influenced by the portrayal of the messianic times in Jewish apocalyptic. His conception of the millennium took on the same paradisal colors. Undoubtedly, however, he was only the recipient of a tradition which had its antecedents in Palestine. His dependence on the oral teaching of the elders in regard to the millennium has been pointed out by Eusebius. Following his lead, other Church Fathers, like Commodian and Methodius, did not limit themselves to the scanty language of Revelation in their representation of the millennium, but resorted, time and again, to apocalyptic speculations of the messianic times. Naturally, under the advocacy of these prominent Church Fathers, this type of chiliasm became most popular in Asia Minor. Its most frequently described features were the reconciliation of the animals, the extraordinary fecundity of the earth, and a human life-span of a thousand years.

The predominance of Jewish apocalyptic in Asiatic chiliasm is not surprising if it is seen in light of the background of a strong Jewish presence in Asia Minor. The Christian communities could not escape being influenced by the hope, cherished even among Jews converted to Christianity, of a temporal reign of the Messiah.[65] This was determined by the fact that the messianic fever in Judaism was kept alive never so ardently as during the time between A.D. 50 and 70. Its passionate articulation did not only influence the formulation of Asiatic chiliasm, but also religious philosophies which, like Gnosticism, were, in many respects, more akin to the speculative system of Jewish apocalyptic than to Christian theology. A brief examination of Cerinthus' millennial views suffices to see how deeply the messianic hope of Judaism penetrated Gnosticism. That this influence was not as virulent elsewhere is probably connected to some extent with the fact that, whereas at Alexandria and Rome the Jewish community had to guard itself against a hostile

---

65 Cf. Bo Reicke, *Diakonie, Festfreude und Zelos*, Uppsala, 1951, pp. 283-287.

environment, in Asia it was allowed to be a prominent social factor.[66]

Asiatic chiliasm distinguished itself by emphasizing the significance of a restored earthly Jerusalem. In this regard there was no difference between Irenaeus' millennial views and Jewish apocalyptic, or for that matter, of Cerinthus and Montanus.

It has been suggested that there are three distinct schools of thought in Asiatic chiliasm. The most materialistic one, that of Cerinthus, understood the millennium as a period when sensual pleasure will be satisfied in the act of procreation and in the enjoyment of the fruitfulness of the earth; the moderate group, that of Papias and Irenaeus, allowed for an exceptional fecundity of the earth during that time, but was silent about the possibility of the continuance of human procreation (this view seems to concur best with the idea of Adam's thousand years); and the third school, that of Methodius, disputed both the idea of human procreation and the fruitfulness of the earth. The latter viewpoint seems to coincide more with a new chiliastic concept, which sees the millennium as the seventh day of the cosmic week, during which God ceases his work of creation.

---

66 Cf. Gregory Dix, *Jew and Greek*, Dacre Press, Westminster, 1953, pp. 53-62.

Chapter 5
Chiliasm of Justin Martyr

5.1. Introduction 138
5.2. Millennium 140
5.3. Conclusion 145

5. Chiliasm of Justin Martyr

5.1. Introduction

Flavius Justinus[1] was probably born into a Greek family in Neapolis in the province of Samaria around A.D. 89.[2] His early education and cultural background clearly portrays a Hellenistic influence. As a young man he embarked on an incessant quest for truth and spirituality. He familiarized himself first with the Stoic, then with the Peripatetic and Pythagorean, and at last with the Platonic system of philosophy. The idealism of Plato was most appealing to him, because of its transcendental elements, a fact which helped him later to embrace the Christian faith. Until the day of his death he held the Greek philosophers in high esteem, especially the writings of Plato.[3] Hence, some church historians have called him a Christian Platonist. Although he was never able to divest himself completely from his pagan past[4], the similarity of his theology to Platonic idealism is more appar-

---

1 Tertullian (*Adv. Val.* 5) first called him "philosophus et martyr"; Hippolytus (*Philos.* VIII.16), "Justin Martyr"; Eusebius (*His. Eccl.* 4.12), "a genuine lover of the true philosophy", who "in the garb of a philosopher proclaimed the divine word and defended the faith by writings" (IV.17).

2 There is no conclusive evidence to ascertain Justin's nationality. Both the names of his grandfather, Bacchius, and his father, Priscus, were Greek, whereas his own, Flavius Justinus, was Latin. Although he called himself a Samaritan, it is very unlikely that he was of Jewish or Samaritan decent, because, as he had stated, he was unfamiliar with the Hebrew Bible before his conversion to Christianity. It has also been suggested that Justin grew up in a Roman colony established by the Roman Emperor Vespasian in Samaria after the destruction of Jerusalem.

3 Besides Plato, Justin cited Homer, Euripides, Xenophon, and Menander.

4 Traces of his pagan past can be discovered in Justin's "Logos" theoe logy. He believed that the "Logos" gave human beings the ability to use their rational faculties which remained unaffected by the fall (cf. *Apol.* I.46). Further he taught that, even before Christ's incarnation, God had revealed divine truth to Jews and Greeks alike. In pre-Christian times salvation was based on the obligation to live reasonably and virtuously in obedience to the divine knowledge providentially given to everyone. He regarded the Greek philosopher and poets as the prophets of the pagans.

ent than real, based on external congruence rather than on analogous concepts. Justin subjugated his philosophical reminiscences in many respects to the truth of the Scriptures.

His conversion to Christianity[5] at about A.D. 132 marked a turning point in his life and career. Convinced of the truthfulness of the Christian faith, he developed his literary talents and became a prolific writer. For more than 20 years his apologetic treatises exercised a wide spread influence on Jews and pagans alike. He eventually sealed his faith as a martyr in Rome about the year A.D. 166. A Roman tribunal sentenced him and six other Christians to death after they had refused to sacrifice to the heathen gods.

His most famous writings were the two *Apologies*[6], exhibiting his talents in presenting a cogent defence of the Christian faith against the assault of pagan religions and philosophies.

Once he was engaged in a dispute with Trypho, a respectable Jew, living in Ephesus.[7] At a later time Justin committed this conversation to writing and called it the *Dialogue with Trypho*. It is a storehouse of allegorical interpretations of Old Testament prophecies. Its most striking characteristic is the christological emphasis given to these

---

5 In his *Second Apology*, he mentioned particularly how much he was impressed, while yet still a Platonist, by the steadfastness and fearless courage of Christians, even in the face of death (*Apol.* II., 12,13). Later, as he became a Christian, he drew a clear demarcation line between Socrates and Christ, and between the best pagan and the humblest Christian. No one trusted Socrates, he said, so as to die for his doctrine; but Christ, who was partially known by Socrates, was trusted not only by philosophers and scholars, but also by artisans and uneducated people.

6 The first or larger *Apology* contained in 68 chapters was presumably composed about A.D. 147, the second or smaller *Apology*, extending to 25 chapters, was an addition to the first and perhaps intended as a conclusion. Both were dedicated to the Emperor Antoninus Pius (A.D. 137-161) and his sons.

7 The purpose of the whole conversation was to answer the following two questions by Trypho: How Christians could profess to serve God, and yet break the Law of Moses, and why they believe in a human Saviour who suffered and died? Justin tried to make a plausible case for his claim that the Christian faith constitutes the only true religion and is the rightful heir of Judaism.

interpretations. Justin tried to convince Trypho that the Hebrew prophets were speaking about Christ, either by allusions or direct references, in almost all of their prophecies.

In the following we will focus our attention on Justin's chiliasm. We will also ask the question of whether or not Justin, in formulating his millennial ideas, was influenced by other sources, than that of the passage in Revelation 20. And if so, which sources he used and how he applied them to strengthen his case for a literal millennium.

5.2. Millennium

Justin expressed his chiliastic views in chapters 80 and 81 of his *Dialogue with Trypho*. Touching on many differences between the Jewish and the Christian faith, Trypho remarked that Justin was well versed in the Scriptures and able to argue convincingly for his own position. On the other hand, he questioned the integrity of other Christians who seemed to have taken a partisan view about the millennium. Trypho felt that such a view would put those, including himself, who argue against it into a bad light. In particular he was interested if Justin expected the restoration of Jerusalem among other things. "… be gathered together, and made joyful with Christ and the patriarchs, and the prophets, both the men of our nation, and other proselytes who joined them before your Christ came."[8]

These questions gave Justin an opportunity to clarify any misapprehensions on Trypho's side about the millennium. It also provided him with the opportunity to demonstrate that the predictions of the Hebrew prophets complemented the description of the millennium in Revelation. Thus Justin began to acquaint Trypho with the generally accepted chiliasm current in the Asiatic Church at that time.[9]

---

8 Justin Martyr, *Dialogue with Trypho*, chap. 80 in *The Writings of Justin Martyr and Athenagoras*, trans. by Marcus Dods, George Reith, D.P. Pratten, T. & T. Clark, Edinburgh, 1867.

9 It should be noted that Justin is the only Greek apologist who wrote about the millennium.

Justin introduced his millennial theme by repeatedly mentioning the Second Coming of Christ.[10] He believed that this event would be preceded by the manifestation of impostors and false teachers in the ranks of the Church "... who are called Christians, but are godless, impious heretics, teach doctrines that are in every way blasphemous, atheistical, and foolish."[11] By pointing out that his motives were pure he assures Trypho that he has no intention to deceive him.[12] Although he admits that there are some true and pious Christians who reject the idea of a literal millennium[13], he regards it as the cornerstone of orthodoxy.[14] Again, at the end of chapter 80, he asserts that many other Christians share his convictions: "[He] and others, who are right-minded Christians on all points, are assured that there will be a resurrection of the dead, and a thousand years in Jerusalem, which will then be built, adorned, and enlarged, as the prophets Ezekiel and Isaiah and others declare."[15]

His chiliasm resembles that of Papias and, to a lesser degree, of Cerinthus and Montanus. Hence, it was not only shared by "right-minded Christians", as he maintains, but also by heretics and schismatics. The allusions to the restoration of Jerusalem in splendor and glory, the participation of the saints in the millennial dominion of Christ, and the reference to the prophecies of the Hebrew Bible constitute the common stock of millenarianism which flourished, as we have seen, in Asia Minor. One element of Asiatic chiliasm, however, is missing - the description of the extraordinary fruitfulness of vegetation. Justin might have discounted it, because of its grotesqueness.

---

10 Cf. *op. cit.*, chs. 32,51,110.

11 Ibid., chap. 80.

12 Ibid.

13 Ibid.; It is interesting to note that already at the end of the second century A.D. the controversy about the millennium had affected the Christian Church in Palestine and Asia Minor.

14 Ibid.

15 Ibid.

Justin's reference to the prophets is of particular interest to us, because it indicates his reliance on the Old Testament as the primary source of his chiliasm. He did not shy away from utilizing different passages from the Hebrew Bible to strengthen his argument in favor of a literal millennium. This was the most viable approach to explain and defend his cause against the probing questions of a skeptical Jew.

Justin must have especially liked the description of the new heavens and the new earth in Isaiah 65. The portrayal of the glorious future awaiting God's chosen people contained in this passage was conducive of reminding Trypho about the similarities of their hope.[16] Contrary to Trypho, however, who would not have seen a millennial significance in this prophecy of Isaiah, Justin interprets this passage according to his chiliastic views. "For Isaiah spoke thus concerning this period of a thousand years."[17] Yet he must have realized that the millennium, in the strict sense of the word, did not appear in this passage. In an attempt to justify himself, he tries to convince Trypho that the expression "according to the days of the tree [of life] shall be the days of my people,"[18] obscurely predicts a thousand years. The translators of the LXX added this phrase to the passage of Isaiah, thus indicating that they may have already understood this prophecy as an allusion to the Golden Age.

That Justin used the word "obscurely" in reference to this statement might indicate that he himself felt uncomfortable with this interpretation. The only elaboration which he provides as an explanation is found in the following two statements: "As Adam was told that in the day he ate of the tree he would die, we know that he did not complete a thousand years"[19] and "We have perceived, moreover, that the expression, 'The day of the Lord is as a thousand years,' is connected with this subject."[20] Therefore we might suspect

---

16 Ibid., chap. 81.
17 Ibid.
18 Ibid.
19 Ibid.
20 Ibid.

that he used a Jewish source which mentioned the concept of a thousand years in the context of a legendary account about Adam's life-span in paradise.

Indeed, we find in this one passage many of the arguments of Jewish apocalyptic which had been used in the interpretation of Ps. 90:4. Since Justin regarded the millennium as a return to the once lost Paradise, he believed that the length of life will be the same as that of Adam. The writer of *Jubilees* used the same argument to show that life in Paradise lasts for a thousand years.[21] Justin connects this idea with the passage in Isaiah which also seems to equate the life-span in messianic times with that of life in Paradise.

After acknowledging the Apostle John's authorship of Revelation[22], Justin emphasizes the importance of the millennial passage in Revelation by pointing out that it coincides with Christ's own words. He also argues for continuity between the prophecies of the Hebrew prophets and those revealed to John.

In describing the sequence of events following the establishment of the millennium he almost quotes verbatim the passage in Revelation 20:1-6. Christ would reign on earth in the midst of his resurrected saints. After the millennium the second and general resurrection would occur culminating in the judgment of the world.[23] He leaves out the account of Satan's short release and the rebellion and final destruction of Gog and Magog.

It will remain a matter of conjecture why Justin used the millennial passage in Revelation only sparingly. He might not have been convinced that even a tolerant Jew, like

---

21 Cf. *Jubilees* 23:27 (?) 4:30.

22 Cf. Justin, *1. Apol.* 11.28.52; *Dial.* 80f.; Euseb., *Hist. Eccl.* 4.18.8."He also writes that even up to his own time prophetic gifts illuminated the church, and quotes the APocalypse of John, saying clearly that it is the work of the apostle."

23 Justin, who on the basis of Revelation 20:5 taught that the saints would rise first, and that the resurrection of unbelievers to judgement would take place at the end of the thousand years (chap. 81), stands at variance with the simpler arrangement of Irenaeus. The latter did not differentiate between two resurrections.

Trypho, would have accepted any divine revelation outside his own religious context.

In another passage Justin mentioned the conquest of Canaan by Joshua and the subsequent distribution of the land among the tribes of Israel. He saw in this story an analogy to the conversion of the diaspora at Christ's Second Coming and the allotment of the world among the believers. It should be indicated, however, that Justin definitively understood the latter as the bestowal of the eternal inheritance and not as an award of earthly possessions. It is difficult to perceive this passage as a further representation of his millennial views. There are two possibilities to explain the ambiguities of this text. Either he slightly contradicted himself from what he had taught earlier in chs. 80, 81 or he expected that the establishment of the millennium would occur after the destruction and final restitution of the world. To settle this question we do best to take Justin's clear statements about the millennium in chs. 80, 81 as our primary guide. This is also necessary because some scholars have argued that Justin did not believe in a chiliasm of a pure character, as if he looked for a millennium not in this world, but in the eternity. They have based their arguments on Justin's interpretation of the verse in Isaiah 65:17, "Behold I create new heavens and a new earth". It is claimed that the millennium, which Justin expected, would be established after the general resurrection and the restitution of all things. If this would be true, Justin would not have quoted at length verses speaking of the earthly character of the messianic times before the final restitution. We might be justified to assume that he believed in an earthly millennium before the restitution.[24] The ambiguity was certainly caused by the passage in Isaiah itself which does not clearly distinguish between the terrestrial manifestations of messianic times and the new creation. The discussion is further complicated, as it is disputable whether Justin believed in a complete annihilation of the world or if he expected the earth's resto-

---

24 See quotation of Is. 65:18ff in *Dial.*, 81.

ration.[25] In the final analysis it will remain unclear if Justin expected the establishment of the millennium before or after the final restitution.

5.3. Conclusion

It is generally recognized that Justin represents the transition from the Jewish Christian view of the millennium to the one which became prominent among Gentile Christians. It will be remembered that the dialogue with Trypho takes place at Ephesus. Therefore, an analysis of this conversation has to take its Asiatic context into consideration. Justin was certainly connected with a group of Asiatic millenarians and is simply reflecting their chiliastic views of a literal millennium on earth equalling the original Paradise. He based most of his arguments on either the prophetic books of the Hebrew Bible and, to a lesser degree, on Revelation 20 and Jewish apocalyptic.

If Justin Martyr tended to view the millennium more literally, the writer of the *Epistle of Barnabas* preferred to interpret it allegorically. The Asiatic influence on Justin's chiliastic views is as noticeable as the penetration of Alexandrian mysticism on the thinking of Barnabas. Gnosticism, in its many forms, was more prevalent in the Egyptian metropolis in the second century A.D. than in Asia Minor. Thus we should expect at least some traces of its teaching in Barnabas' millennialism.

---

25 In *Dial.*, chap. 113 Justin says that God, through Christ, will renew the heaven and the earth; in the *Apologies*, he represents the common view of a general resurrection and judgment which is followed by a total destruction of the world by fire. Although there is no mention of the millennium in the *Apologies*, this does not mean that he excluded it from his eschatological teaching altogether.

Chapter 6
Chiliasm of the Epistle of Barnabas

6.1. Introduction 148
6.2. Authorship 149
   6.2.1. Content 149
   6.2.2. Date 152
6.3. Millennium 153
   6.3.1. Cosmic Week 154
   6.3.2. Sabbath of Rest 155
   6.3.3. Eighth Day 155
6.4. Conclusion 157

6. Chiliasm of the Epistle of Barnabas

6.1. Introduction

The earliest attested Christian expression of a millennial concept is found in the *Epistle of Barnabas*. The epistle itself presents a true picture of the state of early Jewish-Christian theology. Barnabas[1] wrote this epistle in the form of a general address to a Christian community. He adduced evidence from the Scriptures and other writings which, in contrast to the works of Philo[2], was presented in favor of Christianity.[3] While disclaiming to be a teacher, he saw the purpose of the epistle in bringing joy to his readership.[4]

---

1 The name Barnabas is a 'nom de plume'. As will be explained later, I do not believe that the author of the *Epistle of Barnabas* is identical with Barnabas, the companion of Paul (see footnote #4). In the following, however, I will call the author Barnabas for convenience.

2 It has also been pointed out that the *Epistle of Barnabas* not only stands in contrast with the writings of the Jewish scholar Philo, but also closely resembles them. Indeed the author of the epistle must have been intimately familiar with the works of Philo and agreed with him in many ways.

3 The author does not discriminate between passages from canonical and non-canonical books, as far as the Canon of the Hebrew Bible is concerned. He quoted profusely from the LXX, especially from Isaiah and Daniel, but does not hesitate to call the writer of *Second Esdras* "another prophet" (chap. 12) or to introduce *I Enoch* 16:5 as "the Scripture says". Barnabas alluded to many passages from the New Testament. The words of Matthew 22:14 "many are called but few are chosen" are cited in chap. 4:14. "He came not to call the righteous but sinners" (chap. 5:9) is taken from another passage in Matthew (9:13) or possibly from the parallel passages in the synoptic gospels (Mk. 2:17; Lk. 5:32). The list of New Testament allusions can be further prolonged. The following examples, however, should suffice. (Cf. chap. 4:12 with Rom. 2:11 and 1 Pet. 1:17; chap. 5:6 with 2 Tim. 1:10; chap. 7:9 with Rev. 1:7; chap. 12:11 with Mk. 11:37 [Mt. 22:45; Lk. 20:44]; chap. 15:4 with 2 Pet. 3:8 concerning a thousand years being with the Lord as one day.)

4 *The Epistle of Barnabas* chap. 1.

6.2. Authorship

Barnabas' identity is shrouded in mystery. No personal information about him has come down to us. That he called himself by the same name as the close companion of the Apostle Paul does not necessarily intimate that he was identical with him, since there is no indication of that in the epistle itself. Thus it seems more likely that he was a Christian of Jewish background simply by the name of Barnabas.[5] This accounts best for the fact that the content of his teaching deviated from the Christian doctrines of the Pauline epistles.

6.2.1. Content

The author's main concern could be summarized under three different headings: "Righteousness, the hope of life, and the love of joy."[6] He believed that the Law of Moses has not been superseded by Christ, and that salvation is just as much dependent on its observance as on the Lord's sufferings. Works of righteousness[7] assume a greater importance in the theology of Barnabas than they do in Paul's writings. Emphasizing the importance of the Mosaic Law, he expressed himself in these words: "I cherish the hope that, according to my desire, you have omitted none of those things at present which are necessary for salvation."[8] Thus it should not surprise us that Barnabas based the attainment of eternal life both on baptism and the hope of the cross.[9] Yet he can also

---

5 Patristic scholars generally assume a different identity from the author of the epistle and the companion of Paul. See G.G. Walsh, "Introduction to the Letters of St. Ignatius of Antioch", in *The Apostolic Fathers*, trans. by F. Glimm, J.M.F. Marique, G. G. Walsh, Cima Publ., New York, 1947, pp. 84, 85.

6 *Op. cit.*, chap. 1:6.

7 This righteousness should become evident, for example, in a genuine concern for the hungry.

8 *Op. cit.*, chap. 17:1.

9 Ibid., chap. 9:11.

say that Jesus Christ has put the seal of his covenant on the hearts of believers. Their sanctification is brought about by the 'sprinkled blood' of Christ, i.e. his death on the cross. This high calling, however, should not make them impertinent towards others.

Furthermore, he asserts that the Pentateuch is filled with many figures of speech. In general he favors an allegorical approach to the interpretation of the Scriptures betraying a noticeable influence of Hellenistic ideas on his thinking. This indicates a possible affinity between him and the proponents of the Alexandrian school of theology. It has been suggested that he might have even resided in Alexandria. A close geographical proximity is at least likely.

In the epistle Barnabas habitually quoted specific passages from the Old Testament, especially from Isaiah. He blamed the Jews, however, for their rigid observance of the literal sense of Scripture.[10] What God really asked of his people was not bloody sacrifices, as the Law seemed to prescribe, but a contrite heart; not bodily fasting, but the practice of good works; not abstention from certain forms of food, but the avoidance of vices symbolized by them.[11] He enforced the moral strength of his teaching by admonishing his readers in these words: "The man perishes justly, who, having a knowledge of the way of righteousness, continues in the way of darkness."[12] Judged by the amount of space Barnabas devoted to the exposition of prophecy, it must have been one of his particular interests. Already in the first chapter he mentioned prophecy in a favorable light. "For the Lord has made known to us by the prophets both the present and the past, giving us also the first-fruits of the knowledge of things to come."

One prophetic theme, in particular, seems to have been most intriguing to him – the prediction of Christ's death on the cross. He pointed out repeatedly that Christ endured to

---

10 Ibid., chs.4,7.

11 Ibid., chap. 9.

12 Ibid., chap. 5.

suffer at the hand of men.¹³ Recollecting that not only the prediction of Christ's death had been fulfilled, but many of the other Old Testament prophecies, he reminds his readers that they should approach God "with reverence, the greatest richness of faith and elevation of spirit".¹⁴

Barnabas identifies the fourth beast of Daniel with Rome, the then-ruling empire and anticipates the division of Rome into ten kingdoms. Referring to "the Prophet Enoch", he interprets the little horn as a little king who, at his appearance, would bring about the demise of three other kings. This, in turn, would indicate the imminence of the last offence. Thus he exhorts his audience "to inquire diligently into those things which are able to save us".¹⁵ In even stronger terms he continues to say: "Let us then utterly flee from all works of unrighteousness lest they captivate us; and let us hate the error of the present times, that we may set our love on the world to come."¹⁶ In pursuing this thought to its logical end, he charged the believers to prevent the coming of the "Black One" by "fleeing vanity", hating "evil works", and by "becoming spiritual, a perfect temple of God".¹⁷ This can only be accomplished by fearing God, keeping his commandments, and rejoicing in his ordinances.

In chapters 20 and 21 of his epistle he elaborates further on the description of the Black One as one whose "way is crooked and full of curse, for it is the way of eternal death and punishment". In passing, the author mentions the resurrection of the dead and the accompanying recompense. At last he reminds them to wait expectantly for the manifestation of the day of the Lord. Being convinced that this day was near, he points out that God would make a clear distinction between the righteous and the wicked. The former would be rewarded according to their deeds. The wicked,

---

13 E.g. ibid., chap. 5.
14 Ibid., chap. 1.
15 Ibid., chap. 4.
16 Ibid.
17 Ibid.

however, would meet their doom. Just as the Evil One, they will perish, because of their willful opposition to God.

6.2.2. Date

The *Epistle of Barnabas* was widely circulated among the Christian churches. Its early composition is firmly attested, although it is impossible to determine the exact date.[18] The author does not give any indisputable evidence as to the time when he wrote the epistle. There is, however, a passage alluding to the destruction of the Jewish Temple in Jerusalem in A.D. 70 and its impending reconstruction.[19] As it is difficult to determine what the author meant by referring to the rebuilding of the temple, a precise time of this event cannot be set.[20] Modern scholars have proposed different dates as to the time of its composition. Yet none of these dates are indisputable and range from the years A.D. 70 to 150. Most scholars, however, tend to favor a later date in proximity to the year A.D. 150.[21]

---

18 The earliest citations appear in the writings of Clement of Alexandria and Origen at the close of the 2nd century. Clement of Alexandria quoted it as canonical, and it seems as if Origen had the same opinion calling it "the Catholic *Epistle of Barnabas*". Both of them testified to its high esteem among the early Church Fathers. At a later time, however, Jerome and Eusebius treated it as "apocryphal", i.e. non-canonical.

19 "Furthermore he says again, 'Lo, they who destroyed this temple shall themselves build it.' That is happening. For on account of the war it was destroyed by the enemy; now even the servants of the enemy will build it again" (chap. 16:3-4).

20 As to this day the Jewish temple has not been rebuilt, since it was destroyed in A.D. 70, Barnabas' reference to the reconstruction of the temple by the "enemies" (the Romans?) will remain enigmatic. It might have been an allusion to the building of a pagan temple on the temple site during the reign of Hadrian.

21 Lightfoot tended to prefer an early date. Yet he did not commit himself to one specific year. Other scholars have speculated about a date in the third decade of the second century (see Introductions to Barnabas, in J.B. Lightfoot, J.R. Harmer ed., *The Ante-Nicene Fathers*, Macmillan and Co., London, 1926, pp. 239-242; in *ANF*, vol.1, pp. 133-135; and in *ANF*, Glimm's transl., Cima, New York, 1947, pp. 137-189). The date circa A.D. 130 seems to be the one most frequently suggested in modern publicati-

Having thus surveyed the authorship, content, and date of the *Epistle of Barnabas*, we will present now the author's millennial ideas, paying special attention to his analogy of the six creation days representing six thousand years and the seventh day of rest with the last millennium.

6.3. Millennium

Among the Apostolic Fathers Barnabas is the first ecclesiastical writer who spoke of the six ages of the world and the seventh millennium of rest at the Second Coming of Christ. He considered the Mosaic history of the creation a type of six ages of labor for the world, each lasting a thousand years, and of a millennium of rest. The millennial sabbath on earth will be followed by an eighth and eternal day in a new world, of which the Lord's Day, called by Barnabas "the eighth day", is the type.[22]

The original idea of a millennium which permeated the thinking of the Asiatic Church has been located in the cosmic week speculations of Jewish apocalyptic literature. This fact has been established in one of the previous chapters. However, it would be wrong to assume that only the Jewish-Christian community in Asia Minor directed its thoughts toward a speculative contemplation of the cosmic week. As we have noted earlier, the Barnabas belonged almost certainly to the Jewish Christian community which flourished in Alexandria. Thus he lived in a completely different environment from that of Asia Minor. Considering the fact that his chiliastic views are partially based on verses from the Old Testament[23], and that he frequently quoted passages from apocalyptic writings, makes the contention

---

ons of the *Epistle of Barnabas* (e.g. Introduction to *The Epistle of Barnabas*, in *Early Christian Writings: The Apostolic Fathers*, trans. by Maxwell Staniforth, Penguin Books, Harmondsworth, 1968).

22 *Op. cit.*, chap. 15.

23 In regard to the cosmic week speculation the verse in Ps. 90:4 seems to be the most important of the Old Testament.

plausible that the Alexandrian Christians were equally acquainted with the same Jewish source material.

It should also be noted that Barnabas did not equate, as might be expected, the chiliasm of Revelation 20 with his seventh millennium. He does not even quote the Apocalypse, although he might have been familiar with it. On the whole he appears to have been independent of any concept of Christian chiliasm.

Two main ideas dominate his millennialism. First, by establishing the analogy between the creation week and the duration of the world he emphasized the correlation of the Sabbath with the eschatological rest. Secondly, he pointed to the significance of the eighth day.

6.3.1. Cosmic Week

Barnabas' use of this analogy does not determine whether or not he attributed any millennial importance to the Jewish speculations about the cosmic week. The theme of an eschatological Sabbath could be understood, as Origen obviously did[24], to signify eternal life. There is no need to look for another motive behind this analogy except for the six days of creation representing the time of this world, and the seventh day, the eternal world.

It was a common practice among the ancient Jews to interpret the six Alephs in the first verse of Genesis, which in the Jewish arithmetic stand for 6 times 1000, to mean that the world would last 6000 years. The six days of the creation week and the following seventh day, the Sabbath, were understood as outlining the duration of the world, in which one creation day counted for one thousand years. The seventh and last millennium was thought to be eternity.[25] So

---

24 Origen, *Hom.* XXIII, 3.

25 The idea that the history of the world would come to an end after six "days" of a thousand year each, was not only limited to the Jewish literature. The cosmic week speculation, which had been an early Jewish tradition, has also been attested in pagan literature (e.g. in the *Sibylline Oracles*). In fact the Chaldeans, according to Plutarch, believed in a struggle between good and evil for the time of 6000 years. Afterwards

far as it is possible to trace the influence of Jewish literature on Barnabas' thinking, we are able to say that he embraced the same concept of a cosmic week.

6.3.2. Sabbath of Rest

The idea of rest on the seventh day must have been equally important to him. Again he might have taken this concept from a Jewish source, like the *Ascension of Isaiah*. The latter source, however, does not include Ps. 90:4 as part of its description of the Golden Age, nor does it associate the idea of rest with speculations about the cosmic week. Barnabas might have exercised some editorial alterations to combine both concepts with each other.

Yet another, even more convincing, explanation for the origin of the "millennial rest" motif in the *Epistle of Barnabas* might be found in the primarily Gnostic concept of the eighth day.

6.3.3. Eighth Day

The eighth day, the "ogdoad", was an important part of the Pythagorean number-mysticism. It cannot be conclusively established that Barnabas was familiar with this kind of pagan mysticism. He might have encountered the same idea in the writings of Hellenistic Jews. Philo, for example, had incorporated certain aspects of Pythagoras's numerology into his own system of interpretation. He was, however, cautious about placing too much significance on the speculations about the numerical value of biblical letters and words.

Hades would cease to exist and all mankind would enjoy a state of happiness. Plutarch also believed, although without giving any substantiation of his belief, that Zoroaster taught the same. Theopompus, who lived in the 4th century B.C., relates that the Persian Magi taught that the present state of things would continue 6000 years, after which Hades would be destroyed and mankind would live happily thereafter.

His partial indifference towards the idea of the "ogdoad", however, stands in sharp contrast to the great importance which the Gnostics attributed to it. The latter gained a hearing in Alexandria at approximately the same time that Barnabas wrote his epistle. They might have "enlightened" him about the significance of the eighth day. However, most of the material which the Gnostics used was borrowed from other sources. The high regard for the eighth day, as it came to be known among them, was clearly a reflection of the Christian practice to venerate the day after the sabbath, the Sunday, in remembrance of Christ's resurrection. Originally it was this practice, probably more than any other, which distinguishes the Christians from the Jews. This fact might have motivated the Gnostics to use the same concept, although in a mystical sense, in order to elevate themselves on a supposedly higher spiritual plateau than the ordinary Christians. Thus the importance of the "ogdoad" assumed extraordinary proportions in Gnosticism. It was one of the most fundamental ideas of their alleged superior knowledge.

The affinity of this gnostic analogy to the ideas expressed in the *Epistle of Barnabas* is obvious, especially if we consider that its author introduced a type of chiliasm which differed substantially from that of Asia Minor. Apparently Barnabas placed a special emphasis on the seven millennia followed by the eighth day, rather than on a pure concept of the millennium which was current in the Asiatic churches. It is, however, questionable to what extent Barnabas depended on these gnostic speculations about the "hebdomad" and "ogdoad". The minimal amount of evidence prevents us from making any definite statement. In closing it might be helpful to add that the true Alexandrian typology of the week of creation is the one found in Philo, Clement, Origen and the Valentinians, which indeed contrasts the "hebdomad" as the world of time with the "ogdoad" as the world of eternity.

6.4. Conclusion

Instead of postulating that there was a direct exchange of chiliastic ideas throughout the early Church, as was surely the case in later times, it is perhaps better to look for the origin of millenarianism in Egypt at the same place from which Asiatic millennialism drew its inspirations, namely from the teaching of the Old Testament and Jewish apocalyptic literature.

The contribution of Barnabas to the chiliastic doctrine of the early Church is seen in his efforts to relate the concept of the eschatological rest to the speculations on the cosmic week. Moreover Barnabas was to retain the Hellenistic idea of the seven millennia as the duration of the world and the Jewish concept of the prominent place of the sabbath, the seventh day, as a time of rest. The notion of the eighth day, the "ogdoad", as symbolizing eternal life, might have come from Gnosticism. The Christian hope of heaven, a future conscious existence in the presence of God, has only secondary significance in the *Epistle of Barnabas*. The millennium itself is simply conceived as an extended time of rest. As we will see, Augustine was to defend this kind of chiliasm for a long time, although condemning the "carnal" conceptions of Asiatic millenarianism.

Chiliasm in its strict sense had no place in the Alexandrian world, whether orthodox or Gnostic. Although some Alexandrian theologians did not completely divest themselves from the influence of Asiatic millenarianism, they overtly tended to disregard its validity. The influence which it later assumed in the provincial regions of Egypt is noticeable, though minimal, in the writings of Clement of Alexandria who speaks of "a time which, through the seven ages of the world, effects the restoration of the perfect rest" (*Strom.* IV, 25:159). Gradually, however, the Alexandrian theology, both in its orthodox and heretical forms, was to substitute a strictly historical understanding of the cosmic week with a cosmological one. The "hebdomad" symbolized the mundane affairs of the world ruled by the seven planets, and the "ogdoad" the eternal state in heaven. In this respect there was hardly any difference in views between the Gnostic

Valentinians[26] and Clement of Alexandria[27]. How far Barnabas actually participated in these Gnostic speculations is a matter of conjecture.

It seems certain that Barnabas did not directly contribute to the dramatic changes in the chiliastic debate which occurred in the Eastern Church under the theological auspices of Origen and Dionysius of Alexandria. He merely paved the way for a more allegorical interpretation of the millennium, not its rejection.

---

26 Cf. Irenaeus, *Haer.* I, 5:3.

27 Clem. Alex., *Strom.* VI, 14:7, 10.

Chapter 7
Anti-Millennialism of Alexandria

7.1. Introduction 160
7.2. Origen 161
   7.2.1. Introduction 161
   7.2.2. Allegorical Interpretation 162
   7.2.3. Aversion against Millennialism 163
   7.2.4. First and Second Resurrection 164
   7.2.5. Second Coming 165
   7.2.6. Origen's Influence on the Church 166
7.3. Dionysius of Alexandria 167
   7.3.1. Introduction 167
   7.3.2. Chiliastic Dispute 167
      7.3.2.1. Origin 168
      7.3.2.2. Intent 169
7.4. Conclusion 170

7. Anti-Millennialism of Alexandria

7.1. Introduction

Progressive divergence from the original position on the millennium occurred during the third, fourth, and fifth centuries. The most definitive steps in this process centered in the teaching of Origen, Dionysius and, as will be seen later, Augustine. The ascendancy of the Alexandrian school of theology, which is inextricably connected with Origen, its most famous proponent, marks a turning point in church history. This does not mean that all the changes in the Church, away from the apostolic standards of doctrine and worship, began with Origen and reached full development with Augustine. Nor does it mean that the drift from the original dogmas of the Church manifested itself in the abandonment of the earliest views on the prophecies, especially those on the Second Coming and the millennium. It only means that during this period the Church opened itself up to mystical influences which gradually began to alter the prophetic interpretation of the Scriptures. There was, in fact, considerable interaction of various doctrinal streams in the Church prior to the major shifts in the prophetic point of view. For example, as early as the second century, the infiltration of religious concepts from outside the bounds of apostolicity were justified by Tertullian (A.D. 160-240) on the basis of doctrinal tradition. These incursions of extra-biblical dogmas were not sudden or complete, but nevertheless decisive in altering a complex system of biblical doctrines of the Church. They became clearly noticeable for the first time at the Council of Nicaea (A.D. 325).

In the following pages we will describe these changes in the early Church, especially in regard to chiliasm, by focusing our attention on the eschatological teaching of two Alexandrian theologians, Origen and Dionysius.

7.2. Origen

7.2.1. Introduction

Origen (c.185 - c.254 A.D.) was probably born in Alexandria of Greek parentage. He was considered the most gifted scholar of his age. Although his expertise was in the area of textual criticism, he possessed an excellent knowledge of philosophy, philology, and theology. His familiarity with Greek literature was only surpassed by his erudition in the Scriptures. His position as a leading figure of Christian spirituality was unrivalled among his contemporaries. In the interpretation of the biblical text he probed its "inner sense", deeming its literal meaning of lesser value. Eusebius, who describes the early life of Origen in his *Ecclesiastical History*[1], tells us that Origen's father, Leonides, rebuked his son sternly for this tendency and discouraged him for inquiring into things beyond his youthful capacity.[2]

In 202 Origen commenced his studies at the catechetical school of Alexandria under the tutelage of Clement. In the same year the Roman emperor Septimius Severus launched a severe persecution upon the Christians. Fearing for his life Clement fled from Alexandria, abandoning the catechetical school. At once Origen was given the opportunity to instruct its students in the Christian faith.

One year later the bishop of Alexandria, Demetrius, invested him with the authority to lead the school. Under his leadership the school, already famous, rose even more in prominence as many students came to listen to his lectures. Thinking to fulfil his office better, he devoted himself to an exhaustive study of all the heresies of his age, until he became steeped in Greek philosophy and heretical Gnosticism.

He brilliantly refuted the opponents of Christianity, but impaired the very religion he defended by mixing it with the currently popular Neoplatonism. Origen thus contributed

---

1 Eusebius, *Ecclesiastical History*, VI.2-3, in *NPNF*, 2nd series, vol. 1, pp. 249-252.

2 Ibid., VI.2, p. 230.

tragically to the corruption of the Christian faith. Instead of enlightening the minds of his students with the truth of the Scriptures, he introduced a form of syncretism into the Church which combined elements of pagan mysticism and Greek philosophy with those of Christianity.

After Origen had taught thirteen years at Alexandria, though still a layman, he was asked by the bishops of Jerusalem and Caesarea to teach theology in a public gathering. Demetrius, incensed about this unprecedented occurrence, demanded his return to Alexandria. Origen complied and, after reassuming his tasks at the catechetical school, began to write his famous expositions of Scripture, distinguishing himself for the next fifteen years as the foremost instructor of theology in the Eastern Church.

About the year 230 he was ordained a presbyter at Caesarea earning his again the displeasure of his bishop. His ordination was pronounced invalid, and his authority over the Alexandrian school revoked. Following this incident Origen took up permanent residence in Caesarea and founded a theological school similar to that in Alexandria. Under the persecution of Decius, he was imprisoned in Tyre. Although later released, he never recuperated from the injuries inflicted upon him and died a broken man a few years later.

Either at the Fifth Ecumenical Council or at an earlier synod in Constantinople in 543 he was charged, although dead, with heresy and branded as a false teacher. His teaching, however, lived on, and exercised a profound influence on the succeeding centuries. From the days of Origen to those of Chrysostom there was not a single eminent commentator who did not borrow largely from his works.

7.2.2. Allegorical Interpretation

Origen declared prophecies in general as enigmatic and unintelligible.

> And what need is there to speak of the prophecies, which we all know to be filled with enigmas and dark

saying? ... And who, on reading the revelations made to John, would not be amazed at the unspeakable mysteries therein concealed, and which are evident (even) to him who does not comprehend what is written? And therefore, since these things are so, and since innumerable individuals fall into mistakes, it is not safe in reading (the Scriptures) to declare that one easily understands what needs the key of knowledge, which the Saviour declares is with the lawyers.[3]

He did not deny that the Scriptures, if taken literally, taught a corporeal resurrection, an earthly millennium, and the personal Second Coming of Christ. Being convinced, however, that prophetic texts must be interpreted allegorically he altered their meaning significantly in his search for the true and inner sense of Scripture.[4] The gates of the New Jerusalem became, for example, the various modes by which souls enter the better world.[5] His rejection of a literal hermeneutic immediately undermined the argumentation of the millennialists.

7.2.3. Aversion against Millennialism

The mixture of rationalism and mysticism which dominated the Alexandrian school exercised such a great influence on the interpretation of the Scriptures in general that it affected also the exposition of the chiliastic passages. Origen was particularly zealous to counteract the spread of Asiatic chiliasm which he deemed inimical to the high standard of the Christian ethic on account of its pronounced sensuality. It is significant that Origen never spoke of millennialism except to condemn it.[6] He opposed chiliasm as a Jewish dream, and spiritualized every Scriptural passage, which, if taken liter-

---

3 Origen, *De principiis*, book 4, chap. 1, sec. 10, in *ANF*, vol. 4, p. 358.

4 Allan Menzies, *Commentaries of Origen. Introduction*, in *ANF*, vol. 9, p. 293.

5 Origen, *Against Celsus*, book 6, chap. 23, in *ANF*, vol. 4, p. 583.

6 Ibid., book 2, chap. 11, sec. 2, in *ANF*, vol. 4, p. 297.

ally, would support a millennial view.[7] His own philosophical presuppositions did not allow him to concede any biblical validity to the argument of his chiliastic opponents. By allegorizing the first and second resurrection he struck an irrevocable blow at the heart of chiliasm.[8]

7.2.4. First and Second Resurrection

Origen contends for the orthodox belief of the Church concerning the actual resurrection of the body, quoting such texts as 1 Thes. 4:15, 16 and 1 Cor. 15:39-42.[9] Yet he teaches that the resurrected spiritual bodies must undergo gradual, perhaps age-long purification in the next world, perhaps many worlds, becoming more spiritual and less material until the saints attain the highest spiritual condition, that in which "God shall be all in all".[10] Although he elsewhere treats the subject allegorically, and speaks of a spiritual resurrection from spiritual death, Origen distinctly mentions the two resurrections.[11]

Yet he vitiates the whole point, purpose, and distinction of the two resurrections by assigning the possibility of ultimate salvation also to those who have part in the second resurrection, after the purifying "refiner's fire".[12] Furthermore, he asserts that as soon as one believes in the immortality of the soul, he can place his hope in Christ without

---

7 Origen, *De prin.*, book 2, chap. 2.

8 Ibid., pp. 611,619.

9 Ibid., book 2, chap. 10, secs. 1-3, and book 3, chap. 6, secs. 4-9, in *ANF*, vol.4, pp. 293-295 and 346-348 respectively; Origen, *Against Celsus*, book 5, chs. 17-19, 22, 23, in *ANF*, vol.4, pp. 550-53; *Selections from the Commentaries and Homilies of Origen*, part 7, chap. 88, pp. 232,233.

10 Ibid., book 3, chap. 6, secs. 8-9, in *ANF*, vol.4, pp. 347, 348; cf. ibid., book 1, chap. 6, pp. 260-262, and fragments translated by Jerome, appended to book 1, p. 267.

11 Origen, *Commentary on John*, book 1, chap. 25, in *ANF*, vol. 9, p. 312; *Selections from the Commentaries and Homilies of Origen*, part 7, chap. 87, pp. 228.

12 Origen, *De prin.*, book 3, chap. 6, sec. 5, and *Against Celsus*, book 4, chap. 13, in *ANF*, vol. 4, pp. 346 and 502 respectively.

believing in a bodily resurrection.[13] He thus effectively renders meaningless a literal concept of the millennium in which the resurrected saints reign with Christ on earth. Taking his stance against chiliasm in regard to the first and second resurrections, he was constrained also to allegorize the Second Coming.

7.2.5. Second Coming

Origen speaks of the two advents of Christ[14], but does not connect the Second Coming with the resurrection or the millennium, or recognize it as marking the climax of prophetically foretold human history.[15] Rather, the effects of that transcendent event are set forth as the ultimate reign of Christ, brought about by a gradual process, through successive worlds and long ages of purification.

> At the consummation and restoration of all things, those who make a gradual advance, and who ascend (in the scale of improvement), will arrive in due measure and order at the land, and at that training which is contained in it, where they may be prepared for those better institutions to which no addition can be made. For, after his agents and servants, the Lord Christ, who is King of all, will himself assume the kingdom; i.e., after instruction in the holy virtues, he will himself instruct those who are capable of receiving him in respect of his being wisdom, reigning in them until he has subjected them to the Father, who has subdued all things to himself, i.e., that when they shall have been made capable of receiving God, God may be to them all in all.[16]

---

13 Origen, *Selections*, part 7, chap. 89, p. 237.

14 Origen, *Against Celsus*, book 1, chap. 56, in *ANF*, vol. 4, p. 421.

15 Ibid.

16 Origen, *De prin.*, book 3, chap. 6, sec. 8, in *ANF*, vol. 4, p. 348.

Origen first gives the traditional, literal interpretation of our Lord's promise of returning in the clouds of heaven with power and great glory, but he turns from that to the allegorical "prophetic clouds" of the prophets' writings. He compares those exegetes who hold to a literal or "corporeal" interpretation of this passage to children and insists on a spiritual sense alone for the enlightened Christian. The supreme event of the plan of salvation is spiritualized away, with the observation that the literal understanding is only for the simple. He was only able to speak about the Coming of Christ as a double advent into the souls of individual Christians.

Origen contested the opinion of the ante-Nicene fathers who held that the ultimate triumph of Christianity over the world would be inaugurated at the Second Coming of Christ. In spite of severe persecution, Origen, as the only Christian exegete of his time, seems to have believed that the Church would gain the dominion of the world by its gradual expansion. He initiated these doctrinal changes concerning the eschatological hope of the Church and succeeded finally in setting it aside.[17]

7.2.6. Origen's Influence on the Church

Origen's views were not widely disseminated until after his death. During his lifetime only a minority of Christians accepted them fully. In later years he even rejected some of his own more extravagant earlier speculations. The majority of believers clung to the historic prophetic positions, in spite of the increasing tendency, following Origen's precedent, to allegorize the Scriptures. With the passing of time, however, this tendency became widely accepted, as the Church diverted its attention from the Second Coming and the future millennium to secular aggrandizement in this present world. The biblical doctrines of the early Church on the bodily resurrection, the judgment of the Antichrist, and the establishment of the millennium were abandoned on

---

17 Origen, *Against Celsus*, book 8, chap. 68, in *ANF*, vol. 4, p. 666.

account of Origen's allegorical interpretations. The ambiguous influence of mystical philosophy on the Church supplanted considerably the truth of scriptural eschatology.

7.3. Dionysius of Alexandria

7.3.1. Introduction

After an encounter with Origen, Dionysius of Alexandria (A.D. 190-265) was converted from a pagan background to Christianity. Following his student days, he was put in charge of the Alexandrian school in 231 or 232. About 247 he succeeded Heraclas as bishop of Alexandria, which at that time was the greatest and most powerful see of Christendom. Yet the time of his episcopate was filled with doctrinal strife and political oppression. He was driven into the Libyan desert by the Decian persecution, in 257, he was banished by the perfect of Egypt and died eight years later.

7.3.2. Chiliastic Dispute

Origen's allegorical interpretations, however speculative they might have been, did not impugn the common belief in the divine inspiration of Scripture. He was convinced of the canonicity of Revelation.

His immediate successors, however, showed less restraint and cast doubt on the inspiration of certain books of the Bible. Dionysius, as bishop of Alexandria, was one of those leading theologians who began at about A.D. 255 to question the inclusion of Revelation into the New Testament canon. In contrast to the chiliasts, he refused to believe in the apostolic authorship of Revelation, thus providing a fertile ground for the growth of scepticism over its canonicity. The resulting controversy can only be understood against the background of its historical origin and intended purpose.

7.3.2.1. Origin

From its very beginning the tendency of the Alexandrian school to harmonize biblical truth with Greek philosophy emulated the example of the Jewish scholar Philo, a former resident of Alexandria. The earlier Alexandrian theologians, like Clement or Origen, did not reject Revelation as an uninspired book, which would have deprived the chiliasts of this important support; they only opposed its literal interpretation. The question of inspiration and canonicity did not concern these theologians. Only to their successors it seemed necessary to oppose millenarianism along those lines.

Dionysius went beyond Origen in his attack on the apostolic authorship of Revelation. He believed that the validity of millenarianism could best be impugned by adopting such a strategy. The Alogi in the second century had already directed their attacks against the inspiration of Revelation.[18] The Roman presbyter Gaius, specifically, singled out the doctrine of the millennium as the object of contention and became prominent in his attack against the chiliastic Montanists.[19] And, as we have seen, Origen allegorized the prophetic passages of Revelation to avoid a literal interpretation of the millennium. Dionysius now joined the ranks of these anti-chiliasts in attempting to negate the canonicity of Revelation. He could not entirely follow the Alogi, who had set aside the entire book of Revelation, pronouncing it without sense; yet he modified their radical approach to suit his own purpose. Dionysius did not dare to reject the book, because many Christians esteemed it highly. Yet by advancing some critical observations, such as an alleged difference in style and diction from John's Gospel and epistles, he ascribed its authorship to another John - some "holy and inspired man" - but not the apostle John.[20]

---

18 Eusebius, *Hist. Eccl.*, VII.25, in *NPNF*, 2nd series, vol. 1, p. 309.

19 Ibid., III.28, p. 160; cf. ibid., II.25 (against the Montanist Proclus).

20 Ibid., VII.25; cf. S.D.F. Salmond, *Translator's Introduction Notice to Dionysius*, in *ANF*, vol. 6, pp. 78,79; and Dionysius, *Extant Fragments*, part 1, chap. 1, "From the Two Books on the Promises", sec. 4, in *ANF*, vol. 6, p. 83.

7.3.2.2. Intent

The influence of the Alexandrian school did not immediately spread from the place of its inception to the other regions of Egypt, which, lagged, in regard to cultural refinement, far behind that flourishing seat of academia. As the anti-chiliastic mode of Origen and his successors became gradually known in the provincial districts of Egypt, it caused a strong conservative reaction.

Nepos, a bishop of Arsinoe in Egpyt, defended millenarianism, in his book, *A Refutation of the Allegorists*, against the Alexandrian school. Basing his chiliastic convictions on a literal method of interpretation, he ignited the fires of controversy in Egypt. His book was circulated widely among the churches in the region of Arsinoe. The doctrinal frictions sprang up which caused several Arsinoean churches to disassociate themselves, on this account, from the metropolitan church at Alexandria.

Bishop Nepos had insisted on the interpretation of Revelation 20 as referring to a literal "millennium of bodily luxury" on earth.[21] Bishop Dionysius of Alexandria was not disposed to exercise his ecclesiastical authority rigorously, but handled the affair with shrewd moderation. An absolute condemnation of the chiliastic dogma would probably have laid the foundation of a lasting schism; and its adherents would, in all probability, have become only the more fanatical. He summoned the parochial clergy who held a millennial position, and, for three days, disputed with them over the contents of Nepos's book. According to the account given by Eusebius, he patiently listened to all of their objections, and tried to answer them from the Scriptures.[22] As the final outcome of this debate proved, Dionysius succeeded tactically by convincing the chiliasts of the soundness of his argumentation. The assembled clergy thanked him for his instructions. Even Coracion, who, after Nepos's death, had

---

21 Ibid., VII.24.1-5.

22 Ibid.

taken the lead of the chiliastic party, made a volte face, in the presence of all, by reversing his former opinions.[23]

Dionysius thus restored the unity among the churches in Egypt. For the purpose of confirming those who had been convinced by his arguments, and for the instruction of others, who still held fast to the opinions of Nepos, he wrote his work, *On Promises*. In this book Dionysius expressed his personal admiration, despite the controversy, for the deceased Nepos. "On many accounts," says he, "I esteemed and loved Nepos; on account of his faith, his untiring diligence, his familiar acquaintance with the Holy Scriptures; and on account of the great number of church hymns composed by him, which to this day are the delight of many of the brethren. And the more do I venerate the man, because he had already entered into his rest. But dear to me, and prized above all things else, is the truth. We must love him, and, wherever he has expressed the truth, agree with him; but we must examine and correct him in those passages of his writings where he seems to be in the wrong."[24]

7.4. Conclusion

Thus the Alexandrian Church leaders began to recede from millennialism in precisely the same proportion as philosophical theology became ascendant. In this sense the later uprooting of the millennial expectation is one of the most momentous factors in the history of early Christianity. With the loss of millennialism, the Church lost a living faith in the impending return of Christ, and the prophetic Scriptures, pointing to the reign of Christ, came to be applied to the current age and to the Church, with far-reaching results.

Origen's doctrine of the progressive, final triumph of the Church on earth, his speculations which undermined the fundamental Christian concepts of the expected kingdom of God, and his ridicule of the current beliefs in the

---

23 Ibid.

24 Ibid.; cf. Johannes Quasten, *Patrology. The Ante-Nicene Literature after Irenaeus*, vol. II, Sectrum Publishers, Utrecht-Antwerp, 1964, p. 104.

future millennium extreme as some of them were, helped to pave the way for the later Augustinian idea of the millennium as the Christian Era, and the earthly Church as God's kingdom. The latter idea led to the rise of the papal hierarchy and the full-blown Catholic system of the Middle Ages.

Since Dionysius was taught by Origen, he also refuted the chiliastic doctrine. Dionysius sought to combat it by undermining confidence in the apostolic character of the Revelation. His influence was felt in subsequent doubts concerning the canonicity of Revelation causing much discussion in the Church. At about A.D. 255 Dionysius succeeded through his oral and written efforts in checking an Egyptian revival of chiliasm. From then on millennialism was never again able to assert itself among the proponents of the Alexandrian school of theology, leaving its distinctive mark on the pages of history as the stronghold of anti-chiliasm in the early Church.

Now that we have looked at the reaction against the millennial concepts of the Asiatic Church Fathers at Alexandria, we will turn to the study of Augustine's amillennialism.

Chapter 8
Amillennialism of Augustine

8.1. Introduction 174
8.2. Millennium 177
   8.2.1. Overview 177
   8.2.2. Second Coming of Christ 178
   8.2.3. First Resurrection is Spiritual 179
   8.2.4. Thousand Years 180
   8.2.5. Binding of Satan 184
   8.2.6. Abyss 185
   8.2.7. Devil's Short Release 186
   8.2.8. Church Authorities govern the Church. 187
   8.2.9. Church represents the Kingdom of Christ. 188
8.3. Conclusion 189

8. Amillennialism of Augustine

8.1. Introduction

Augustine (Aurelius Augustinus), the most famous of the Latin Church Fathers, was born in Numidia, North Africa, in A.D. 354. Although his mother was a Christian, he grew up under the tutelage of a pagan father. After his graduation from the schools in Madaura and Carthage, he taught rhetoric in Rome and Milan. In his younger days he led a licentious life-style which was only partially checked by his later devotion to Platonic idealism and his subsequent attachment to Manichaeanism. Essentially a sceptic, he spent his time in speculating about the origin of mankind and the source of evil. His initial fascination with astrology and divination turned into an empty pursuit of pagan religiosity.

The call to the professorship of rhetoric at Milan in the year A.D. 384 launched a promising academic career. This period of his life was marked by personal achievements and political disturbances. The Visigoths had crossed the Danube and begun ravaging the Roman Empire. In 410 Rome was sacked by these Germanic warriors who had set out to destroy the Roman hegemony. These political and social upheavals caused many people to believe that the end of the world had come. Augustine lived, therefore, at a time in history which was transitional in the sense that the old Roman civilization was vanishing under the invasion of barbarians, but the new order of things had not yet emerged. In the last year of his life, he witnessed the invasion of North Africa by the sweeping hordes of Genseric, king of the Vandals. In A.D. 430, while the Vandals were besieging the city of Hippo, his eventful life came to an end in the midst of his friends. Within a few decades the Roman Empire completely succumbed to the marauding invaders.

In 387, after a period of intense inward struggles, he converted to Christianity as a result of reading the Scriptures and listening to the preaching of Ambrose, bishop of Milan. After his baptism at the age of thirty-three he renounced all worldly allurements which, in his eyes, included his lucrative vocation as a professor of rhetoric. After living in Rome for some time, he returned to Africa, where he spent three years in contemplative study. Against his own volition he was made a presbyter in 391. Four years later he became bishop of Hippo. For the next thirty-five years he was the most influential ecclesiastical administrator of the Roman Church.

Augustine produced a vast collection of literary works which fill sixteen volumes in the Migne collection. His most famous work, *De civitate dei* (On the City of God)[1], a theodicy and philosophy of history, distinguished him as the theological authority of Christianity in North Africa and in the Western Church at the close of the 4th and the beginning of the 5th century. Beginning in 413, shortly after Alaric's conquest of Rome, Augustine took thirteen years, the most productive phase of his life, to write this remarkable treatise. The immediate circumstances demanded a definitive Christian answer to the taunts of pagans who attributed the fall of Rome to the neglect of pagan worship. In his capacity as the foremost theologian of the Roman Church, Augustine dedicated his literary talents to creating a new concept of history depicting two antagonistic governments, the domain of God and that of the devil. His main objective was to establish a new interpretation of prophecy, in which history was perceived as the period of God's dealings with the Church in the world. Augustine argued that God's kingdom was established in the "city" and as such this kingdom is different from that of the world in its character, constituency, privileges, present state, and destiny. Its citizens were thus perceived as pilgrims and strangers in this world. He maintained that the "kingdom of God" would outlast the final destruction of "the kingdom of this world" and then exist for ever.

Augustine was repelled by a literal hermeneutic, and advocated a system of allegorical interpretation. At first he might have been influenced by Philo's rule that all seemingly

---

1 It should be noted, however, that the expression "civitas", has a more comprehensive meaning than simply "city". It rather describes a community or state populated by its citizens.

unorthodox passages in Scripture must be interpreted mystically. Later, however, he championed the unrestricted application of Tychonius' Rules to the extent that whole portions of his writings were an almost verbatim reproduction of the arguments of his Donatist rival.

Tychonius' "Seven Rules" exerted a powerful influence for they became the governing principles of almost all biblical interpreters for hundreds of years: (1) *De domino et corpore ejus*, that is, "About the Lord and his Body", or church; (2) *De domini corpore bipartitio*, or "On the twofold Body of the Lord"; (3) *De promissis et lege*, "*On the Promises and the Law*"; (4) *De specie et genere*, "*Concerning species and genus*"; that is, it is permissible to take a "species" of the text, and to understand its "genus" to which it belongs – to reach the abstract thought from the concrete picture (this led away from all reality to fanciful, symbolic or mystical interpretations); (5) *De temporibus*, or "*Concerning times*", which, he held, reveal the mystic measure of time in the Bible – a part of time standing for the whole, as in the three days between the death and the resurrection of Christ - or the mystical value of numbers, especially 7, 10, and 12; (6) *De recapitulatione*, "*On Recapitulations*", which states, for instance, that in the book of Revelation the narrative is not continuous, but repeats itself and goes over the same ground under new and different symbols (it was this principle carried to excess, that soon led to the full premise of Augustinianism); (7) *De diabolo et ejus corpore*, "*On Satan and his Body*", an exact analogy to Christ and his body. As Christ, he is represented in the *corpus malorum*, the evildoers, or the body of the rejected.[2]

With the ascendancy of Augustine as the authoritative voice in the exposition of the Scriptures, the allegorical method gained substantially in popularity in the Western Church. He also strengthened the position of the Roman

---

[2] The rules appear in Augustine, *On Christian Doctrine*, book 3, chs. 30-37, in *NPNF*, 1st series, vol.2, pp. 568-573. Probably the best discussion is to be found in F. C. Burkitt, *The Book of Rules of Tyconius*, TaS, III, 1, Cambridge, 1894.

Church by insisting that the Bible has to be interpreted in harmony with Church orthodoxy.[3]

In what follows we will discuss Augustine's positions on the millennium, specifically the prophecies regarding the resurrection and the kingdom. First, we will present a panoramic picture of his basic views, before attempting to analyze his chiliastic argument in detail.

8.2. Millennium

8.2.1. Overview

In *De civitate dei* Augustine presents a new view of the millennium, as a present reality, not a future expectation.[4] Instead of referring to the Second Coming of Christ, he believed that the passage in Revelation 20 is descriptive of the first advent. By applying Tychonius's Rule of recapitulation, Augustine concluded that the beginning of the millennium coincided with that of the Christian dispensation, which was ushered in by Christ's ministry. The first resurrection is interpreted spiritually, meaning the rebirth of a person into the family of God at the moment of conversion; the second is corporeal, the general resurrection of the body at the end of the world. Augustine equates the expulsion of the dragon from heaven (Rev. 12:9-13) with Satan's imprisonment in the Abyss (Rev. 20:3). The Abyss is identified with the "non-Christian nations".[5] The thrones of judgment are presented as ecclesiastical sees. In Augustines' chiliastic scheme Christ's first advent is of greater significance than his Second Coming. He interprets the camp of the saints as the universal Church of Christ, thus equating the Church mili-

---

3 See Augustine, *On Christian Doctrine*, book 3, chap. 10, vol.3, sec.15 and *Against the Epistle of Manichaeus*, chap. 5, in *NPNF*, 1st series, vol.2, p. 561, and vol.4, p. 131.

4 Aurelius Augustinus, *De civitate dei contra paganos*, Liber XX, chs. 5-14.

5 Ibid., book XX, chap. 7.

tant with the Church triumphant. Under such conditions the 144,000 (Rev. 14:1-5) become simultaneously the Church, the saints, and the city of God. The promises given to the Jews in the Hebrew Bible are applied to the Church. Thus, in order to participate in these promises, the Jews have to convert to the Christian faith. The imperial Church is identified with the stone which demolishes all earthly kingdoms and will eventually dominate the entire world. The close relationship of Church and state becomes the blueprint for Augustine's interpretation of the millennial kingdom which, in its function as a present politico-religious phenomenon, marks a new era in prophetic exposition. The Augustinian theory of the millennium influenced the interpretation of Revelation 20 for about thirteen centuries long.

After having looked at the main features of Augustine's millenarianism, we will proceed to a detailed discussion of its individual facets, beginning with his view of the Second Coming of Christ.

8.2.2. Second Coming of Christ

After discussing the last judgment, Augustine mentions certain "ambiguous" texts[6], which seem to refer either to this judgment or to the "Second Coming of the Saviour".[7] Although he does not indicate which specific passages he has in mind, he interprets the Second Coming as follows: "For example, to that coming of the Saviour which occurs throughout our age in his church, that is, in his members, piece by piece and little by little, since the whole church is his body."[8] Obviously he must have understood the Second Coming figuratively as the gradual realization of "Christ's

---

6 Ibid., book XX, chap. 5: "Multa praetereo quae de ultimo iudicio ita dici videntur, ut diligenter considerata reperiantur ambigua vel magis ad aliud pertinentia." ("Many passages I pass over the seem to refer to the last judgment but that on careful consideration are found to be ambiguous or to bear rather on some other matter.")

7 Ibid.

8 Ibid.

Coming" manifested in the expansion of the Church during this age. This interpretation, however, stands at variance with other statements in the same book, expressing his belief in a literal Second Coming. In *De civitate dei*, book XVIII, chap. 53, he states, for example, "... from the Lord's ascension to his final coming."; or, again, in book XX, chap. 8, "... from the first coming of Christ to the end of the age, which will be his Second Coming." Augustine's contrary interpretations of the Second Coming cannot merely be excused as accidental inconsistencies on his part, for they do raise a question in regard to his understanding of prophecy in general. The only explanation for this phenomenon appears to be the change of his hermeneutical system which affected, especially, his eschatological views. This change can be observed in his preference of allegorizing prophetic passages, which grew out of his increasing dependence upon Tychonius's Rules. However, it seems that he was not prepared to cast aside completely his view of a literal Second Coming. He retained it even to the point of appearing contradictory. In regard to the millennium, he was less restrained about discarding his earlier convictions in favour of a figurative interpretation. But not even here did he dismiss all facets of a literal millennium, as can be readily shown by pointing to his insistence of a thousand year period for the duration of the present age. Still, Augustine's tendency to allegorize prophetic passages became gradually more prominent, as evidenced by his exegetical treatment of the first resurrection.

8.2.3. First Resurrection is Spiritual

Augustine suggests that the significance of Matthew 8:22 - "Let the dead bury their dead!" - lies in its reference to the first resurrection. He explains that there are two different groups of dead, the dead in soul and the physically dead. The former are still alive, but need to be resurrected spiritually in order to live in righteousness. Thus the first resurrection occurs when a living person, though dead in sin, is raised to a spiritual life through the act of regeneration. Furthermore, he states that the verse in John 5:25, "The hour is coming and now is." indicates that the first resurrection is a present reality, not a future event. Christ, so he explains, is the active agent in bringing about this resurrection in the life of sinners. He summarizes this whole process thus: "So it is of those who are dead in soul, because of impiety and wickedness, that he says: 'The hour is coming, and now is, when the dead shall hear the voice of the Son of God; and they who hear it shall live.'"[9]

In contrast to the allegorical meaning of the first resurrection he understands the second resurrection literally, as a bodily resurrection. He expected a single, simultaneous physical resurrection of all the dead at the last day, instead of a literal first and second resurrection.

Augustine's distinction of interpreting one resurrection allegorically and the other literally had an immediate effect on the traditional chiliastic position. His identification of the first resurrection with regeneration meant that the beginning of the millennium would coincide with the inception of the Church at Pentecost, or perhaps, with Christ's earthly ministry. According to this view, the inauguration of the millennium at the dawn of this present age necessitated a revision of the traditional millenarianism. One thing was clear; it could no longer be taken literally. A new understanding of the thousand year reign of Christ was about to revolutionize the Christian doctrine of eschatology.

8.2.4. Thousand Years

Augustine rejects the simplistic concept of the "chiliasts"[10], as he calls them, who maintained that the millennium would be a holy sabbath, a time of enjoyment, in which all the saints, after a life of hardship and trouble, are entitled to participate. With reference to Revelation 20:1-6, he summarily deals with the arguments of Asiatic millenarianism:

---

9 *Op. cit.*, book XX, chap. 6.

10 Ibid., book XX, chap. 7: "Those who are spiritually minded call those who believe these things, in Greek, chiliasts, and we may in Latin translate the term literally as 'millenarians'."

> Since the creation of man and his expulsion, deserved by his great sin, from the felicity of paradise into the hardships of this mortal life, so that, since Scripture says, 'One day with the Lord is like a thousand years, and a thousand years like one day' (2 Peter 3:8), there should follow after the completion of the six thousand years, which are like six days, a kind of seventh-day sabbath during the succeeding thousand years, and the saints were to rise again precisely to celebrate this sabbath.[11]

In astonishing frankness he concedes that he was once in agreement with this view[12], and would be tolerant enough to accept it even now, if it were not for certain sensual expectations in regard to the millennium on the side of "carnal" chiliasts. He would not object to the interpretation of the millennium as a period of a "holy rest"[13] in which the saints would receive spiritual blessings in the presence of God. His anti-chiliastic protest was, therefore, solely directed against

---

11 Ibid.

12 Cf. Augustine, *Sermons 259*. Augustine preached this sermon at about A.D. 393. His early chiliasm was built on the scheme of the creation week analogy (see footnote 24). He taught that the sixth day, representing the present age, began with the first advent of Christ. Its conclusion will be marked by the Second Coming of Christ which will usher in the seventh day, also called "the sabbath of the saints on earth". If this day still belongs to the old creation, the eighth day will be part of the new: "Octavus ergo ipse dies in fine saeculi novam vitam significat." Yet, strangely enough, Augustine reverts the eighth day back (*"tunc velut ad caput reditur"*) to the first day of the creation week (*"Quomodo enim cum peracti fuerint isti septem dies octavus ipse est qui primus"*). Gerhard Maier, in *Die Johannesoffenbarung und die Kirche*, J.C.B. Mohr (Paul Siebeck), Tübingen, 1981, p. 135, summarizes this interpretation, contrary to Jean Daniélou‹s view (in »La typologie de la semaine au IVe siecle«, *RSR* 35 (1948), p. 403), as follows: »Gerade der Analogiebezug läßt deutlich werden, daß der 8. Tag kein Übergang, sondern ein Neubeginn sein soll. Denn eben die 7 vorhergehenden tragen im Gegensatz zum 8. Tag das Merkmal des Vergänglichen ... Es scheint auch, daß Augustin bemüht war, eine Verbindung zu der seit Irenäus im Raum stehenden Recapitulationstheologie herzustellen, und daß dieses Bemühen ebenfalls im Hintergrund des Vergleiches von 1. Tag und 8. Tag steht."

13 Lit.: "a rest, although, holy"; the force of the "scilicet" is the "although"; it is a rest/holiday, it is holy.

the exaggerated view of the millennium as being a "holiday of most immoderate carnal feasts."[14] He deplores the fact that, in the popular mind, the millennium was seen as a time of luxurious feasting, of which he gives the following description: "... in which food and drink will be so plentiful that not only will they observe no limits of moderation but will also exceed all bounds even of incredulity, all this can be believed only by the carnally minded."[15] Deeming it unnecessary to refute the position of his opponents in detail, Augustine presented his own chiliastic views.[16] Availing himself of Tychonius' Fifth Rule he begins his exposition by first looking at the meaning of the thousand years:

> Now the thousand years may be understood in two ways, so far as I can see: either because this event takes place in the last thousand years, that is, in the sixth millennium, the latter parts of which are even now passing, as if it were a sixth day, to be followed by a Sabbath without an evening, which is the rest of the saints without an end, so that by the figure of speech which speaks of the whole, meaning a part (the reference is to the rhetorical figure called synecdoche), he calls the last part of the millennium, or day, which remained before the end of the world, a thousand years as the equivalent of the whole period of this number the fullness of time.[17]

Augustine offers two possible meanings for the occurrence of the one thousand year period. The first is expressive of the whole period intervening between Christ's earthly ministry and the end that the time between the Lord's ascension and his Second Coming may be four or five hundred, or even a thousand years[18], he believed that the sixth millen-

---

14 Cf. Hans Bietenhard, *Das tausendjährige Reich. Eine biblisch-theologische Studie*, 2.Aufl., Zürich, 1955, p. 8.

15 *Op. cit.*, book XX, chap. 7.

16 Ibid.

17 Ibid.

18 Ibid.: "(Quos tamen alii) quadringentos, alii quingentos, alii etiam mille ab ascensione Domini usque ad eius ultimum adventum compleri

nium was more than half gone, and he expected the end in less than a thousand years.[19] In his calculation he followed the Septuagint chronology which was based on the creation week analogy.[20] The second is descriptive of the thousand years as the equivalent of the whole period of world's history.[21] Augustine's argument is based on the assumption that the number "one thousand", possessing perfect properties, symbolizes the fullness of time.[22] Then, in the attempt to counter any objections, he concludes his line of reasoning in the following words: "Furthermore, if a hundred is sometimes used as the equivalent of totality ... how much more is a thousand the equivalent of totality, since it is the cube of ten, rather than the square."[23] Although he leaves the question open as to which of these two views he himself espoused, it seems that he favoured the first.

From this stage in his treatise he goes onto interpret Satan's binding. In this context one question must have primarily occupied his mind. If Satan is continuously bound in the present age, and only released shortly at the end of

---

posse dixerunt."

19 Ibid.

20 Augustine did not regard the six days of creation as literal, but as a step-by-step revelation to the angels of the various phases of a creation which really occurred all at once (Augustine, *De genesi ad litteram*, book 4, chap. 35, sec.56, and book 5, chap. 3, sec.5, in Migne, *PL*, vol.34, col. 320, 322, respectively). But he symbolized the events of the six days by the ages of the world. His later enumeration of these ages, which differed, in regard to the seventh age, decisively from his earlier writings, was followed by later writers through the

Middle Ages and into modern times; they were used, with slight modification, by Ussher and incorporated into various Bible chronologies. These periods of Augustine are: (1) Adam to Noah, (2) Noah to Abraham, (3) Abraham to David, (4) David to the Captivity, (5) The Captivity to Christ, (6) Christ to the end, (7) The Second Coming and the eternal rest (Augustine, *De genesi contra Manichaeos*, book 1, chap. 23, in Migne, *PL*, vol. 34, cols. 190-193).

21 *Op. cit.*, book XX, chap. 7: «Aut certe mille annos pro annis omnibus huius saeculi posuit.»

22 Ibid.: "Ut perfecto numero notaretur ipsa temporis plenitudo."

23 Ibid.

time, how could he still be active and hinder the full realization of Christ's kingdom on earth? He knew that this question needed to be addressed, before he could convincingly demonstrate that the present Church is, indeed, the kingdom of Christ.

8.2.5. Binding of Satan

The crux of Augustine's argument is that the duration of Satan's binding dates from Christ's first advent to his Second Coming. Here is how he expressed himself about this point:

> So during the whole time that the Apocalypse embraces, that is, from the first coming of Christ to the end of the age, which shall be his Second Coming, the devil is not bound in the sense that during this interval, called the thousand years, he does not lead the Church astray, since not even when loosed is he to lead it astray.[24]

Thus the extent of Satan's incapacitation needed to be defined in harmony with this view. By pointing out that Satan was not able to prevent the spread of the Church, Augustine suggests that Satan's binding could not be described as one single historical act, but must rather be understood as a reoccurring phenomenon. He believed that it was taking place even at the moment of his writing and would continue to the end of the age. That Satan was constantly in the process of being bound could be observed in the reoccurring conversion experience of human beings: "... because even now human beings are being converted from the unbelief in which he held them into faith, and beyond doubt they will go on being converted to the end of the age."[25] This interpretation, however, compelled him to allegorize the meaning of the Abyss also. He called it "the innumerable multitude of the irreligious."[26]

---

24 Ibid., book XX, chap. 8.

25 Ibid.

26 Ibid., book XX, chap. 7.

8.2.6. Abyss

It is obvious that Augustine could not retain the interpretation of the Abyss, as an inescapable prison, after he had defined Satan's binding as the inability to hinder the spread of the Church. It was not possible for him to view it as a complete incapacitation. Therefore, he was compelled to spiritualize the meaning of the Abyss as depicting "the innumerable multitude of irreligious" instead of seeing it as a literal bottomless pit. He went on to describe these irreligious as those whose hearts advance far "into malignity against the Church of God."[27] In an explanatory note, he observes that Satan was active in the hearts of unbelievers even before the Church's inception. Now, however, he is all the more agile, because he lost access to the hearts of the believers.[28] Therefore, in referring to the seal which God places on Satan, he interprets this verse in keeping with his general understanding of the millennium:

> For he is more completely possessed by the devil who not merely is alienated from God but goes out of his way to hate those who serve God. 'And he shut him up,' he says, 'and put a seal upon him, so that he could no longer seduce the nations until the thousand years should be ended.' 'Shut him up,' that is, forbade him to go forth. And the added words, 'put a seal upon him,' seem to me to mean that God wished it to be unknown who belonged to the devil's party and who did not.[29]

It is interesting to note that Augustine does express some uncertainties about the meaning of the seal placed on Satan. He suggests that the seal symbolizes God's wish to keep the identity of those who belong to "the devil's party" secret. He qualifies this statement in the next sentence thus: "For in this world this is indeed unknown, since it is uncertain whether he who seems to stand is about to fall, and whether he who

---

27 Ibid.

28 Ibid.

29 Ibid.

seems to lie prone is about to rise again."[30] This thought lead him to consider the importance of the devil's short release from the Abyss.

8.2.7. Devil's Short Release

The devil will be released for a short time at the end of time. Augustine asserts this very succinctly: "But then he shall be loosed, when it will be also a short time" or "... when there will be even a short time." The Latin is rather ambiguous.[31] He dismisses immediately any suggestion which would make room for the possibility that Satan, after his release, could lead the Church astray. This, so he asserts, would be a gross misunderstanding of this passage. He emphatically declares that such a possibility could never happen. Stating his reasons in the next sentence, he says: "God forbid, for never shall that Church be led astray by him which was predestined and elect before the founding of the world."[32] The predestined and elect believers would not fall prey to the beguiling influence of Satan. Because he had previously defined Satan's binding as the prohibition to draw human beings to his side, by either compulsion or delusion[33], he now explains why Satan had to be set loose. By referring to the Scriptures (cf. Rev. 11:2; 13:5) Augustine believes that Satan, upon his release, joins his allies in order to combat the saints for three and a half years. In the end, however, the saints prove to be invincible. God wanted to show the Church that it cannot be vanquished, even if assaulted by all the powers of hell. Satan, in all his might, has to concede to his final defeat. Augustine finishes this passage by glorifying God: "And in the end he will loose him, so that the City of

---

30 Ibid.

31 Ibid., book XX, chap. 8.

32 Ibid.

33 Ibid.

God may perceive how strong an adversary it has vanquished, to the great glory of its Redeemer, Helper, Deliverer."[34]

By referring to Mark 12:29, "Who enters into the house of a strong man, to take his goods, unless he first binds the strong man?"[35], Augustine is doubtful whether there will be any conversions – "No one will be added to the Christian community."[36] – during these three and a half years. Satan will prevent anyone, who has not previously been a Christian, to join the Church. At the same time some nominal Christians will apostatize and, in so doing, indicate that they never really belonged to the predestined number of the believers.

Augustine raises another question, namely whether this short interlude of persecution is included in the thousand years, and concludes that it is neither deducted from the whole time of Satan's imprisonment, nor added to the whole duration of the reign of the saints.[37]

8.2.8. Church Authorities govern the Church.

As a summary statement of what the Church is going to do during the millennium, Augustine mentions the text in Rev. 20:4, "And I saw thrones and those who sat upon them, and judgment was given" (cf. Rev. 20:7).[38] It is not to be supposed, claims Augustine, that this verse refers to the last judgment; it must be understood as a reference to both the ecclesiastical sees and the Church authorities by whom they are now governed.[39] In his opinion there is no verse in Scripture which better explains this situation than Mt. 18:18, "Whatsoever you bind on earth shall be bound in heaven; and whatsoever you loose on earth shall be loosed in heaven."

---

34 Ibid.

35 Ibid.

36 Ibid.

37 Ibid., book XX, chap. 13.

38 Ibid., book XX, chap. 9.

39 Ibid.

After quoting more Bible passages and adding further deliberations he comes to the conclusion that the Church begins its reign among the living and the dead now.

8.2.9. Church represents the Kingdom of Christ.

> Accordingly, the Church even now is the kingdom of Christ and the kingdom of heaven. And so even now his saints reign with him, though otherwise than they shall then reign.[40]

Augustine intimates that the Church is presently enjoying the blessing of the millennium. This period is doubtless to be understood as the time between the first and the Second Coming of Christ.[41] He makes a clear distinction between the millennium and the eternal kingdom. The former is only seen as a prelude to that kingdom, in which the invitation of Christ, "Come, blessed of my father, take possession of the kingdom that is prepared for you."[42] will find its fulfilment. But for now those who follow the Apostle's directive in Col. 3:1,2, Since, then, you have been raised with Christ, set your hearts on things above, where Christ is seated at the right hand of God. etc.", will be co-regents with Christ on earth. Being thus endowed with ruling power they should not think, however, that they would be exempted from combating their enemies nor be freed from the obligation to subdue their sinful tendencies. The present age, although being the millennium, is still called a "militant kingdom".[43] This state

---

40 *Op. cit.*, book XX, chap. 9.

41 Ibid.: "Interea dum mille annis ligatus est diabolus, sancti regnant cum Christo etiam ipsi mille annis, eisdam sine dubio et eodem modo intellegendis, id est isto iam tempore prioris eius adventus." ("While the devil is bound for a thousand years, the saints reign, together with Christ, also for a thousand years, which are doubtless to be understood as the same period, that is, as that between the first and the Second Comings of Christ (lit.: ... of the first coming of Christ).")

42 Ibid.

43 Ibid.

of things will continue "until that most peaceful kingdom is attained where our King shall reign without a foe."[44]

8.3. Conclusion

Augustine, who himself had formerly entertained chiliastic hopes, turned against millenarianism, because he was appalled of the "carnal" interpretations of some of its adherents. He framed the new theory which reflected his own theological change, and was generally accepted. The apocalyptic millennium he understood to be both the present reign of Christ in the Church and the Church's ruling on earth. Consequently Augustine saw the Church as the object and recipient of all the promises given to the people of Israel in the Old Testament.

The idea of the millennial kingdom, as a present reality, was a resplendent vision. Yet it led the Church away from her historic course. The dream of a present spiritual resurrection and an earthly millennium introduced through the first advent, together with a spiritualization of the prophecies and the New Jerusalem became the accepted view of Christian eschatology.

Augustine, in his *De civitate dei*, did more than all the Fathers to idealize the Roman Church as the Christian Zion. It is true that he did not foresee the system that would be built upon that concept. Nevertheless, he provided the materials from which, in later times, was built the medieval theory and policy of the religio-political state church. With the adoption of this world-church ideal of Augustine the Church abandoned the idea of the millennium separating two literal resurrections; and the future, general resurrection and judgment at the Second Coming were pushed out of range – beyond a "thousand years" of indefinite duration. The millennium was therefore no longer a *desideratum*; it was already a realization. This resulted in a restricted eschatology which blurred the vision of the future kingdom of Christ to be inaugurated at the Second Coming. It was

---

44 Ibid.: "... ad illud pacatissimum regnum ubi sine hoste regnabitur."

consistent with this theory that towards the close of the first millennium of the Christian era there was a wide-spread expectation in Western Europe that the final judgment was at hand.

Shirley Jackson Case summarized this radical shift in the interpretation of the millennium appropriately: "Augustine laid "the ghost" of millenarianism so effectually that for centuries thereafter the subject was practically a closed question."[45] From the time of Constantine and Augustine, chiliasm took its place among the heresies, and was rejected subsequently even by the Protestant reformers as a Jewish dream.

---

45 Shirley Jackson Case, *The Millennial Hope*, University of Chicago Press, 1918, p. 179.

Chapter 9
Conclusion

9.1. Principles of Biblical Interpretation in the Early Church 192
9.2. Asiatic Millennialism 195
    9.2.1. Categorization of Revelation 195
    9.2.2. Jewish Apocalyptic 196
    9.2.3. Apocalyptic Influence on Asiatic Millennialism 197
    9.2.4. Similarity of Modern Premillennialism with Asiatic
            Millennialism 198
9.3. Millennialism of John 199
9.4. Millennialism of Justin Martyr 202
9.5. Millennialism of the Epistle of Barnabas 203
9.6. Anti-millennialism of the Alexandrians 204
9.7. Amillennialism of Augustine 206
    9.7.1. Modern Amillennialism 208
    9.7.2. Modern Postmillennialism 209
    9.7.3. Modern Premillennialism 210

9. Conclusion

9.1. Principles of Biblical Interpretation in the Early Church[1]

The key to understanding the chiliastic controversy, both in its theological and historical contexts, can be found in the different hermeneutical principles employed by the Church Fathers. As has been shown in the foregoing pages, a comprehension of these principles is essential if we are to unlock the intricacies of various opposing millennial concepts in the main centers of early Christianity [chap. 4].

A cursory acquaintance with the Church Fathers reveals that, for all the exegetical variations, they undoubtedly shared the same basic understanding. Relative to both the Hebrew Bible and the New Testament, this understanding can be summarized under the rubric of prophecy and fulfilment. Taught by Jesus Christ, the apostles, and the NT writers, the Church found in the gospel of Christ's life, death and resurrection and in the outpouring of the Holy Spirit, a striking fulfilment of the Hebrew Bible. Not only was a distinctive prophetic meaning found for the Scriptures, but the Hebrew Bible and the New Testament were seen together in indissoluble unity as the one book of the one God, inspired by the one Spirit and testifying to the one Son.

The Christian interpretation of the Hebrew Bible, and the concept of the unity of the Hebrew Bible and the New Testament, found frequent expression during the patristic period. Justin Martyr told Trypho the Jew that Scripture belongs more to Christians than to Jews because the latter read it but do not understand it (*Dial.* 29). Justin himself was particularly impressed in his reading of the Old Testament by the way in which detailed prophecies had found fulfilment in Christ. Origen used the metaphor of a symphony (*On John* 5:8), to illustrate the relation between the Testaments, and insisted that, while the mode of presentation changed, the content remained substantially the same

---

1 Specific references to relevant thesis chapters are given square brakkets e.g. [chap. 5].

(*Comm. on Mt.* 14:4). Augustine summed up this whole line of patristic thinking in his famous dictum that the New Testament is latent in the Old Testament and the Old Testament is patent in the New Testament (*Quest. in Hept.* 2 qu.73).

The themes of unity and fulfilment found their focus for the Fathers in the conviction that Christ himself is the true and final subject of Scripture. Whether they looked at the individual prophecies of the Hebrew Bible or at the themes and factors that figured prominently in its history and message, the Fathers saw all the lines converging upon the incarnate Son who, with the Father and the Holy Spirit, formed the core of Christian faith and proclamation. Christ in fact provided the hermeneutical key that enabled patristic exegetes to see the whole of Scripture in its divinely given unity and to achieve a convincingly integrated understanding. The Epistle of Barnabas, in its more restrained typology, discerned in Christ and his work both the true temple and the true sabbath (chs. 15-16). Irenaeus found in Christ the higher righteousness intimated but not yet declared in the law (*Haer.* 4,12-13).

The Fathers realized that not all readers of the Hebrew Bible, nor indeed of the New Testament, enjoyed the same understanding as they did. Jews on the one side and pagans on the other, both failed to see the Bible as the book of Christ or obstinately refused to do so. Difficult though individual portions of Scripture might be, this could hardly be ascribed to an ultimate obscurity of the divinely inspired message. The Fathers, then, were led to another important hermeneutical principle, namely, that only as people read the Bible in the enlightening power of the Holy Spirit, with faith and spiritual understanding, can they come to a true appreciation of its meaning. Justin had something of this in mind, when he told Trypho that Christians let themselves be persuaded as they read (*Dial.* 29). Chrysostom pleaded for faith in the reading of Scripture so that one may hear the voice of the Spirit and thus be enabled to perceive heavenly things (*Hom. on John* 1).

Consensus reigned among the Fathers that Holy Scripture, inspired and illumined by the Spirit, is in its unity and totality the book of Christ. The Alexandrians and their successors, however, favoring a more allegorical line of interpretation disagreed with the Antiochenes and their supporters, who pleaded for a more strictly historical interpretation.

Displaying a remarkable ingenuity, Origen established a mode of approach that appealed to many who succeeded him. Even the scholarly Jerome did not reject the threefold method (*Epistle* 120), while Augustine, who in his early Christian period achieved an inventiveness comparable to that of Origen, expanded the threefold sense into a fourfold: the historical, etiological, analogical, and figurative (cf. *De. doct.* 3, 27, 38 etc.). Yet Augustine recognized the danger of unchecked speculation. All allegorical interpretation needs the support of other plain passages of Scripture. It must also correspond to the rules of faith and love. Within these limits, however, allegorizing could still flourish, and Augustine's fourfold division developed later into the familiar historical, allegorical, moral, and anagogical senses.

Nevertheless, the exegetes of the Antioch school, Diodore of Tarsus, Theodore of Mopsuestia, and Theodoret, offered an important theoretical and practical alternative to the Alexandrian allegorical exegesis. They accepted the validity of typology, the type being for them a form of prophecy. They insisted, however, on strict adherence to the historical form in biblical exposition, even in the discernment and unfolding of the type. Nor would they accept an arbitrary imposition of types where none seemed to exist. Some passages must be taken solely in their historical sense. Allegory meant the introduction of a supposedly hidden meaning to the detriment of the natural sense and was thus to be differentiated from the authentic typology. In their commentaries the Antiochenes made a serious effort to put the various texts in their historical settings, to explain the primary meaning of the texts, and to bring out their prophetic significance only where it was plainly indicated either by direct reference in the New Testament or by the general tenor of the Christian message.

9.2. Asiatic Millennialism

The application of these hermeneutical principles in exegeting the millennial passage in Revelation 20 brought forth a rich diversity of chiliastic views in the patristic literature. In the ante-Nicene age the belief in a literal millennium was one of the most important aspects of Christian eschatology. It was a viewpoint widely held among many early Church Fathers, such as Papias, Justin Martyr, Irenaeus, Barnabas, and Tertullian [chap. 5].

Eusebius, in his attempt to denigrate the grotesque elements of chiliasm, tells us that Papias, the bishop of Hierapolis, disseminated this doctrine far beyond the bounds of his own bishopric, attributing it to the oral teaching of the elders.

9.2.1. Categorization of Revelation

The Johannine tradition of a future millennium was certainly similar to the Jewish apocalyptic concept of the messianic kingdom. The skilled employment of apocalyptic symbolism in the book of Revelation bears witness to that fact. Its author must have been well versed in the apocalyptic lore of Jewish literature [chap. 2]. Yet, in many respects, it also demonstrated his creative originality. Therefore many New Testament scholars have adopted a mediating position in categorizing the Apocalypse. They agree to classify it both as an extension of the apocalyptic genre and as a unique work of Christian eschatology.

To underline the continuity of the book of Revelation with the Jewish apocalyptic we briefly summarized the theme of the Syriac Apocalypse of Baruch (*Syr.Bar.* 24-28; 29-30; 32; 39, 50-52).

At first the cup of divine wrath is poured out on the unrighteous which is followed by the appearance of the Messiah; the righteous will come to life in a partial resurrection while the godless people will meet their doom; Jerusalem will be reconstructed repeatedly until at last it arises in splendor to exist for all eternity; the Messiah will establish his earthly kingdom in whose rule the righteous will participate; this event will be preceded by a general, universal resurrection and the subsequent judgment of the world; at last, salvation will be the lot of the pious whereas torment will await the wicked.

In general the book of Revelation occupies a unique place among apocalyptic writings. For example, it is not pseudonymous. Its author was John (Rev. 1:1,4,9; 22:8). He does not pose as an illustrious figure of Jewish history to give special credence to the book. Unlike the authors of Jewish apocalyptic literature, he does not venture into mysterious revelations of cosmogony, astrology, or ancient history. The most important aspect of his book is a Christocentric view of history culminating in the description of the New Jerusalem, descending from heaven, as the abode of the righteous in God's presence. This heavenly vision is, however, preceded by a thousand-year reign of Christ on earth.

Not limiting themselves to the millennial passage in Revelation 20:1-10, the Asiatic Church Fathers incorporated many prophetic and apocalyptic concepts into the fabric of their chiliastic views. Jewish apocalyptic literature, in particular, became a primary source of information about the nature of the millennium.

9.2.2. Jewish Apocalyptic

If the Hebrew prophets had occasionally described the calamitous events leading up to the coming of the Messiah and the Golden Age which followed, it became one of the main religious themes during the intertestamental period [chap. 2]. During this period, lasting about three hundred years, the Palestinian Jews had to face recurring struggles against intruding Gentile nations. Military defeat at the hands of their enemies violated repeatedly their national pride and religious sentiments. They yearned for deliverance and national independence. The apocalyptics captured the imagination of their compatriots by setting forth the glories of an approaching Golden Age. This concept of a future paradise was the result of a compromise between two different eschatological perspectives. According to the more primitive view, the Jews expected, the restoration of the old Davidic kingdom. The Messiah would assume his royal authority at his appearance and govern the world from Jerusalem.

Gradually this perspective changed into the magnificent vision of a transcendent kingdom, comprising a renewed heaven and earth. God would exercise his ultimate authority over the whole realm of the universe. The wide dissemination of popular Greek philosophy in the 2nd century B.C. induced Jewish scholars, primarily in Alexandria, to adapt their understanding of the kingdom of God to the ideas of an eschatological dualism.[2] These scholars began to make a clear distinction between the present and the future world. They could no longer accept the former teaching of the messianic kingdom, but introduced another change. By appropriating elements from the two earlier views, they constructed a concept in which a preliminary earthly kingdom is followed by an eternal kingdom (*4 Ezra* 7:28f). In a theocratic kingdom, the old world order would be changed by God to create an earthly paradise. Apocalyptic literature is filled with many splendid accounts about the heavenly blessings bestowed upon the people of God.

9.2.3. Apocalyptic Influence on Asiatic Millennialism

The blissful world of Jewish apocalyptic not only shaped the content of Asiatic chiliasm, but also penetrated the esoteric systems of Gnosticism [chap. 5]. If we take Eusebius' account of Cerinthus' teaching at face value, we see the famous Gnostic expressing his carnal phantasies of a nuptial feast at the time of the millennium in apocalyptic terminology. For instance, the theme of a great wedding banquet is portrayed in *The Testament of Isaac* (8:11, 20; 10:12). It is also reminiscent of biblical passages like Is. 25:6-8; 65:13f and Rev. 19:9. The schismatic Montanists shared the same chiliastic convic-

---

2 Cf. Gerhard von Rad, in *Old Testament Theology*, II, London, 1965, p. 301.

tions with only minor deviations. They placed, for example, the specific location of the restored Jerusalem inside their native Phrygia.

Irenaeus, Commodian and Methodius were equally responsible for a broadening of the millennial concept. They described repeatedly the change of nature during the millennium, especially the phenomenal fecundity of vegetation, a concept derived directly from the Jewish apocalyptic. The author of *I Enoch*, for example, described the abundant fruitfulness of mankind (10:17) and of the vegetation (10:18f; cf. *II Baruch* 29:5-8). *The Book of Jubilees* speaks of the longevity of mankind (*Jub.* 23:27; cf. *Syr.Bar* 49f; 73:3). The author of the *Secrets of Enoch* (32:2; 33:1-2) taught that the natural environment would be changed by God's blessings during the last of seven millennia of world history in which the Messiah would rule his earthly kingdom. Afterwards an eighth millennium, eternity itself, would begin (*cf. 4 Ezra* 7:28f). Sometimes, as in *4 Ezra*, the end of the millennium and the beginning of eternity would be marked by the death of the Messiah. These apocalyptic concepts were supplemented by the Asiatic Church Fathers with two other features, namely, the reconciliation of the animal world and the human life span of a thousand years.

9.2.4. Similarity of Modern Premillennialism with Asiatic Millennialism

In our modern era, premillennialism, both in its historical and dispensational variations, has rediscovered many of the concepts of the early Asiatic chiliasm [chap. 3] Most characteristically it is committed to the concept of an earthly reign by Christ of one thousand years representing him as physically present during that time; it believes that he will return personally and bodily to commence the millennium. This being the case, the millennium must be seen as still to take place in the future.

It is also important to observe the nature of the millennium. Whereas the postmillennialist thinks that the millennium is being introduced gradually, perhaps almost imperceptibly, the premillennialist envisions a sudden, cataclysmic event. In the premillennialist view, the rule of Christ will be complete from the very beginning of the millennium. Evil will have been virtually eliminated.

The key passage for premillennialism is Revelation 20:1-10. Premillennialists observe that here is evidence of a thousand-year period and two resurrections, one at the beginning and the other at the end. They insist on a literal and consistent interpretation of this passage.

9.3. Millennialism of John

In the opening verses (vv. 1-3) of this passage John saw an angel coming down from heaven, holding in his hand the key to the Abyss and a great chain. The angel took hold of Satan, bound him, and cast him into the Abyss. Then he locked it to prevent Satan from deceiving the nations for a thousand years [chap. 3].

An important interpretive question is whether Satan was bound at the first coming of Christ, as is frequently argued by amillenarians, or will be bound at his Second Coming, as is asserted by premillenarians. Revelation 20:1-3, if taken literally, contradicts the amillennial interpretation that Satan was bound at the first coming of Christ. According to the testimony of the Scriptures Satan exerts great power both against the unbelievers and Christians (cf. Lk. 22:3; Acts 5:3; 1 Peter 5:8; Rev. 12:2, 17).

In this regard amillenarians advance the opinion that Satan is limited by the power of God. They spiritualize the passage in Rev. 20:1-3 as well as many other New Testament references to Satan's power and present agility. There is, however, no evidence today that Satan's present situation has been locked in the Abyss and is unable to deceive the nations for the duration of a thousand years.

Next in the sequence of revelations John wrote in verse 4 that he saw thrones on which were seated those who had been given authority to judge. He further perceived the souls of those who had been beheaded because of their steadfast witness to their Lord and his word.

Though he could see the souls, he was informed that they had been beheaded because they had neither worshipped the beast or his image, nor did they receive his mark. John was not told the identity of the persons seated on the thrones. They were distinct from those who had been martyred. Christ had foretold in Luke 22:29-30 that the 12 apostles would "eat and drink at my table in my kingdom and sit on thrones, judging the 12 tribes of Israel". The apostles, as the representatives of the Church, were probably those individuals to whom it was granted to sit on these thrones.

John recorded that the martyrs were resurrected and reigned with Christ for a thousand years. Subsequently to receiving this vision, John was informed as to the meaning and character of the judgment that was passing before his eyes.

In verse 5 John was also informed that the rest of the dead remained in the grave until the thousand years were completed. The second resurrection refers to the resurrection of the unrighteous explained in detail later on (vv. 11-15).

Since the same verb – "ἔζησαν" – is used in reference to both resurrections, they must be of the same kind. If this is not the case, as both amillennialists and postmillennialists maintain, then the exegete, as Henry Alford pointed out, would be at a loss to interpret the meaning of Scripture. He contended that if one resurrection is a spiritual coming to life, and the other a physical coming to life, "then there is an end of all significance in language, and Scripture is wiped out as a definite testimony to anything."[3]

The two examples of "ἔζησαν" occur in two subsequent verses. Nothing in the context intimates any alteration in meaning. Thus the two resurrections must both be physical, involving two distinct groups of people at an interim of a thousand years. If taken literally, the context does not suggest that those who take part in the first resurrection are also participating in the second, which will be reserved for 'the rest of the dead'.

---

3 Henry Alford, *The Greek New Testament*, IV, 1894, revised by Everett F. Harrison, Moody Press, Chicago, 1958, p. 732-33.

It should be evident, however, that the first resurrection, which John mentions here, is not the first chronologically because Christ was the first, historically, to be raised from the dead and to receive a resurrected body. There was also the resurrection "of many", recorded in Mt. 27:52-53, which occurred on the day of Christ's crucifixion. In what sense then can this resurrection in Revelation 20:5 be "first"?

As the context which follows indicates, "the first resurrection" (vv.5-6) contrasts with the last resurrection (vv.12-13), which is followed by "the second death" (vv. 6, 14). It is "first" in the sense of "before". All the righteous, regardless of when they are raised, take part in the resurrection which is first or before the final resurrection (of the unrighteous dead) at the end of the millennium. Those who participate in the first resurrection are said to be blessed and holy, because the second death will have no power over them. They will reign as priests of God with Christ for a thousand years (v.6). It should be mentioned that the term "a thousand years" occurs six times in chapter 20. While amillenarians and others have tended to view this as not literal, there is no evidence to support this conclusion. This is the only chapter in Revelation where a period of a thousand years is mentioned, and the fact that it is mentioned six times and is clearly noted as a period of time before, which and after events take place, lead to the conclusion that it means a literal thousand-year period.

Besides the duration of the millennium as a period of a thousand years, there are no further details given in regard to the reign of Christ on earth except the statement that it is a time of great blessing.

John recorded also the events that will occur at the end of the thousand years. Satan will be released from the Abyss, where he had been imprisoned, and will again try to deceive the nations, called Gog and Magog, provoking them to rebel against Christ (vv. 7-8). This last worldwide rebellion will be directed against the millennial authority of Christ. The armies will be so vast in numbers that they are said to be like the sand on the seashore.

They will surround the camp of God's people, the city he loves (v.9). This city is most likely Jerusalem. The result is immediate judgment. Fire will come down from heaven and devour them.

After Satan's followers are annihilated, he himself will be thrown into the lake of burning sulphur (v.10). Being cast into the lake prepared for him and his angels is the final judgment on Satan. He and his primary human instruments, the beast and the false prophet, will be tormented day and night forever and ever.

9.4. Millennialism of Justin Martyr

As a prominent proponent of the early premillennial view, Justin has been generally recognized as representing the transition from the Jewish Christian view of the millennium to the one which became prominent among Gentile Christians [chap. 6]. It will be remembered that the dialogue with Trypho took place at Ephesus. Justin was simply reflecting the chiliastic views of the Asiatic millenarians holding to a literal millennium on earth. He also reflects on the themes of the New Jerusalem, the reconciliation of the animal kingdom and the subject of longevity. It seems as though the essential characteristic of Asiatic millenarianism lies in its application of the prophecies of Isaiah 65:17-25 in the LXX version to the doctrine of the first resurrection. The only chiliastic element missing from his discourse with Trypho is the story on the fruitfulness of the vine. Nevertheless, the millennium, in the strict sense of the word, does not appear in this passage of Isaiah, even though Justin asserts that the reign of a thousand years is there foretold. Justin shows that life in Paradise is for a thousand years; and since Isaiah makes the span of life in messianic times equal to that of life in Paradise, it is clear that the length of life in the messianic kingdom will also be a thousand years. This he explicitly associates with the millennium of Revelation. In fact, at this point all the themes of Asiatic millenarianism converge. Since the Asiatic Church Fathers, following the lead of the apocalyptics, regarded the messianic reign as a return to Paradise, it was natural that the corresponding length of life should be the same as Adam's should have been in Eden (cf. *Jub.* 23:27).

It is clear, however, that in the context of ideas, the chronological aspect of the millennium is secondary; what really matters is that it points to a paradisal state of existence. Hence Asiatic millenarianism may be said (1) to derive from speculation on the paradisal character of the messianic age, and (2) to signify that after the first resurrection the just will live a thousand years on a new earth, but after an earthly manner. Then, following the judgment, they will be translated to heaven. This is exactly how Justin substantiates his chiliastic argument, in the conversation with Trypho, explicitly referring to the text of *Jubilees* (cf. *Dial.* 80, 4; 81, 1-2).

9.5. Millennialism of the Epistle of Barnabas

The first work in which the doctrine of the seventh millennium is found is the *Epistle of Barnabas* (15, 3-8) belonging to the Jewish Christian community of Alexandria [chap. 7]. It is important to distinguish some of its principal features. The repose on the seventh day is a Jewish contribution whereas the seven millennia is a Hellenistic one. In this epistle a relationship is established between the eschatological rest and the sabbath. All that is involved here is a typology of the week in which the six days of creation represent the time of this world, and the seventh day, the world to come. Thus a system is set up in which seven millennia constitute the total time of the world. Whereas the duration of the world is "six days", "the seventh day" represents eternal life.

In *Barnabas* a third element intervenes – "the eighth day". Attempts have been made to find Hellenistic origins for this component. It is certain that the "ogdoad" plays some part in the Pythagorean number-mysticism, to which Philo is indebted, but it is not an important one; on the other hand, in Gnosticism it is of the highest importance. However, like most of the material used by the Gnostics it is borrowed from other sources. It was Christianity that gave the eighth day its importance; Christ rose on the day after the sabbath, and hence the eighth day is the day of the resurrection, the Sunday.

It will be seen that the originality of *Barnabas* lies in his relating the primitive data of the eschatological repose to speculations on the cosmic week inherited from Judaism, Hellenism and Christianity. *Barnabas* was to retain the Hellenist notion of the seven millennia as constituting the sum of history, the Jewish idea of the privileged character of the seventh day as a time of rest, and the Christian concept of the eighth day as eternal life. Here millenarianism appears rather as an answer to the speculative problem of the passage from the "hebdomad" to the "ogdoad" than as a concrete hope. The millennium itself is conceived simply as rest. Augustine was to defend this kind of millenarianism for a long time, although condemning the Asiatic type.

The text of Barnabas, then, introduces a type of speculation on millenarianism which is quite different from that of the Asiatic Church Fathers. In it the emphasis is placed on the seven millennia followed by the eighth day, rather than on millenarianism in the strictest sense.

In this elaborate complex of ideas the *Epistle of Barnabas* is reminiscent, to a remarkable degree, of the *Ascension of Isaiah*, with its idea of repose (except that, in the *Ascension*, this repose was not associated with speculations about the week). In Barnabas, there is also a millenarian feature which did not appear in the *Ascension*, namely the quotation from Ps. 90:4.

9.6. Anti-millennialism of the Alexandrians

The chiliastic doctrine of the Asiatic Church Fathers was challenged, on exegetical and philosophical grounds, by the Alexandrian school of theology in the third century, personified in Origen and Dionysius [chap. 8]. It is also significant that Origen spoke disparagingly of Asiatic millennialism (Origen, *Against Celsus*, book 2, chap. 11, sec. 2). Until his time, belief in the second, personal, premillennial coming of Christ was general, being held together with the millennial reign of the saints with Christ after their literal resurrection from the dead at the advent. It was due in great measure to Origen's formative influence, that millennialism began to wane. He opposed it because it was incompatible with his interpretation of Scripture.

As concerns the resurrection, inseparably related in Scriptures to the Second Coming, Origen is ambiguous. He contends for the orthodox belief of the church in the actual resurrection of the body, quoting such texts as 1 Thes. 4:15, 16 and 1 Cor. 15:39-42 (Origen, *De principiis*, book 2, chap. 10, secs. 1-3, and book 3, chap. 6, secs. 4-9). Yet he also teaches that the resurrected spiritual bodies must undergo gradual, perhaps age-long, purification in the next world, perhaps many worlds, and become progressively more spiritual and less material until the saints attain to the highest spiritual condition in which "God shall be all in all" (ibid., book 3, chap. 6, secs. 8-9). Although he elsewhere treats the subject allegorically, and speaks of a spiritual resurrection from spiritual death, Origen distinctly mentions the two resurrections (Origen, *Commentary on John*, book 1, chap. 25). Yet he vitiates the whole purpose of the two resurrections by assigning the possibility of ultimate salvation also to those who have part in the second resurrection (ibid., book 3, chap. 6, sec. 5). He thus effectually renders meaningless the Second Coming of Christ.

Origen speaks of the two advents of Christ (Origen, *Against Celsus*, book 1, chap. 56), but does not connect the Second Coming with the resurrection or the millennium, or recognize it as marking the climax of prophetically foretold human history (ibid.). Rather, the effects of that transcendent event are set forth as the ultimate reign of Christ, brought about by a gradual process, through successive worlds and long ages of purification.

Origen first gives the traditional, literal interpretation of our Lord's promise of returning in the clouds of heaven with power and great glory, but he turns from that to the allegorical "prophetic clouds" of the prophets' writings. He likens to children those who hold to a literal or "corporeal" interpretation of this passage, and insists on a spiritual sense alone for the enlightened Christian.

In the same century, Dionysius, bishop of Alexandria, following in the footsteps of Origen, refuted the chiliastic doctrine. But he went beyond his master, even impugning the apostolic authorship of the Apocalypse in his attempts to discredit the millenarians. His influence was felt in later doubts concerning the canonicity of the Apocalypse, which caused much discussion in the Church, and which lingered in the East for several centuries. It seems that the doctrinal controversy was the basis for his attack, although he offered some critical grounds, such as an alleged difference in style and diction, from John's Gospel and epistles. Yet he was convinced that the Apocalypse was written by a man inspired by God.

Already there had been an attack on the Apocalypse by the Alogi in the second century (Eusebius, *Hist. Eccl.* 7.25.), and by the presbyter Gaius against the millennium (ibid., 3.28.), as well as Origen's spiritualization of the prophetic symbols. It was about A.D. 255 that dispute arose concerning the chiliastic opinions taught in a book entitled *Refutation of Allegorists*, by Nepos, a bishop in Egypt. Dionysius succeeded through his oral and written efforts in checking this Egyptian revival of chiliasm.

9.7. Amillennialism of Augustine

Augustine exerted, doubtless, the most powerful, permanent, and extensive influence of all ecclesiastical writers since the days of the apostles. His remarkable treatise, *De civitate dei* (*On the City of God*) discussing the "kingdom of this world", as doomed to destruction, and the "kingdom of God", as destined to last forever, took thirteen years in the making, during the most mature period of his life [chap. 9].

A new theory is here presented, asserting that the millennium is a present fact, with Revelation 20 referring to the first, instead of to the Second Coming. Tychonius' Rules and his essential exposition are adopted. It should be borne in mind that, following Tychonius, Augustine regarded the thousand years as a figurative numeric expression of the whole period between Christ's earthly ministry and the end of the world (*De civitate dei*, book 18, chap. 53).

It is well to remember that Augustine followed the Septuagint chronology; he believed that the sixth millennium was more than half gone, and it is natural that he would expect the end in less than a thousand years (ibid., book 20, chap. 7). However, the thousand-year idea later came to prevail.

The theory of the allegorical first resurrection lies at the foundation of Augustine's structure, the resurrection of souls from the death of sin to the life of righteousness (ibid., chap. 6). According to Augustine, there is a single, simultaneous physical resurrection of all men at the last day, instead of a first and a second literal resurrection. Once this thesis was accepted, the Asiatic millennialism was vanquished.

The description in Revelation 20 of Satan's being bound and cast into the Abyss, is identified with the casting down of the dragon of chapter 12, and is considered as already accomplished. The Abyss is the "non-Christian nations". The thrones of judgment are present ecclesiastical sees. Thus the emphasis is shifted back to the first advent and away from the second, which is increasingly relegated to the background. The Church militant is the Church triumphant. The camp of the saints is the Church of Christ extending over the whole world. The Old Testament prophecies are claimed for the new ecclesiastical empire.

A new era in prophetic interpretation was thus introduced; this specious Augustinian theory of the millennium, spiritualized into a present politico-religious fact, fastened itself upon the Church for about thirteen centuries. Abandoning the idea of the millennium separating the two literal resurrections, the future, general resurrection and judgment at the Second Coming were pushed out of range, beyond a "thousand years" of indefinite duration. This resulted in a blurred vision of the future kingdom of Christ to be inaugurated at the Second Coming.

From the time of Augustine onwards, chiliasm became a rejected doctrine. Even the Protestant reformers regarded it as merely a Jewish dream.

9.7.1. Modern Amillennialism

Still today most theologians are committed to an amillennial position. In dealing with the millennium, they have come up with a wide variety of explanations. As the term "amillennialism" already indicates, its proponents do not believe in a literal millennium. The final judgment will occur subsequent to the Second Coming of Christ and determine the ultimate states of the righteous and the wicked [chap. 3].

When amillennialists interpret Revelation 20, they usually take the message of the whole book into account. They see several, mostly seven, sections in the book of Revelation which do not describe successive periods of time, but rather recapitulate the events occurring during the time between Christ's first and Second Coming. Each of these sections, it is said, are narratives of the same story seen only from different angles. The author merely elaborates, though progressively, on its different subplots. If this is the case, Revelation 20 does not refer to a future Golden Age, but describes the entire history of the Church.

Amillennialists also point out that the book of Revelation, in its entirety, is very symbolic. If the bowls, seals, and trumpets are interpreted as symbols, why not also interpret the "thousand years" of Revelation 20 in such a way? They contend that the figure of a thousand years, if taken symbolically rather than literally, would convey to our minds the idea of absolute completeness.[4]

The exegetical problem which presents the most difficulty to amillennialists is not the interpretation of the phrase "one thousand years", although that is difficult enough, but the nature of the two resurrections. While there are different amillennial views about the two resurrections, the common factor to all of them is the contention that Revelation does not indicate two physical resurrections operative on two different groups. The most recurrent amillennial interpretation is that all human beings participate in the second, bodily, resurrection, but only a few will partake of the first,

---

4 Benjamin B. Warfield, „The Millennium and the Apocalypse", in *Biblical Doctrines*, Oxford University Press, New York, 1929, p. 654.

or spiritual, resurrection, commonly known as regeneration.

A common criticism of the amillennial view is its inconsistency in interpreting the identical terms ("ἔζησαν") used in the same context (Rev. 20:4-5), first as a spiritual resurrection and then as a physical resurrection.

Another feature of amillennialism is a more general view of prophecy, especially of Old Testament prophecy, than is found in premillennialism. In contrast to premillennialists, who tend to interpret biblical prophecy quite literally, amillennialists often treat prophecies as historical or symbolic rather than futuristic. As a general rule, prophecy occupies a much less important place in amillennial than in premillennial thought.

9.7.2. Modern Postmillennialism

In agreement with amillennialism, postmillennialists do not interpret the millennium to mean a literal one thousand years [chap. 3]. They believe it to be an extended period of indefinite time during which Christ, even though physically absent, will gradually establish his kingdom on earth. Advocates of both views often insist on regarding the church age as the millennium. They differ, however, in that postmillennialists, unlike the amillennialists, believe in an earthly reign of Christ. Postmillennialism rests on the belief that the preaching of the gospel will be so successful that the world will be converted. The reign of Christ in human hearts will be complete and universal. Jesus said on several occasions that it would be preached universally prior to his Second Coming (Mt. 24:14). Peace will prevail and evil will be virtually banished. At that moment when the gospel has come to its complete fruition, Christ will return. According to postmillennial ideas, a positive transformation of social conditions will follow mass conversions of people. Wars will cease to exist. As time passes on, economic injustice, racial conflicts and other forms of violence will simply fade away. In this scheme, the kingdom of God is viewed as a present reality, here and now, rather than a future heavenly realm.

Postmillennialists are prepared to cope with what appears to be setbacks, since they anticipate the ultimate triumph of the gospel in due time.

The most distinguishing feature of postmillennialism is its anticipation of nearly paradisal conditions immediately prior to Christ's return. Thus, in its essence, it is an optimistic view.

This view has much less support at the present time than it did in the late nineteenth and early twentieth centuries. The confidence of postmillennialists regarding a wide acceptance of the gospel seems somewhat unjustified.

There are also strong biblical grounds for rejecting postmillennialism. Jesus's teaching regarding the increase of lawlessness and the apostasy of many before his return seems to conflict quite clearly with postmillennial idealism. Another major weakness of this position is the lack of any scriptural basis of an earthly reign of Christ without his physical presence.

9.7.3. Modern Premillennialism

The issue in deciding which millennial view seems to be preferable to us depends on the interpretation of the biblical references to the millennium. Are there sufficient grounds for adopting the more complicated premillennial view rather than the simpler amillennial or postmillennial conceptions? It is sometimes contended that premillennialism rests upon a single passage of Scripture, and that no doctrine should be based upon a single passage. But if one view can account for a specific reference better than any other, and both views explain the rest of Scripture equally well, then the former view must certainly be judged more adequate than the latter.

We note here that there are no biblical passages which premillennialism cannot adequately interpret. We have seen, on the other hand, that the reference to two, presumably bodily, resurrections (Rev.20:4-5) are a source of irritation to both amillennialists and postmillennialists. Their explanations that we have here two different types of resurrections strain some of the most basic exegetical rules. The premillennialist case appears to be preferable here. This is why the author believes that the interpretation which accounts best for the language and context of Revelation 20:1-10, is the system of premillennialism.

Bibliography

Primary Sources

Augustine, *Sermons 259*.
--, *De genesi ad litteram*.
--, *De doctrina christiana* (*On Christian Learning*).
--, *Confessiones* (*Confessions*).
--, *De genesi contra Manichaeos*, in Migne, *PL*, vol.34.
--, *De civitate dei*.
--, *Quaestionum in heptateuchum libri VII*.
Chrysostom, *Homily on the Gospel of John*.
Clement of Alexandria, *Excerpta ex Theodoto*.
--, *Stromateis*.
Commodian, *Instructiones*.
--, *Carmen apologeticum*.
Dionysius, *Extant Fragments*, part 1, chap. 1, "From the Two Books on the Promises", sec. 4, in *ANF*, vol. 6.
Eusebius of Caesarea, *Ecclesiastical History*, William Heinemann, London, 1926, vol.1.
--, *Historia ecclesiastica*, books 3, 6 and 7, in *NPNF*, 2nd series, vol. 1.
Irenaeus, *Adversus Haereses*, in Glimm, Francis X. and Marique, Joseph M.F. and Walsh, Gerald G., trans., *The Ante-Nicene Fathers*, Cima Publishing Co., Inc., New York, 1947.
Jerome, *Commentariorum in Zachariam prophetam*.
--, *Epistolae*.
Josephus, *Antiquitates Judaicae* (*Jewish Antiquities*).
Justin Martyr, *Apology, I,II*.
--, *Dialogue with Trypho*.
Hippolytus, *Philosophumena*.
Lactantius, *Divinae institutiones*.
Maccabees I-IV
Methodius of Olypmus, *Convivium decem virginum* (*The Banquet of the Ten Virgins*).
--, *De resurrectione* (*About the Resurrection*).
Origen, *Hexapla*.
--, *De principiis* or *Peri archon* (*On the Principal Doctrines*), books 1, 2, 3 and 4, chap. 1, in *ANF*, vol. 4.
--, *Homilies*.

--, *Scholia.*
--, *Contra Celsum* (*Against Celsus*), books 1, 2, 4, 5, 6, and 8, in *ANF*, vol. 4.
--, *Commentary on John*, book 1, chap. 25, in *ANF*, vol. 9.
--, *Series commentariorum Origenis in Mattheum*, chs. 32 and 50, in Migne, *PG*, vol. 13.
--, *Selections from the Commentaries and Homilies of Origen*, part 7, chs. 87, 88 and 89.
Philo, *De ebrietate.*
Plato, *Respublica* (*The Republic*).
Syriac Apocalypse of Baruch, or *2 Baruch.*
Tertullian, *Adversus Marcionem* (*Against Marcion*).
--, *Adversus Valentinianos* (*Against the Valentinians*).
The Book of Jubilees.
The Sibylline Oracles.

Secondary Sources

Ackroyd, P.R. and Evans C.F., (ed.), *Cambridge History of the Bible*, Vol.1: *From the Beginnings to Jerome*, Cambridge University Press, New York and Cambridge, 1970.
Adams, Jay E., *The Time is at Hand*, Presbyterian and Reformed Publishing Co., 1970.
Aland, Kurt, *A History of Christianity*, 2 vols., Fortress Press, Philiadelphia, (1980) 1985.
Alford, Henry, *The Greek New Testament*, IV, 1894, revised by Everett F. Harrison, Moody Press, Chicago, 1958.
Allis, Oswald, *Prophecy and the Church*, Presbyterian and Reformed, Philadelphia, 1945.
Altaner, B., *Patrology*, tr. H.C. Graef from the 5th German ed., Nelson, Edinburgh and London, 1960.
Barnard, L.W., *Justin Martyr. His Life and Thought*, University Press, Cambridge, 1967.
Bauer, Walter, *A Greek-English Lexicon of the New Testament etc.*, 2 ed., The University of Chicago Press, Chicago, 1958.
Bauer, Walter, *Orthodoxy and Heresy in Earliest Christianity*, Fortress Press, Philadelphia, and SCM Press, London, 1972.

Baus, Karl, *From the Apostolic Community to Constantine*, Herder, Freiburg, 1965.
Beasley-Murray, G.R., *The Book of Revelation*, Wm. B. Eerdman Publ. Co., Grand Rapids, Mich., 1974.
Beckwith, Isbon T., *The Apocalypse of John*, Baker Book House, Grand Rapids, Mich., (1919) 1967.
Bietenhard, Hans, *Das tausendjährige Reich*, Eine biblisch-theologische Studie, 2.Aufl. Zürich, 1955.
Blackman, E.C., *Biblical Interpretation*, Westminster Press, Philadelphia, 1959.
Bloch, J., *On the Apocalyptic in Judaism*, JQR Monograph 2, 1952.
Böcher, Otto, *Die Johannesapokalypse*, Wissenschaftliche Buchgesellschaft, Darmstadt, 1975.
––, *Kirche in Zeit und Endzeit*, Aufsätze zur Offenbarung des Johannes, Neukirchener Verlag, Neukirchen-Vluyn, 1983.
Boettner, Loraine, *The Millennium*, Presbyterian and Reformed Publishing Co., Philadelphia, 1957.
Bousset, Wilhelm, *Die Offenbarung Johannis neu bearbeitet*, Vandenhoeck & Ruprecht, Göttingen, 1896.
Bouyer, Louis, *The Spirituality of the New Testament and the Fathers*, Burnes & Oates, London, 1960.
Bruce, F.F., *This is That. The NT Development of some OT Themes*, Paternoster Press, Exeter, 1968.
––, *The Canon of Scripture*, IVP, Downers Grove, 1988.
Caird, G. B., *The Revelation of St. John The Divine*, Hendrickson Publishers, Peabody, Mass., 1987 (1966).
Carrington, Philip, *The Early Christian Church*, 2 vols., Cambridge University Press, Cambridge, 1957.
Case, Shirley Jackson, *The Millennial Hope*, University of Chicago Press, 1918.
Chadwick, H., *The Early Church*, Penguin, Harmondsworth, 1967.
Charles, R. H. *Religious Developments between the Old and New Testament*, 1914.
––, *The Apocrypha and Pseudepigrapha of the Old Testament*, I-II, Oxford University Press, New York, 1913.
––, *The Revelation of St. John*, T.& T. Clark, Edinburgh, 1920.

Charlesworth, James H., *The Old Testament Pseudepigrapha*, Doubleday Co., Garden City, New York, 1983.

Clouse, Robert (ed.), *The Meaning of the Millennium. Four Views*, InterVarsity Press, Downers Grove, Ill., 1977.

Cohn, Norman, *The Pursuit of the Millennium*, Paladin, London, (1957) 1972.

Collins, John J., *The Apocalyptic Imagination*, Crossroad, New York, 1984.

Conzelmann, H., *An Outline of the Theology of the New Testament*, Harper and Row, New York, 1969.

Cross, F. L. and Livingston, E.A., (eds.), *The Oxford Dictionary of the Christian Church*, Oxford University Press, New York, Toronto, 1974.

--, *Early Christian Fathers*, Studies in Theology No.57, Duckworth, London, 1960.

Cunningham, William, *A Dissertation on the Epistle of S. Barnabas*, Macmillan and Co., London, 1877.

Daley, Brian, *Eschatologie in der Schift und Patristik*, Handbuch der Dogmengeschichte, Bd. IV, Herder, Freiburg, 1986.

Daniélou, Jean, *A History of Early Christian Doctrine*, Darton, Longman & Todd, London, 1964.

Dix, Gregory, *Jew and Greek*, Dacre Press, Westminster, 1953.

Feinberg, Charles L., *Millennialism. The Two Major Views*, 3 ed., Moody Press, Chicago, (1936) 1980.

Ferguson, E., (ed.), *Encyclopaedia of Early Christianity*, Garland, New York, 1989.

Ford, J. Massynberde, *Revelation*, The Anchor Bible, Doubleday, London, 1975.

Frend, W.H.C., *Saints and Sinners in the Early Church*, Darton, Longman & Todd, London, 1985.

--, *Martyrdom and Persecution in the Early Church*, Blackwell, Oxford, 1965.

--, *The Rise of Christianity*, Darton, Longman & Todd, London, 1984.

--, *The Early Church from the Beginning to 461 A.D.*, SCM Press LTD, 3 ed., London, 1991.

Froehlich, Karlfried, (translator/editor), *Biblical Interpretation in the Early Church*, Fortress Press, 1984.

Froom, LeRoy E., *The Prophetic Faith of our Fathers*, Vol.1, Review and Herald, Washington, D.C., 1946-1954.

Frost, S. B., *Old Testment Apocalyptic: Its Origins and Growth*, Epworth, London, 1952.

Fuller, R. H., *A Critical Introduction to the New Testament*, London, 1966.

Grant, R. M. and Tracy, D., *A Short History of the Interpretation of the Bible*, 2 ed., SCM Press LTD, London, 1984.

, *The Letter and the Spirit*, Macmillan Co., New York, 1957.

Guthrie, Donald, *New Testament Theology*, InterVarsity Press, Leicester, England, 1981.

Hamilton, Floyd, *The Basis of Millennial Faith*, Eerdmans, Grand Rapids, Mich., 1942.

Hanson, Paul D., *The Dawn of Apocalyptic*, Fortress, Philadelphia, 1975.

Harrison, R. K., *Introduction to the Old Testament*, Wm. B. Eerdman Publishing Com., Grand Rapids, Mich., 1969.

Hazlett, I., (ed.), *Early Christianity*, SPCK, London, 1991.

Hebblethwaite, Brian, *The Christian Hope*, Marshall, Morgan & Scott, Basingstoke, Hants, 1984.

Hendriksen, William, *More Than Conquerors*, Baker Book House, Grand Rapids, 1939.

Hoekema, Anthony A., *The Bible and The Future*, The Paternoster Press, Exeter, 1979.

Horne, Edward H., *The Meaning of the Apocalypse*, S.W. Partridge, London, 1916.

Hughes, P.E., *Interpreting Prophecy*, Wm. B. Eerdman, Grand Rapids, 1976.

Hyldahl, Niels, *Philosophie und Christentum. Eine Interpretation der Einleitung zum Dialog Justins*, Prostant Apud Munksgaard, Kopenhagen, 1966.

Jackson, G.A., *The Apostolic Fathers and the Apologists of the Second Century*, D. Appleton and Comp., New York, 1879.

Keil, C.F., *Introduction to the Old Testament*, Vol.2, Hendrickson Publishers, Peabody, Mass., (1869) 1991.

Kelly, J. N. D., *Early Christian Doctrine*, Adam & Charles Black, London, 1958.

Kik, J. Marcellus, *Revelation Twenty*, Presbyterian and Reformed, Philadelphia, 1955.

Klausner, Joseph, *The Messianic Idea in Israel from its Beginnings to the Completion of the Mishnah*, New York, 1955.

Körtner, Ulrich H. J., *Papias von Hierapolis*, Ein Beitrag zur Geschichte des frühen Christentums, Vandenhoeck & Ruprecht, Göttingen, 1985.

Kretschmar, G., *Die Offenbarung des Johannes. Die Geschichte ihrer Auslegung im 1. Jahrtausend*, Calwer Theologische Monographien B9, Calwer Verlag, Stuttgart, 1985.

Kümmel, Werner G., *Heilsgeschehen und Geschichte*, N.G. Elwert Verlag Marburg, 1965.

Kuyper, Abraham, *The Revelation of St. John*, trans. from the Dutch by J. Hendrik De Vries, Eerdmans, Grand Rapids, 1935.

Ladd, George E., *Commentary on Revelation of John*, Wm. B. Eerdman, Grand Rapids, 1972.

Lawson, John, *The Biblical Theology of Saint Irenaeus*, Epworth Press, London, 1948.

Lebreton, Jules and Zeiller, Jacques, *The History of the Primitive Church*, 2 vols., Macmillan, New York, 1946.

Lenski, R. C. H., *The Interpretation of St. John's Revelation*, Lutheran Book Concern, Columbus, Ohio, 1935.

Lightfoot, J. B. and Harmer, J.R., (ed.), *The Ante-Nicene Fathers*, vol. 1, Macmillan and Co., London, 1926.

Longenecker, R. N., *Biblical Exegesis in the Apostolic Period*, Wm. B. Eerdman, Grand Rapids, 1975.

Lücke, Versuch einer vollständigen Einleitung in die Offenbarung des Johannes, *Bonn*, 1852.

Maier, Gerhard, *Die Johannesoffenbarung und die Kirche*, J.C.B. Mohr (Paul Siebeck), Tübingen, 1981.

Menzies, Allan, *Commentaries of Origen. Introduction*, in *ANF*, vol. 9.

Metzger, Bruce M., *An Introduction to the Apocrypha*, Oxford University Press, New York, 1957.

Morgan, Robert, and Barton, John, *Biblical Interpretation*, Oxford University Press, Oxford, 1988.

Morris, Leon, *Apocalyptic*, Wm. B. Eerdman Publishing Com., Grand Rapids, 1972.

--, *The Book of Revelation*, Inter-Varsity Press, Leicester, England, (1969) 1987.

Mounce, Robert H., *The Book of Revelation*, Wm. B. Eerdman Publishing Co., 1977.

Muilenburg, James, *The Literary Relations of the Epistle of Barnabas and the Teaching of the Twelve Apostles*, Marburg, Germany, 1929.

Norris, Richard A., *God and World in Early Christian Theology. A Study in Justin Martyr, Irenaeus, Tertullian and Origen*, Adam & Charles Black, London, 1966.

Osborn, Eric F., *Justin Martyr*, Mohr & Siebeck, Tübingen, 1973.

Peake, Arthur S., *The Revelation of John*, Holborn Publishing House, London, 1921.

Pentecost, J. Dwight, *Things To Come*, Zondervan Publishing House, Grand Rapids, (1958) 1977.

Quasten, Johannes, *Patrology*, vol. 1 (The Beginnings of Patristic Literature), Spectrum Publishers, Utrecht and Antwerp, 1966.

Ramm, Bernard, *Protestant Biblical Interpretation*, W.A. Wilde Co., Boston, 1950.

Rauh, Horst Dieter, *Das Bild des Antichrist in Mittelalter. Von Tychonius zum Deutschen Symbolismus*, Verlag Aschendorff, Münster, 1973.

Roloff, Jürgen, *Die Offenbarung des Johannes*, Züricher Bibelkommentare, Theologischer Verlag Zürich, 1984.

Rowley, H. H., *The Relevance of Apocalyptic*, Association Press, London, (1944) 1963.

Russell, D. S., *The Method and Message of Jewish Apocalyptic*, SCM Press LTD, London, 1964.

Ryrie, Charles, *Dispensationalism Today*, Moody Press, Chicago, 1965.

Salmond, S. D. F., *Translator's Introduction Notice to Dionysius*, in *ANF*, vol. 6.

Schmithals, Walter, *The Apocalyptic Movement*, trans. by John E. Steely, Abingdon, Nashville, 1975.

Schoedel, William R., *The Apostolic Fathers*, Thomas Nelson & Sons, London, 1967.

Seiss, Joseph A., *The Apocalypse*, Kregel Publications, Grand Rapids, Mich., (1900) 1987.

Staniforth, Maxwell, trans., *The Epistle of Barnabas*, in *Early Christian Writings*. *The Apostolic Fathers*, Penguin Books, Harmondsworth, Middlesex, 1968.

Sweet, John, *Revelation*, SCM Press LTD, London, 1979.

Thompson, Leonard L., *The Book of Revelation*, Oxford University Press, 1990.

Torry, Charles C., *The Apocryphal Literature*, Yale University Press, New Haven, 1948.

Volz, Paul, *Die Eschatologie der jüdischen Gemeinde im neutestamentlichen Zeitalter nach den Quellen der rabbinischen*, apokalyptischen und apokryphen Literatur, Tübingen, 1934.

Walvoord, John F., *The Millennial Kingdom*, Findlay, Dunham, Ohio, 1959.

Warfield, Benjamin B., *The Millennium and the Apocalypse*, in Biblical Doctrines, Oxford University Press, New York, 1929.

Werner, M., *Die Entstehung des christlichen Dogmas*, Leipzig, 1941.

Wood, A. S., *The Principles of Biblical Interpretation*, Zondervan Publishing House, Grand Rapids, Michigan, 1967.

Articles

Aland, Kurt, »Der Montanismus und die kleinasiatische Theologie«, *ZNW*, XLIV 1955, pp. 113-114.

Bailey, J. W., "The Temporary Messianic Reign in the Literature of Early Judaism", *JBL* 53 (1934), pp. 170-187.

Bauer, Walter, »Chiliasmus«, *RAC* II (1954), col. 1073-1078.

Billerbeck, Paul, »Vorzeichen und Berechnung der Tage des Messias«, in Strack, Herman L. and Billerbeck, Paul, *Kommentar zum Neuen Testament aus Talmud und Midrasch*, IV 2, Munich, 1928 (7 ed. 1978), pp. 977-1015.

Billerbeck, Paul, »Diese Welt, die Tage des Messias und die zukünftige Welt«, in Strack, Herman L. and Billerbeck, Paul, *Kommentar zum Neuen Testament aus Talmud und Midrasch*, IV 2, Munich, 1928 (7 ed. 1978), pp. 799-976.

Bousset, Wilhelm and Greßmann, Hugo, »Die Religion des Judentums im späthellenistischen Zeitalter«, *HNT* XXI (1966), Tübingen.

Crutchfield, Larry V., "The Apostle John and Asia Minor as a Source of Premillennialism in the Early Church Fathers", *JETS* 31/4 (Dec.1988), pp. 411-427.

Daniélou, Jean, «La typologie de la semaine au IVe siecle», *RSR* 35 (1948), p. 403.

Lohse, Eduard, "Chilias Chilioi", *TWNT* IX (1973), pp. 455-460.

Löwy, M., *Messiaszeit und zukünftige Welt*, Dogmengeschichtliche Studien, MGWJ 41, 1897, pp. 392-409.

Schäfer, Peter, »Die messianischen Hoffnungen des rabbinischen Judentums zwischen Naherwartung und religiösem Pragmatismus«, in Lauer, Simon und Thoma, Clemens, *Zukunft in der Gegenwart. Wegweisungen in Judentum und Christentum*, Bern, 1976, pp. 95-125.

Wikenhauser, Alfred, »Weltwoche und tausendjähriges Reich«, *ThQ* 127 (1947), pp. 399-417.

——, »Herkunft der Idee des tausendjährigen Reiches in der Johannes-Apokalypse«, *RQ* 45 (1937), pp. 1-24.

Shepherd, Norman, "Postmillennialism", in Tenney, M.C., (ed.), *The Zondervan Pictorial Encyclopedia of the Bible*, Zondervan, Grand Rapids, 1975, IV, pp. 822-823.

Index

Abraham	16, 20, 56, 70, 100, 183, 218
Abyss	XXIV, 34-35, 41, 59-61, 63-64, 66-67, 69, 72, 83-84, 88-89, 173, 177, 184-186, 199, 201, 207
bottomless pit	60-61, 185
Alogi	168, 206
Antichrist	75, 85, 125, 166, 219
The Beast	32, 34-35, 41, 48, 61, 63, 65, 73, 75, 88, 151, 200, 202
Antiochus (Epiphanes) IV	21
Antiochus III	21
Apocalypse of John	XI, XV, xix, 2, 4-6, 9, 13, 16, 21, 24-28, 32, 36, 46, 48, 62, 84, 143, 154, 184, 195, 206, 208, 214-215, 217, 220
apocalypticism	7-10, 17, 19
apocalyptic ideas	XIV, 11-12, 22
apocalyptists	4, 15, 20, 23, 26, 28
Apollinarius	130, 134

Apostle John	III, IV, IX, XI, XIII, xviii, xix, XXII, XXV, 2-3, 6, 13, 24-27, 31-36, 38-39, 48, 50, 52-53, 55, 59, 61-62, 64-65, 67, 69-70, 73, 75-79, 81-82, 84-85, 87, 89, 96-97, 99, 104, 110-112, 114, 126, 129, 134, 143, 163-164, 168, 179, 191-193, 196, 199-201, 205-206, 213-216, 218-221
Ascension of Isaiah	118, 121, 134, 155, 204
Asia Minor	XVI, 32, 39, 73, 111, 116-117, 119, 127, 130-135, 141, 145, 153, 156, 221
Babylon	32, 35
Battle of Armageddon	65
Bible	IV, V, XVI, 6, 10, 15-16, 18, 21, 36-37, 45-46, 50, 52-53, 58, 66-67, 82, 87-88, 92-93, 95-106, 112, 138, 141-142, 145, 148, 167, 176-178, 183, 188, 192-193, 214, 216-217, 221
canonicity	XXII, 1, 6, 15-16, 167-168, 171, 206
Hebrew Bible	10, 15-16, 18, 21, 93, 95-99, 101, 104-106, 138, 141-142, 145, 148, 178, 192-193

New Testament	V, XV, xviii, 2, 8, 20, 25, 36, 40, 50, 56-59, 63, 66, 68, 71, 76, 80, 93, 95-99, 101, 103-105, 107, 113, 115, 124, 148, 167, 192-195, 199-200, 214-217
Old Testament	xviii, XXIII, 3, 5, 11, 17, 27, 50, 52-58, 78, 81-82, 95-96, 103, 109, 113, 116-117, 123-124, 131, 139, 142, 150-151, 153, 157, 189, 192-193, 197, 207, 209, 216-218
Boettner, Loraine	42-46, 215
Caird, G. B.	77-80, 85-87, 215
Cerinthus	128-130, 133-136, 141, 197
Charles, R. H.	3, 5, 16-17, 20, 26, 87
Christianity	XIV, 17-18, 98, 100, 127, 135, 138-139, 148, 161-162, 166-167, 170, 174-175, 192, 203-204, 214-217
Christian faith	XIV, XVI, 93-94, 99, 104, 106, 111-112, 138-140, 161-162, 178, 193
Christians	III, XIII, XV, 17, 41, 57, 68, 97-99, 101, 105, 139-141, 145, 154, 156, 161, 166, 168, 187, 192-193, 199, 202

Church	II, III, IV, V, XI, XIII, XIV, XV, XVI, XVII, xxi, XXIII, XXIV, XXV, 7, 32, 37, 39-40, 42-44, 46, 50, 52, 54-55, 58-60, 64, 66-69, 71-72, 74, 79-80, 82, 86, 89, 91-95, 97-103, 105-107, 111-113, 115-118, 122, 124, 127-132, 134-135, 138, 140-141, 143, 152-153, 157-160, 162, 164, 166-167, 169-171, 173-180, 184-189, 191-192, 195-196, 198, 200, 202, 204-209, 214-218, 221
Church Age	40, 42, 46, 209
Eastern Church	XVI, XVII, 158, 162
Latin Church	XIII, XVII, 100, 174
Western Church	XVI, XVII, 100, 111, 175-176
Church Fathers	III, IV, V, XI, XIII, XIV, XV, XVI, XVII, 89, 92-95, 98-100, 102, 105-107, 113, 115-118, 127-130, 132, 134-135, 152, 171, 174, 192, 195-196, 198, 202, 204, 221
Alexandrians	XI, XXV, 94, 102-104, 191, 194, 204
Ambrose	174
Antiochenes	94, 102-104, 194

Aurelius Augustine	V, XI, XIII, XVII, xix, XXIV, XXV, 66, 71, 96-97, 99-102, 107, 118, 157, 160, 171, 173-191, 193-194, 204, 206-207, 213
Chrysostom	XI, xix, 97, 99, 162, 193, 213
Clement of Alexandria	XVI, xix, 99, 152, 157-158, 213
Commodian	xix, 117, 120, 126, 135, 198, 213
Diodore of Tarsus	103, 194
Dionysius of Alexandria	XVII, XXIV, 128, 158-159, 167, 169
Hippolytus	XVII, xx, 138, 213
Irenaeus	XV, XVI, xx, 93-94, 97, 110-116, 119-126, 128-131, 136, 143, 158, 170, 193, 195, 198, 213, 218-219
Jerome	XI, XIII, XVII, xx, 101, 121, 152, 164, 194, 213-214
Lactantius	xx, 117-118, 120-121, 213
Methodius of Olympus	119-120, 134

Origen	XVI, XVII, xx, XXIV, 96, 100-101, 104, 152, 154, 156, 158-171, 192, 194, 204-206, 213-214, 218-219
Papias	XV, XVI, 110-118, 120-121, 127-129, 132-134, 136, 141, 195, 218
Polycarp	XVI, 110-111
Tertullian	XVII, xx, 96, 127, 133-134, 138, 160, 195, 214, 219
Theodoret	103, 194
Council of Nicaea	II, XIII, 160
dispensationalism	53, 58-59, 219
dualism	4, 8, 20, 128, 197
earthly kingdom	XV, 2, 4-5, 46, 51, 57, 196-198
Epistle of Barnabas	XVII, XXIII, XXV, 97, 100, 104, 122, 145, 147-148, 152-153, 155-157, 191, 193, 203-204, 219-220
eschatology	IV, V, XIII, XV, 4, 8, 11, 13, 17, 19, 23, 52, 167, 180, 189, 195

Eusebius	XI, XIII, xix, 110-111, 114, 128-129, 134-135, 138, 152, 161, 168-169, 195, 197, 206, 213
Ecclesiastical History	xx, 110, 161, 213
Gnosticism	111, 124, 129, 135, 145, 156-157, 161, 197, 203
Gnostics	93, 95, 156, 203
Gnostic speculations	112, 156, 158
Valentinians	xx, 156, 158, 214
God	IV, VI, XIV, 2-5, 7-8, 12-16, 20, 22-23, 26-29, 32-35, 42-44, 49-50, 55-61, 63-65, 68-71, 73-76, 78-79, 82-89, 92, 95-99, 101, 105-106, 113-114, 119-120, 125-126, 129-130, 136, 138-139, 142, 145, 150-152, 157, 164-165, 170-171, 175, 177-178, 180-181, 185-188, 192, 196-199, 201, 205-206, 209, 219
Holy Spirit	42, 60, 68, 72, 93, 99-102, 192-193
kingdom	2-4, 8, 13-14, 42, 44, 50, 58, 65, 83, 170, 175, 197, 206, 209
Gog and Magog	83, 85-86, 143, 201

Golden Age	XIII, XIV, XVII, 11, 28-29, 47, 86, 142, 155, 196, 208
Glorious Age	2, 44, 82
Great Tribulation	33, 43, 52-53, 57-58, 75
Hoekema, A. A.	37-41, 43, 46-47, 50-51, 58-59, 66-67, 217
The Bible and the Future	37, 46, 66-67, 217
Israel	III, 2, 9-10, 14, 28, 33, 49-50, 53, 55-59, 74, 85-86, 98, 144, 189, 200, 218
Jerusalem	XXIII, 2, 21, 26, 32, 34-35, 56, 72, 85, 87, 109, 124-127, 129, 133-134, 136, 138, 140-141, 152, 162-163, 189, 195-198, 201-202
New Jerusalem	26, 32, 35, 87, 126-127, 134, 163, 189, 196, 202
Jesus Christ	III, IV, XI, XIII, XIV, XV, XXIV, 17, 27, 32-33, 35-47, 49-58, 60-61, 65-82, 84, 86, 89, 96-100, 102-104, 110, 113-115, 118, 122-123, 129, 132, 138-141, 143-145, 149-151, 153, 156, 163-166, 170, 173, 176-184, 188-189, 192-194, 196, 198-201, 203-205, 207-210

Ascension	58, 72, 118, 121, 134, 155, 179, 182, 204
Lamb	33-34, 75
Second Advent	17, 48, 71
Second Coming	XIV, XXIV, 35-36, 38, 41, 43-44, 46-47, 49-52, 57-58, 69-70, 97, 113, 123, 141, 144, 153, 159-160, 163, 165-166, 173, 177-179, 181-184, 188-189, 199, 205-209
Servant of the Lord	98
substitutionary atonement	96
Jews	XIV, 5, 7, 12, 14, 17-18, 21-23, 28-29, 46, 50, 54, 56, 59, 85, 97-99, 118-119, 121, 125, 135, 138-139, 150, 154-156, 178, 192-193, 196-197
Jewish apocalyptic literature	V, XIV, XVII, 10, 26, 127, 130, 153, 157, 196
Jewish apocalyptists	4, 26
Jewish history	20-22, 196
Jewish mysticism	18
Jewish nation	14, 21-23, 27-28, 57
Jewish orthodoxy	18, 20
Joachim of Fiore	72

Judaism	XIV, 2-4, 6-9, 12, 17-18, 23, 94, 96, 98, 122, 135, 139, 204, 215, 220
Kik, J. Marcellus	43, 46-47, 218
King David	33, 55-57, 85, 183
Kuyper, Abraham	70, 218
Ladd, George E.	28, 49-52, 218
lake of fire	35, 41, 64, 82, 88-89
Maccabean war	21
Maccabeus, Judas	21
Mattathias	21
Manichaeanism	174
Marcion	xx, 127, 214
Messiah	4-5, 13-14, 26, 29, 46, 53-54, 57, 76, 97, 99, 135, 195-198
messianic hope	XIV, 135
messianic kingdom	XV, 2-3, 5, 26-27, 54, 74, 115-116, 118, 128, 195, 197, 202

millennialism	V, XI, XIII, XV, XXII, XXIII, XXIV, XXV, 6, 31-32, 36, 38, 40, 50, 67-68, 71, 89, 109-110, 112-113, 127, 132, 145, 154, 157, 159, 163, 170-171, 191, 195, 197-199, 202-205, 207, 216
Adamic Millennium	XXIII, 109, 120
amillennialism	XI, XII, XVII, XXII, XXIII, XXIV, XXV, 31, 36-37, 40, 42, 47, 49-51, 65, 77, 107, 171, 173-174, 191, 206, 208-209
chiliasm	XIII, XIV, XVII, XXIII, 65, 110, 112-117, 121-130, 132-138, 140-142, 144, 147-148, 154, 156-157, 160, 163-165, 171, 181, 190, 195, 197-198, 206-207
Cosmic Week	XXIII, XXIV, 109, 121-122, 136, 147, 153-155, 157, 204
dispensational premillennialism	XXII, 31, 36, 48-49, 51-54, 56, 58-59
historical premillennialism	XXII, 31, 37, 48-52
millenarianism	XIII, XIV, XV, 107, 110, 114, 117-118, 122, 125, 127-130, 132-134, 141, 157, 168-169, 178, 180, 189-190, 202-204

millennial controversy	IV, V, XIII, XV, XVII, XXIII, 31, 36, 59, 65, 107, 118, 141, 167, 169-170, 192, 206
millennial kingdom	III, XIV, 53, 72, 112-113, 123, 132, 178, 189, 220
millennium	I, II, III, V, XI, XIII, XV, XVII, XXIII, XXIV, 4-5, 26, 35-37, 39-55, 58, 60, 63, 65-66, 70-72, 75, 77-78, 81-83, 86, 88, 109-111, 113-123, 125-130, 134-137, 140-145, 147, 153-154, 156-158, 160, 163, 165-166, 168-169, 171, 173, 177-182, 185, 187-190, 195-199, 201-210, 215-216, 220
one thousand years	XI, XIV, 4-5, 7, 35, 60, 63-65, 70-72, 76, 81-83, 131, 154, 198, 208-209
postmillennialism	XII, XXII, XXV, 31, 36, 42, 44, 46-47, 65, 191, 209-210, 221
premillennialism	IV, V, XII, XXII, XXIII, XXV, 31, 36-37, 42, 47-56, 58-59, 65, 77, 191, 198-199, 209-211, 221
Sabbath of Rest	XXIV, 147, 155
The Eighth Day	153-157, 181, 203-204

The Seventh Millennium	71, 120, 122, 153-154, 203
Montanism	131-134
Montanists	XXIII, 109, 127, 132, 168, 197
Montanus	120, 132-134, 136, 141
Moses	16, 20, 104, 139, 149
Mosaic Law	149
Pentateuch	96, 150
Mount Zion	3, 34
Neoplatonism	161
new covenant	57
ogdoad	155-157, 203-204
pagan mythology	XIV
paradisal Age	XIII
paradise	77-78, 80, 119, 123, 130-131, 134, 143, 145, 181, 196-197, 202
parousia	XV
Pharisaism	17-18
Philo	xix, 100, 148, 155-156, 168, 175, 203, 214
Platonism	XVI, 103

Christian Platonist	138
Plato	xix, 7, 138, 214
Platonic philosophy	94
prophets	III, 2-3, 10, 12, 14-15, 27, 35, 43, 78, 96, 98, 117, 121, 138, 140-143, 150, 166, 196, 205
Amos	xviii, 56, 117
Ezekiel	xviii, 3, 85-86, 141
Isaiah	xviii, 3, 16, 56, 96, 98, 117-118, 121, 123, 128, 130, 134, 141-144, 148, 150, 155, 202, 204
Jeremiah	xviii, 3, 56-57
Micah	xviii, 56, 117
prophecy	XXII, XXIII, 1, 6-9, 11-13, 15, 19-20, 27-28, 40, 48, 50, 55-56, 58, 66-67, 85, 98, 103, 109, 117, 123-124, 133, 142, 150, 175, 179, 192, 194, 209, 214, 217
Rabbinic literature	18
Ramm, Bernard	54, 219

resurrection	XIV, xx, XXIII, XXIV, 3, 11, 13, 26, 31, 46, 51-53, 71, 73, 75-82, 96, 104, 110, 116-120, 125, 129, 133-134, 141, 143-145, 151, 156, 159, 163-166, 173, 176-177, 179-180, 189, 192, 195-196, 200-205, 207-209, 213
Revelation	IV, V, XI, XII, XIII, XVI, XVII, xviii, XXII, XXV, 1-3, 11, 14-15, 18-19, 24-27, 29, 31-32, 35, 37-41, 43, 46-52, 55, 59-60, 62, 64, 69-74, 78, 85-89, 95-97, 106-107, 116, 118, 125-128, 134-135, 140, 143-145, 154, 167-169, 171, 176-178, 180, 183, 191, 195-196, 199, 201-202, 206-208, 211, 215-216, 218-220
Ryrie, Charles	55, 59, 219
Satan	XI, XXII, XXIII, XXIV, 2, 4, 13, 31, 34-36, 40-41, 43, 46, 48, 51, 59-72, 82-84, 86-88, 143, 173, 176-177, 183-187, 199, 201-202, 207
Devil	XXIV, 48, 59, 63, 66, 68-69, 84, 88, 173, 175, 184-186, 188
dragon	32, 34, 39, 48, 59-61, 63-64, 177, 207

Syria	21-22
The Apocalypse of Abraham	16
The Assumption of Moses	16
The Book of Daniel	15-16
The Book of Jubilees	xix, 16, 64, 122, 130-131, 143, 198, 203, 214
The Book of the Secrets of Enoch	5, 16, 198
Theodore of Mopsuestia	103, 194
The Psalms of Solomon	16
The Sibylline Oracles	xix, 16, 120, 154, 214
The Testament of Abraham	16
The Testament of Isaac	5, 197
The Testaments of the Twelve Patriarchs	16
Titus	21
Trypho	xx, 98-99, 139-142, 144-145, 192-193, 202-203, 213
Tychonius	XVII, 176-177, 179, 182, 206, 219
Walvoord, John F.	53, 220
Warfield, Benjamin B.	46, 208, 220
Wellhausen, Julius	22-23

Ecumenical Quest for a World Federation

The Churches' Contribution to Marshal Public Support for World Order and Peace, 1919 1945

In his book, Ecumenical Quest for a World Federation, Dr. Erdmann deals primarily with John Foster Dulles' participation in the ecumenical movement from 1919 to 1945. Dulles' role in shaping the religious, economic and political policies of the Federal Council of Churches in its support of world order and peace, especially in his function as chairman of the Commission on a Just and Durable Peace, was crowned with success in the founding of the United Nations Organisation in 1945. His personal friends Philip Kerr (Lord Lothian) and Lionel Curtis, the principal leaders of the Round Table Group, come into the pictures at various times. By and large they pursued the same objectives as those of Dulles. The book shows the detailed influence of the Round Table Group and its affiliated organisations – such as the Royal Institute of International Affair (London) and the Council for Foreign Relations (New York City) – on the ecumenical movement, using it successfully for their purpose of creating an international community of nations.

Verax Vox Media
225 Barbours Lane • Greenville, SC 29607
VeraxVoxMedia.com
Publication Date: January 2016 • ISBN: 978-069261-793-9